Texas Stories

Texas Stories

Tales of Cowboys, Ranchers, and Assorted Characters

CRAIG SAVOYE

Nobadeer Press
13331 Featherstone Drive
Saint Louis, MO 63131

Cover painting by Caitlin Heimerl:
www.caitlinheimerl.com

ISBN: 978-0-578-07010-0
Printed in the United States of America

Order this book at www.texasstories.net

Contents

Foreword

There's a coupla things you need to know 'fore we get started. A section is a square mile of land. That's six hun'erd forty acres. Other places in the West, they talk about acres or maybe a quarter, a quarter of a section. But this is Texas. Sure, folks'll mention acres, and I will, too, but, for the most part, it's about sections. Such-and-such a ranch is fifty sections.

Lot of ranches don't go by the owner's name. They go by the brand. There's the Frying Pan, the Pitchfork, the Spade, the four 6s. That last one, the brand is 6666. Other ranches do go by surnames like Waggoner or Bivins. Then there's a ranch like Matador, which is just a name they give it. For some reason, cowboys like to make things plural. They'll call the Pitchfork Ranch the Pitchforks, the Waggoner Ranch the Waggoners, or the JA Ranch the JAs. Do the same thing with names sometimes. Like, I'll be tellin' you about a feller named Button Criswell in the book. Some cowpunchers call him Buttons. Do you call your friend Bills? Or Georges? Or Harrys? Course not. Just done out here. No accounting for it. I won't be callin' any Eds Eds, but might call it the Pitchforks just to get in the spirit of things.

A wreck ain't in a car. It's on a horse. It's a rider gettin' thrown, or maybe both rider and mount going down. That's a wreck. A trap ain't something to snare a jackrabbit with, at least not in this book. It's a name cowboys give any fenced pasture or maybe a pen, where cattle are temporary held for whatever reason. A

7

hoodlum wagon carries all the gear that don't fit in the chuck wagon. The hood, or hoodlum, is the feller who drives it. Hood is a name they give to the wrangler way back.

There's a buncha small towns around the Panhandle got names like big cities in other places. I don't feel like writing 'Memphis, Texas' just so you know it ain't Memphis, Tennessee, or 'Miami, Texas' so you know it ain't Miami, Florida. If you see Memphis or Miami, they're in Texas. Kinda the same thing with Canadian. Got nothin' to do with Canada. Folks are nice enough up there, but they ain't got nothin' to do with this here. Canadian is the name of a town in the Northeast Panhandle that gets mentioned a lot in the book. It's also the name of the biggest river flowing west to east across the Panhandle and through the town of the same name.

Tell you about neighboring. That's when you go work for a day or two at a neighbor's ranch, usually during branding season, when they need extra hands. Then they come to your place when you need extra help. Rodeo ropers use a pigging string to tie down calves. Sure enough, cowboys basically use 'em the same way, except it's on wild cattle. Maybe to tie 'em down for doctorin'. But you can do most anything with a piggin' string. 'Bout as wide used as a pocketknife. Them other uses is how it gets mentioned in the book. A knacker is a feller who processes old horses. A pannier is a bag or container with two sides that gets slung over a pack horse or mule for carryin' stuff.

Sometimes, as I'm tellin' a story, I'll explain a word, but I sometimes don't feel like it. Don't wanna stop every ten seconds and explain what something like hoodlum is. Drag on the story-telling. Then, ten seconds later, I'm stoppin' to explain what a remuda is. A remuda is all the extra saddle horses. Could be all the horses on a ranch, all the horses on a trail drive, or just all the horses out workin' cattle for a few days. Just a buncha horses, is all. See what I mean? Brings everything to a standstill just to explain stuff. Disrupts things. Bothersome. I ain't gettin' ornery. I'm just sayin'. Whole point of this foreword is that, if you don't know what a word means, come back here to find it.

When I say ornery, it don't mean 'mean,' typical. Ornery is practical jokin'. It's mostly good-natured, but it's sometimes prankin' with attitude. But ornery can also mean mean, or a little hot under the collar. Just have to figure out on your own when it does. Like in the last paragraph.

All right, that should be enough to getcha started.

The Sobering

Before Button Criswell moved to Texas from New Mexico, he worked on a ranch in the foothills of the Sangre de Cristo Mountains. Wasn't unusual for elk to come down from the highlands, feed on the grass, and sometimes get mixed up with the cattle or horse herds.

Button's nephew was gettin' married. Gonna be an old-fashioned wedding. They still used a chuck wagon in those days, and the ceremony was gonna be out in a pasture by the wagon. Plan was for guests to be rode out there in horse-drawn carriages.

Night before, groom and his three groomsmen had their bachelor party out by the chuck wagon and got drunk. Wedding was at ten in the mornin.'

Not long after dawn, the father of the groom calls Button and says, Them boys are drunk out by the chuck wagon. I've got problems with the reception I gotta fix. Can you bring them boys in and get 'em sobered up?

Button said okay, and gone out there in his pickup. He wasn't drinkin' anymore himself by then. Them boys were so sauced they was crawling-on-their-hands-and-knees drunk. Button had his oldest daughter with him. She was about ten then. He just scratched his head at the spectacle, not sure what to do. Got them loaded in the truck bed and took them back to the barn. Button had to round up some horses and get them penned before the ceremony, so he propped the boys against the side of the barn.

They was semiconscious, movin' a bit, groanin' a lot.

Button saddled up and went and wrangled them horses, about twenty-five of 'em. An elk was in the middle of the herd. Big buck. Twelve points. Antlers still in velvet that time of year. Button drove him into the pen, along with them colts.

By then, the boys was gettin' to where they could speak again. Button figures he'll have a little fun with them drunk young turks.

He says, Boys, if I was you, in my early twenties like you all are, fixin' to lose my freedom, I'd want to go out by bustin' an elk.

They perked up. All of them were cowboys.

They said, Sure. By golly, if you can rope him, we'll ride him.

Button was still horseback. He run at that elk, just standin' there amongst the horses, and threw a loop over his antlers and tightened up around his neck. They go wild when you catch 'em. Button couldn't do nothin' but turn and ride for the boys, draggin' that big 'ol elk, him bouncin' on the end of the rope.

Boys was game. They come to meet Button, one of 'em carryin' a saddle. Got that elk outside the pen and mugged him. He was pawing and kicking, but they got the saddle on him. Funniest thing Button ever seen was that wild elk saddled up for ridin'.

Button says, All right, somebody get on. I'll lope alongside with the rope.

Had to keep that rope on him. If not and he threw a rider, elk would take off for the high country wearin' that saddle as a souvenir.

The boys got to fightin' over who was gonna go first. Button was havin' trouble controllin' that critter.

He says, Quit your fightin'. Someone get on.

One of them boys got on, and that elk bucked like no bull you ever seen. Leaped so high you could see its belly button. And he was making wheezing, whistling noises, unnerving you a bit. Slam-dunked that first boy like a yard dart.

The three others was still feelin' their oats, or maybe they still weren't feelin' nothing at all. They mugged down that elk again, got another rider saddled, and jumped back. Elk was up and buckin' 'fore they was even clear. Done the exact same maneuver, four hops. Then he'd suck back and send the young cowboy flyin' over his antlers.

When the groom got planted face-first in the sage same way, Button's thinkin,' I do believe I have him figured out. I can ride him.

After the fourth kid got thrown, that buck was worn down.

Button's thinkin,' This is my big chance to get famous for ridin' an elk.

Button says to them boys, You all mug him up again. I'm gonna show you how an old man rides an elk.

With Button aboard, that elk did the same thing. Four big jumps. Button held on and was ridin' tight in the saddle. He braced himself for the maneuver. Sure enough, that buck stopped short. Sure enough, he flung Button off like a troublesome bug and sent him rollin' across the pasture.

They declared the elk the victor. Got that saddle off him. He was all skinned up, and a couple points on them antlers was busted off. But he weren't in no worse shape than any of them cowboys. They let him loose. He took off like horizontal lightning and never looked back. Never mixed with that herd of horses again neither.

The groom's father was foreman of the ranch. He come down to the pens to start hitchin' up teams to the wagons and caught a glimpse of that roughed-up elk boltin' for the high country. His son and the groomsmen were startin' to chase down some stray horses, gettin' them into the pens.

Foreman says to Button, What happened to that elk?

Button says, It's a long story, boss. But mission accomplished. Them boys is sobered up.

Remember, Button's ten year old was a witness to events. They'd made a campfire down by the barn. As father and daughter walked back up to the house to get cleaned up for the wedding, she was carryin' a pot of coffee.

She said, Boy, Daddy, them drunk cowboys sure are crazy.

He said, Yeah, they are, honey. You stay away from them kind.

She said, Yeah, Daddy, but you ain't drunk, and you did the same thing they done.

Button didn't make no eye contact with her. He just said, Keep that coffeepot level, little girl. Don't spill none.

The Prankster

Jason Pelham has cowboyed on some of the biggest ranches in Texas. Started on the Broseco in Mount Pleasant. Used to be one of the five largest ranches in the country. Worked on the King ranch in northeast Texas. They run some cattle there. Then he worked down in Borden County for ten years. Now he works on one of the Spade ranches in the northeast corner of the Panhandle. Every place he's ever departed from, he's left behind men wanting to kill 'im.

Well, not really, but Pelham is ornery. One time, he seen a badger along the road, comin' into Miami. Had Lloyd with him. They'd been playin' tricks on some fellers. Stopped his truck and chased the critter on foot across a pasture. Tricky to rope them things. Either got to lead it just right or set the rope down behind it and back him over it. You don't just run up on 'em. That's for sure. They'll turn, and sucker'll bite you. Get a hold of you pretty good.

Finally, they get him caught and put him in a box, an empty cake feeder, and they gone into town. They found Todd's rig, put the badger in the horse trailer, and closed the gate. Todd come along and gone to loadin' his horse in the trailer. Pelham and Lloyd stand back to watch, and that horse ain't going in the trailer. He gets to snortin' and blowin'. Smelled that badger. They got a stink on 'em like a skunk. In a minute, Todd is madder'n hell, and he's yellin' at the horse. And now he's yellin' at Pelham and

Lloyd to whup on the horse's ass and help get him in the trailer. But them boys don't move a muscle. It gone on like that a minute with Todd yankin' on that horse. Finally, he disappears inside the trailer for a second, still pullin'. Next thing you know, he's boltin' out of there, hollerin' to beat the band with reins flyin'. Badger come sprintin' out behind him. Horse nearly run over Todd.

In all the excitement, Pelham captured the badger again and put him in Todd's toolbox a few days later. Got him pretty good that time, too.

One time, Pelham was out lookin' at horses with JD. JD asked what he got in the dog box. Jason says he caught an armadillo. JD didn't think nothin' of it, and they gone on lookin' at horses. JD was ridin' one when Pelham gone over, got that armadillo, and put it loose in the front seat of JD's truck.

JD seen Pelham closin' the door and says, What're you doing?

Pelham says he left him the armadillo, but JD was on the horse and couldn't hear or understand.

He waves and says, Okay. Bye.

Jason leaves, but JD don't call him that night. Pelham figures JD just let the critter loose. But no, he hadn't seen it yet. Next day, JD was drivin' down the road with his trailer and horse in it and felt something hit his foot. He thought it was an empty bottle rollin' out from under the seat, so he give it a kick. Put a fright in that armadillo. Critter dashes forward, jumps over JD's foot and onto the gas pedal and brake. JD lets out a yell and jerks his feet up on the seat. Now he's drivin' with no feet. He gone off the road and down in a ditch. Didn't roll or nothin'. The horse was okay, but fellers give Pelham a hard time about it. Could have killed him and all that kind of stuff. One old-timer was especially ridin' him.

So Pelham was thinkin' on how that whole trick worked out.

Got him a dead snake and put it in a Coke bottle. Got that snake so he's half in the Coke bottle and half hangin' out. Set it on the floorboard of the old-timer's truck. Well, old-timer come out of work and got in his rig after dark. There's no light in his cab. His boot touches that bottle. He reaches down, grabbin' for it, and feels that snake. He come up so fast and so hard he almost knocked himself out on the side of the steering wheel. He about flew out of that pickup. Vowed on his dead momma's and poppa's lives he'd get back on Pelham, but it ain't happened yet.

One time, Todd stole Pelham's refrigerator. The two worked either side of the big Spade Ranch up there north of Canadian. Two new refrigerators got sent out. Todd was supposed to get one and Pelham the other. They keep refrigerators down in the saddle house and put vaccinations and beer in there. Pelham was supposed to get the bigger one, a side-by-side, and Todd the smaller one. But they delivered over to Todd first, and he grabbed the side-by-side and sent the little one on to Pelham. So JD and Jason decide they were gonna fix him. They roped a coyote and gone over there with it. They tried to stuff the coyote in the side-by-side so that, when Todd opened the door, the critter would jump out at him. But there was too much medicine in there. They was pullin' out medicine and stuffin' in coyote, and he was snappin' and hissin' and bitin' on 'em, so they give up on the fridge.

Instead, they figured on the saddle house. Got that coyote on a string. Of course, a saddle rack was in the saddle house, so they tied him to the rack where Todd got a saddle on. They come out, and Todd seen them. Now, any time you see a cowboy at your camp and he don't really have no business being there, alarm bells got to go off. You know he's messin' around somehow—shortening one stirrup or tying your rope in knots. So Pelham had to think fast and figures he'll just get angry.

He says, frustrated as hell, Where's that bit? We've been tryin' to get JD that bit, and it ain't nowheres.

Todd says, It's right there on the wall.

By God, ain't a bit in there. Like to pull our hair out searchin' for that thing.

Todd shakin' his head, wonderin' why Pelham is havin' anger issues. He walks up to that door and starts to open it. He had barn cats around there. They arched their backs and fuzzed up. Hhhhhheeee!

Todd says, What's wrong with you cats?

That's when Pelham pushed him in and closed the door behind him. Coyote lunged at Todd, hissin' and growlin'. He was on the string, so he didn't go nowheres. But Todd don't know that. He come runnin' out of there, like it was a bear instead of a coyote. Eyes were as wide as a Comanche moon. Scared him pretty good.

After Todd been cussin' them a while, all three loaded up some tubs they needed to move to the other side of the ranch and put the coyote in the back of the pickup. When they come into Higgins, the fire siren is going off. Todd is on the volunteer fire department. He run in to see what the matter was. There was a fire down at Grandma's place. Older woman everyone just called Grandma. Well, all of them fire trucks they had was from the forties, old army trucks. But they got them loaded up, and volunteers got in their cars. Todd climbed back in the pickup, and they all gone screamin' down there. A fire in a small town is a bigger deal than a premiere on Broadway in New York. When they left the fire station, they had the Spanish Armada on wheels headed for that conflagration. As they got closer, they could see smoke billowin' up from Grandma's place.

As it turned out, a guy was over by the railroad with a roll of hay in the back of his pickup. The fire started there, maybe a spark off the tracks, and he drove over to Grandma's with that burnin' hay. Figurin' to put it out with her hose.

Way Grandma tells it, she was just mindin' her business one day, and next thing you know, there's a feller with a flamin' roll of hay in her driveway sprayin' it with her hose when about a hun'erd fire trucks, all older'n her, with lights flashin' and sirens blarin', come crashin' down on her. And to add icing on the apparition, three cowboys in a pickup cruised in with a coyote ridin' shotgun.

Anyway, Pelham, JD, and Todd rode off, but they got that perfectly good coyote with them and they need to do something productive with it. They decide the saddle house strategy is a good one and head over to a neighbor's place. Dan was the unfortunate target. Was a Sunday and barely late mornin' by now. Knew Dan was off workin'. With memories still raw, Todd didn't want no part of it. They dropped him off. Way Dan had things set up, he'd take his saddle off his horse and then use his back to push open the door of the saddle house, turn, and put the saddle on the rack. It was dark in there, and the light switch was behind the door, so Dan usually got his saddle up on the rack without ever turnin' the light on. Well, Pelham and JD get there, tie that coyote up in the saddle house, and take off.

Ol' Dan rides in a while later, and he's practically worked a whole day already. Up before dawn, boss chewin' on him 'cause they're shippin' cattle and them cows are spillin' everywhere. And now he's runnin' behind schedule. The wife is in the driveway with three kids loaded up in the mini van and she's screamin' at him that they're late for church. He unloads his saddle as fast as he can, backs into the door of the saddle house, turns, and puts his saddle on the rack. The coyote was chained to the rack by a dog collar Pelham put on him, but, when he saw that light, he bolted for the open door. The chain wraps around Dan's boot, and he gets jerked right off his feet. Lands with a thud. Meanwhile, the coyote hits the end of that chain. Wham! He was rebounding and flyin' back towards Dan. But the door closes. Now it's pitch-dark and Dan don't know what kind of critter it is but he ain't waitin' around to find out. He jumps up on the saddle rack. That animal is hissin' and growlin' somewheres in the pitch-black. Dan's wife ain't seen nothin'. She's layin' on the horn and screamin' for him to hurry up. He finally got out of there, wonderin' all the while who his friends were that done it.

Pelham grew up in eastern Texas, a small town called White-house, just south of Tyler. His father was an engineer for a couple of different companies, but Pelham always knew he wanted the cowboy life. Did some college in Stephenville, but he was one liked to play more than study and didn't last long on campus. Had to make money and wasn't established yet as a cowhand. Landed in the oil fields. Worked as a roughneck on the drilling rigs for three years. Feller there named Heavy. Weighed about three hundred twenty-five. He was a big ol' boy for sure. Was still in his twenties, but his blood pressure could have popped a champagne cork. Just sky high. He'd bring a bucket of fried chicken to work, and he'd get to eatin' it and shakin' from that blood pressure. The roughnecks, led by Pelham, would be tellin' him that his wife was tryin' to kill him for the insurance money with all that fried chicken she fed him. He'd start gettin' mad at them and grab another drumstick. He'd shake it at them, and his body would shake some more, too. After he finished lunch, he'd come after them. They'd wrassle. Them fellers, in their early twenties, worked all day, lifted heavy stuff. They got real strong.

Got to where they could pick up damn near anything. Pelham could lift Heavy off his feet. He done it all the time. Get Heavy riled. Pick him up, shake him, turn him loose. Because Heavy didn't have no air, he couldn't last long. Pelham would get to playin' with him and get him all wound up. Heavy would chase him. They'd wrassle. In no time, Heavy'd be down on all fours, gaspin' for breath. Pelham would be sittin' on him. They loved to get him mad. But they loved him, too.

Pelham hated the oil field work, but lasted long enough to get out of debt and buy a pickup, trailer, horses, and saddle. That's when he got on full-time at Broseco, makin' about one-third what he made on the rig, but weren't no turnin' back. He was livin' the life. There in east Texas, you put hay up all summer long. Then you put it out all winter. Endless cycle. An old cowboy told Pelham he had to go west. That's when he found the job in Gail, in Borden County, south of Lubbock. After ten years, he come up to the Panhandle. Ran yearlings for two years, but got burned out on that. Spade Ranch was hiring. They were a good outfit. Pelham works on two ranches—one north of Canadian that's about five thousand acres and one near Shamrock that's about eight thousand acres. One runs a cow-calf operation, the other runs yearlings.

One time on the ranch at Gail, Pelham was on horseback with the foreman. Bit of a self-important feller, knew everything, and he was tellin' Pelham how to do this and that. It was springtime, and them grasshoppers out there could get big when it turned warm. Three or four inches long. Big as a cigar and juicy. Jumbo grasshoppers. So big they could hardly fly, but they still got some getup.

Well, the wind picks up, forty or fifty miles an hour. They're makin' a big circle route on horseback, and the feller is tellin'

Pelham how to cowboy. Jason had just swapped out some of the old horses on the ranch. Bought new ones. Foreman was on a five-year-old filly and she had a real light mouth. If you barely touch her, she'd stop *now*. Just real sensitive all around. Didn't hardly need spurs on her neither. She had plenty of go. So this feller is talkin' away, and he's got too much spur on her and too much bit. Wind was howling in their faces. He's turns to Pelham, makin' his points and tryin' to be heard over the wind. When he turns back, lookin' straight ahead, one of them big juicy jumbos, abetted by a fifty-mile-per-hour blow, come up and smashed him right between the eyes. Right between 'em. Thing splattered like a water balloon. Foreman jerked on them reins. Filly reared up tall on her hind legs. Feller let out a bloodcurdling scream that could've emptied perdition. Pierced the air like judgment day come. He grabbed that filly around her neck to keep from fallin' and dug in his spurs for no reason known to man. Horse took off like a demon was settin' on its back. Shot out of a cannon. She got about two licks out there, and now he's in front of the saddle, now he's behind it, now he's hangin' off her flank. Looked like he was trick-ridin' in the circus. Pelham was laughin' so hard at the chain reaction that he slumped over and fell off his horse. Tears were streamin' down his face. Feller finally gets control of himself and the horse and rides back over. He's hotter than an empty six-shooter.

He says, I guess you think that's funny.

Pelham hadn't been working there but a week. He'd stopped laughin' by then. He was standin' by his horse, tryin' to be serious and lookin' away out of respect. Aboard the filly, the feller was towerin' over him. Pelham looked up at him. The mess from that blowed-up grasshopper—looked like tobacco juice—was streaked all over the feller's face. He looked like a human windshield. Pelham started laughin' again. In a minute, he was laughin' so hard he had to take a knee. Feller turned and rode off. Pelham come in, put his stuff up, and figured he'd be gettin' a paycheck for the week and shown the door. But, next morning, foreman didn't say a word about it and never did after.

Another time down in Borden County, he gone to see Slick Sneed. Used to be the sheriff there. Itty-bitty guy. Kind of antsy. He'd retired and was raisin' dogs, big Alaskan malamutes. Pelham seen Slick at the dump, and they started talkin'. Slick mentions them dogs, knowin' Pelham had raised some himself. Slick invites him over to see the dogs. Pelham follows him back to his place in his truck, only a half-mile or so from where they was. They get to the house. No dogs in the backyard. Well, Slick used to keep some cows and had a big set of metal pens in the pasture. Pelham looks out there, and a dog was in each of them cow pens. There was also plenty of room for a dog to scoot out from under the horizontal steel pipe side rails.

He says, How in the world do you keep them dogs in there?

Slick says, Oh, they stay out there. Them's the dog pens.

So they walk over, and they're busy visiting the whole time.

Slick says, Be careful now.

Didn't hardly register with Pelham. Had no idea what Slick was talkin' about. There's dogs. There's pens. What's the worry? Talkin' to a cowboy. Not like there are a bunch of ornery bulls to be mindful of.

They opened the big metal gate and stepped in. Pelham is focused on the gate as he closes it. Slick's talkin' away. Pelham backs up, and his spurs hit the jackpot. What was keepin' them big dogs in the pens become abundant clear. Slick had an electric wire set up around the base of every one of them pens. That wire hung on Pelham's spurs and it starts shockin' the piss outta him.

He's wide-eyed, hair on end, standin' there shakin' and vibratin' like the warden just threw the switch. Couldn't move his legs for nothin'. His spurs start spinnin' like a windmill in a tornado from all that juice. He reaches out and grabs at Slick, who was all of about five-foot-six. Like I said, he was a bit of a nervous feller anyway. When Pelham got a hold of him and started transferrin' that current to Slick, now Slick is gettin' the hell shocked out of him, too. That wire still won't quit from Pelham's spurs. The two of them gone down in a heap. Pelham still holdin' on, both on the ground gettin' zapped and floppin' like beached bass. Pelham is screamin' by now, or maybe he had for a while. Slick is screamin' back at him or maybe at the moon. Now they get loose from each other, and Pelham kicks free from the hot wire. They're on their feet, standin' and facin' each other, bent over slightly at the waist, arms forward like two Greco-Roman wrestlers ready to do battle. They're still shakin' and yellin'. Slick gets his head a bit. He's trying to get out the gate and yellin' at Pelham not to touch him. Just then, one of them giant malamutes decides this loco feller presents a danger to society and charges from behind. He jumps up onto Pelham's back. Pelham still ain't recovered from his brush with capital punishment, and now there's a giant furball surgically attached to his back. He screams some more and pulls that dog's head over his shoulder. He bites him in the nose, wrassles him a while, then flings him to the ground. Dog run off. Pelham and Slick so shook up they're quakin' like kittens.

Jason says to him in a hoarse whisper—like they're in the middle of a World War Two firefight with Germans rather than in a cowpen with malamutes—Slick, we gotta get outta here.

Slick yells at the top of his lungs, even though Pelham's only two foot away: Stay right here, I'll open the gate.

He done it. They both got out and closed the gate after them.

Slick and Pelham both bent over, hands on knees, frightened and shakin' like they'd just encountered blood-suckin' aliens in a dark wood. That's when Jason realized he'd relieved himself in a liquid way down both legs of his Levis. Didn't hardly matter. His pride had long since been scattered like feed grain around Slick's pens. Pelham dropped to his knees and thanked everything that was holy he was still alive. Started laughin' and cryin' both.

Months later, seen Slick in town on the other side of the road. Slick looked at Pelham like he was diseased and Jason was gonna cross the street and infect him.

Pelham is a prankster, not a fighter, but he's also a tough cowboy and a pretty big feller. He'll fight if you make him, especially if you try to show him up in front of three girls. He'd just bought them drinks a few minutes before midnight in a bar over in Oklahoma. Soon as the hour strikes, why, the lights went on. A bouncer come over, and he's yellin' at Pelham to get the freak out of there. Done it in front of the girls, the other bouncers, and the whole bar.

Pelham didn't take kindly to that. Got up, walked over to the feller and says, Surely you can come up with a better way of askin' people to leave the bar. Lights come on two minutes after I just bought a whole bunch of beers, and you're yellin' at me to get the freak out.

Now the bouncer is redder than a matador's cape. Rather than yelling, he seems to be imitatin' a volcano on the verge of an historic event. Finally finds his voice again and hollers at Pelham to shut the bleep up and get the bleep out.

Pelham turns to the trio of females and says to them, You girls really don't even know who I am, do you?

What? He don't even know what he meant sayin' it, but by turnin' he was windin' up and divertin' attention. When he uncorked, he threw a haymaker like it was a chargin' bull and caught the bouncer square in the jaw. Feller collapsed like an implodin' building.

The other two bouncers were stunned a minute, too, not sure if they should help their buddy or deal with Pelham. But Jason's thought process was unambiguous. He was gettin' the hell out of there at high speed. He took off runnin'. When he got to the door, he seen another bouncer sittin' on a stool inside by the entrance. He weren't pickin' his nose, but he mighta been for all the attention he was payin' things. He was another big, heavy feller.

As Pelham comes flyin' by, the feller leans forward and says, What's going on? What's going on?

But he ain't about to get up off that stool. As Pelham gone by him, he slaps that feller upside the head at full speed. Whack! Bouncer tumbles off the stool and rolls across the floor. When Pelham burst through the door, he seen a bunch of highway patrol officers and local cops parked out there. He slows to a walk, gives them a big wave, gets in his pickup, and takes off. Later, he circled around and parked his truck on the backside of Denny's. Them girls come in a little later. He was glad they didn't know his name and couldn't tell it to no one.

They said, Oh my God, you're in so much trouble.

Yeah, maybe. Or maybe them bouncers will get a snake in a bottle next time if they ain't nicer.

The summer I met Pelham, he had an intern. Sounds funny, I know. A cowboy with an intern. Like an astronaut havin' an intern. Just don't seem to fit. Kid was from an ag college out East. He'd grown up on a small farm in Ohio. School wants all them ag students to have a full range of experience in the field, and a cattle ranch in the Texas Panhandle certainly gives you one far end of the full range, sure enough. Annnnnnnyway, kid drew the short straw and got assigned to Pelham for the summer. Jason takes me out to his truck with the intern. Inside a Coke bottle he has a live rattlesnake he caught. Calls it his alarm system. Holds that bottle up, and the snake starts to rattlin' and strikin' the plastic shell. Raises the heartbeat a notch.

Pelham wouldn't tell the kid how he caught the snake. Just attributed it to his 'superior herding ability.' But, at my insistence, he demonstrates, using a wooden pole that looks like it was unscrewed from a floor mop. He keeps it in the back of the truck, where it apparently gets regular use. He shows how he comes up behind a snake, dodges its strikes, and keeps jabbin' with that stick until he pins it in the back of the head with the pole. Then he picks it up and stuffs it head first in the Coke bottle—even though its head looks wider than the mouth of the container.

That reminds Pelham of a story. An American Breeders Service feller come out of Wisconsin one year to help with artificial insemination. It was the head guy, name of Wendell. All the cowboys was used to Pelham catchin' a rattler for the visiting ABS guy, so they was on Jason to catch one for Wendell. Pelham done it and put the rattler in a gallon pickle jar. Wendell gets there in a rent car about eight o'clock, but usually them ABS fellers don't show up until ten, after the cowboys got everything sorted out.

Well, one of the other ABS guys that Pelham knows, Max, told Jason previous to have a go at Wendell. So he did.

Pelham says to him, Those damn ABS guys don't ever get here until noon. Worthless suckers are drunk and laid out most of the time. Don't know what the hell you're doing here so early. You tell them this time, by God, when they get here, we're gonna kick their asses.

Pelham just kept eatin' on him.

Wendell's eyes were big as dinner plates. Wendell says, Well, I'm gonna call 'em. I just can't get any service here.

Pelham says, Course you can't get any service down here by these damn pens. Get your ass up on top of that hill. Get up there. You'll have service. Anybody got any sense can do that.

So Wendell scurries up the hill. He calls Max and tells him he's dealin' with a crazy cowboy who is pissed off about everything and to watch himself when he gets there.

Max says, No, no. It'll be all right. I'll be there in a few minutes.

Wendell lingered on that hill a while but he come back down and Pelham eatin' on him some more until Max shows up. Now Max and Pelham get into it, and it looks like they're fixin' to have a big fight. But then, they couldn't hold it in no more, and their screamin' turned to laughin'.

Wendell realized he'd been had, but was still a little wary of things when Max asked Pelham if he'd given Wendell his present yet. Pelham reaches around and hands Wendell that pickle jar with the live rattlesnake inside. Wendell holds it out, a little shaky, not wantin' to offend his hosts. Straining, cringing, serious, he says, God, I just don't think I can take it on the plane with me.

Cowboys got a laugh out of that. Wendell wanted to know how Pelham got the snake in the jar. So Jason showed him how to work the snake with the pole and got him pinned. Lifted him up by the head and held him high for pictures. But you hold a rattlesnake long enough, they get to corkscrewin' their body. When they get turned around, those fangs gonna come out and get you in the finger. That can make a mess of your whole day. After you've held a few rattlers in your life, you develop a clock in your head, tellin' you when it's time to turn loose. The time comes all of a sudden.

Alarm clock gone off in Pelham's head.

He says, Back up, Wendell. Back up quick!

Pelham drops the snake on the ground and that rattler wants to leave pretty bad. He could have gone any of three hun'erd sixty degrees, but he chose the one degree that pointed right at Wendell. He gone that way hissin' and strikin'. Wendell took off runnin', headin' for cell phone high country.

Hope the intern kid survives the summer.

The Outlaw Riley Bradstreet

Riley Bradstreet's life was defined in a brief moment when he was barely more than a kid.

Been around guns all his life. Family had a place north on Sweetwater Creek from where he lives now in Mobeetie. At night, they'd go huntin' turkeys that roosted on the Thorten's place, the ranch that bordered theirs on the north—him, his brother, and Little Joe Kelly, on horseback. There were no roads between the ranches, so no one could usually catch them. But one night, there were no turkeys on the south side of Thorten's place so they had to cross a county road onto the north side of his ground. Only one place along the whole fence line—on both sides of the road for several miles—where there were gates directly opposite one another. Everywhere else, them gates was offset, meanin' you had to ride in the road for a spell if you wanted to cross from the south pasture onto the north. Riley maybe done a little huntin' out of season before, and he knew you didn't never want to get caught in the road with contraband and no place to go when the game warden drove up sudden.

Annnnnnnyway, they rode through them gates to the north pasture, went over a rise, found some turkeys roosting in the trees, shot into them, and got three. All of that took some time and raised a ruckus, what with shots fired and turkeys gobbling. So, by the time they'd gathered up them turkeys and tied them onto the horses and then come back over that rise, why, the game warden was parked in the road, right between them two gates. Ol' man Thorten heard the noise and give the warden a call. It was pitch-black so the warden couldn't see them. Riley was usually one step ahead of the law, even as a kid. So he takes Little Joe Kelly's turkey and tells him to ride west a spell, punch the sky fulla holes, and then come a hailin' it.

Little Joe done that. He rode west a mile on Trigger Foot and then cut loose like it was him and Davey Crockett at the Alamo with Santa Anna bringin' it. Bam! Bam! Bam! The game warden fired up his car and squealed out of there, headin' west. Riley and his brother Clifford, with them turkeys tied on, trotted down to the road and had both gates open when Little Joe come a flyin' down that hill on Trigger Foot, like he was makin' for the finish at the Kentucky Derby. Blew through them open gates. Riley closed 'em up behind. They made it home and climbed up onto the barn roof. For a while, they could hardly keep their sides from splittin' as they watched the headlights of the game warden's car pacing back and forth, up and down the road and all around Thorten's place, tryin' to figure out what in tarnation was going on.

Growin' up, Riley's father always had horses. When he was away, 'fore they were even teens, Riley and his two brothers would ride an old mare named Flicka. Their towheads didn't even reach up to the middle of Flicka's flank, so gettin' a saddle on the old girl was never part of the plan. Ridin' bareback was no problem, except they needed to find a way to mount the horse, which looked as tall as a windmill to a ten year old. They'd get themselves a coffee can from their mother's kitchen, fill it with milo, and set it in the trough. While Flicka was busy feedin', two of the brothers would give the smallest one a boost up on to Flicka. Then Riley would give his other brother a boost while the youngest was pullin' him up. Finally, Riley would get up on the edge of the trough and leap aboard. Using baling twine as a bridle, the three brothers would be off on an adventure around the countryside.

Riley's great-grandfather was Joseph Riley Bradstreet from Georgia. Fought in the Civil War for the South but was captured. He got tuberculosis and was fixin' to die in prison, but the Yanks said they'd turn him out if he agreed not to carry a gun and become a freighter—which is drivin' a supply wagon. He done the deal. After the war, ended up drawin' a pension from both the North and the South. Married a preacher's daughter when he got back to Georgia, but the carpetbaggers made life hell, and he left for parts West. Ended up in Montague County, Texas, just south of the Red River, where they raised ten kids plus three more by an older daughter whose no-account husband run out on her. From there, members of the family began migratin' west and north into the Panhandle. Riley's grandfather was William Riley. Truman Olin was his dad. He is Truman Riley.

When Riley was a kid, he used to practice fast drawing his pistol like a gunfighter. Not sure why he done it with a loaded gun, but, late one Friday afternoon when he was sixteen, pistol fired off 'fore it cleared his holster, and he shot himself through the thigh. Bullet come out on the underside of his leg, above the back of his knee. He was outside at the time. He hid the gun and holster. Blood hadn't spread much yet, so, except for a slight limp and his face twisted in pain, he was able to walk by his father like nothin' had happened. Only thing he feared more than the physical consequences of shootin' himself in the leg were the physical consequences of tellin' his father he had shot himself in the leg.

He got inside and gone to his mother. She was at the sink.

Told her he'd shot himself in the leg. Had to tell her twice 'fore the message got through. She put him on a divan, pulled down his pants, and spun him over to see where the bullet gone in and come out. When she pulled off his boot, the lead fell out. When the bullet exited the wound, it hit a seam in his pants and dropped down into his boot. She got him to the hospital in Shamrock. They dressed the wound, but Riley didn't like it there. Every time he hopped to the bathroom to take a leak, three nurses were watchin' him. If he shuffled around that toilet to block their view, they could see his butt pokin' out the back of that smock they made him wear. So he called his mother and told her to bring him some clothes. She brought him pajamas instead. He waited until it was dark, put on them pajamas, and got the hell outta Dodge. Every law in the country was lookin' for him, the barefoot, pajama-wearin' hospital escapee with a bullet wound in his leg. Riley walked over to his grandpa's house there in Shamrock.

Grandpa took one look at him—barefoot, wearin' pajamas, sweatin' from the walk, and blood seepin' through the bandage and stainin' the pajamas—shakes his head and says, Only you, Riley.

Riley says, Got any clothes fit me, Granddad?

Grandpa got him some clothes, and Riley talked him into takin' him up to Wheeler, where he met some friends. It was Saturday night. While the law and the rest of his family was out searchin' for him, he was at the picture show.

Riley made it through the ninth grade. Hired out after that. Worked for Thorten in the summers because he was familiar with his ground. Then worked for the Rafter Seven Ranch along-side some legendary cowboys. Tints Williams was one. Know it sounds like he was named for some kind of Renaissance painter, but that ain't it. Variation of Tiny. The i in Tints said like an i. Course, Tints wasn't Tiny at all. Riley punched cows with him a spell. Some of the pens they'd use during spring roundups only got a workout once a year, so weeds would grow up in them rest of the time, and the heelers couldn't hardly throw their loops. See, a heeler tosses his lasso just ahead of a calf's hind legs, and the calf pretty much steps into the loop. Cowboy then drags the calf by its hind legs to the fire, where it gets branded. But the weeds were so high in them pens that they was scratchin' the bellies of them calves, and you couldn't hardly throw a loop normal.

Tints says, Them weeds too tall. We gonna have to shuck it for a while.

Riley was still a young man then, but he'd been workin' cattle for a spell. Ain't never heard of shuckin'. So he just nodded his head like he knew all about it and kept an eye on Tints so he could do whatever it was Tints was about to do. What Tints done was build a loop bigger than normal and toss it over the calf's head, not drag his slack. Let the calf walk through it. And then Tints would pick it up on their back feet. Shuckin'. Weren't long before the weeds got all beat down, and they could go back to heelin' normal. Tints was a ring roper. Won a lotta money doing rodeo. But Riley liked him 'cause he was a real hand. He was a cowboy. Roped in the pasture as good as he roped in the arena.

Toots South was known in them parts for cowboyin', too. Worked for Brainards. I'll be tellin' you about them later. Toots taught Riley how to let a horse learn how to cow. A good cuttin' horse will respond to a cow without waitin' for directions from a rider. Toots taught Riley how to let his horse develop cow sense. Too many riders is too controllin'. Toots taught him how the horse can develop an instinct for dealin' with cows if you let it. But it ain't quite that easy. You have to have cow in you to help a horse get cow.

Roy B. Sessions was one of a kind. Worked for Brainards, too. He was a magician with a rope. He'd walk through a herd and never disturb it. His horse looked like it was half-asleep, and he'd toss his rope left and right. It would sound just as soft as wind through a pine tree while it was finding its mark. Nowadays, them boys whoopin' and ridin', raisin' heck, and churnin' up the herd. None of that from Roy B. He could throw overhand on both sides of his horse or toss underhand. Them fellers like Roy B. knew a thing or two about people as well as livestock. One spring, after Roy B. been ropin' colts and branding for twenty-five years, he, Riley, and the owner of the ranch were standing out there in the round pen.

Roy B. says, Mr. Brainard, this kid is gonna rope the horses this year.

Roy B. been teachin' Riley how to rope. Riley was ready, but Roy B. didn't tell him the week before what he was plannin'. Didn't tell him the night before neither. Didn't tell him that morning. Didn't want the kid sweatin' it. So when the time come for him to step up, time come. Riley didn't miss a loop that day. Threw forty-eight loops and roped forty-eight colts. There was one where he roped both a colt and the top of a post the horse was up agin in that round pen, but that don't hardly count as a miss.

Roy B. was old school when it come to lettin' a horse know who was boss. One time, Riley was breakin' a horse and got bucked off. Roy B. was in the pen on horseback. As he come by Riley, who was dustin' himself off, Roy B. was buildin' a loop.

He says, Is your saddle on good?

Riley nodded, not sure what was fixin' to commence.

Now picture that bronc, riderless but still buckin' and brawlin'.

Roy B. roped the saddle horn while it was tossin' like a cork on an angry sea. Then he parked his horse. Brought it to a full stop. When that colt reached the end of the rope, it was in midair. Roy B. jerked him to the ground. Bronc fell hard. Knocked the wind out of him and the stuffing, too. He was a lot easier to ride after that.

One time, Riley was ridin' a young bronc they were thinkin' about keepin' for a stud. This was on a spread north of the Canadian River. They'd been sortin' cattle all mornin' and the bronc been givin' Riley trouble that whole time, too—wallowin', balkin', doing a bit of everything.

Roy B. seen it. He says, Well, you go ahead and gather them cattle, and then make it over to the corral.

As quick as Riley finished up and rode through that gate, Roy B. jumps off his horse and closes the gate with Riley inside that pen on the troublesome bronc.

Roy B. picked him up a cottonwood limb about six foot long and says, You ride. I'll whup.

He give the bronc a bath with that club. Beat him good on the hindquarters, right behind the saddle. Give Riley an eventful ride. That colt bucked into the water trough and out of it and back into it and back out of it. Looked to Riley like about every blow gonna come down on his own head, but Roy B. never did brain him. That sort of trainin' ain't something the Humane Society would endorse, but Roy B. sure took the balk outta that bronc. Made a good stud horse after that.

Riley ended up being a pretty good roper. Looped a couple coyotes in his day. Had one serious wreck though. Bunch of cowboys was ridin' out for the day on high ground. Riley was the first one they dropped off. Meanin', he was the first to peel off and drop down to a creek to round up strays. Well, he no sooner

fell out and started down the hill when he spotted a coyote in the
tall clover along a creek bank. Built a fire in his horse, and the
chase was on. They were on the same side of the creek, so Riley
didn't give the creek no mind. It was runnin' east and west, and
the coyote was runnin' east. They were flyin'. Riley almost got the
jump on him and got a loop ready to throw.

Sudden, that coyote took a hard right turn and dove down
into the creek. Stream was about as wide as a country road with
five-foot banks on both sides. Talked before about a horse got
some cow in him. Riley was ridin' a big yellow horse that had
some coyote in him. Had the spirit of the chase in him, too.
When that critter made a hard right turn, so did the horse. Only
problem is, ain't no horse alive could've cleared that creek and
made it over to the other side. Instead, ol' yeller, he gone soarin'
over that creek, but his arc weren't high enough or long enough.
When he come down, he crashed into the far bank. Vertical wall
is a better description of that midget cliff on the other side of the
stream. Riley went over the top of yeller and got to skiddin' on
his belly. Got a mouthful of prairie in the process. The show sure
entertained them cowboys watchin' it all from the high ground.
When Riley finally stopped slidin', he wasn't none the worse for
wear, 'cept a thumb got bent back he used for a brake. Yellow
didn't fare so well. Knocked his shoulder down, but he was good
in a few days.

Happened early one mornin' after he'd been out the night
before huntin' coyotes with Daryl and his best friend, Butch.
Coyote crossed the road. Daryl was in the front seat and shot
twice with Riley's gun. He cocked a third time, but the coyote
crossed out of the light so he didn't shoot. Uncocked it instead.
In a six-gun that skips one round. They were out almost 'til dawn.

When they were comin' home, Riley picked up that revolver and was shootin' stop signs until it was snappin'—until it was empty. The hammer was hittin' on empty cylinders. Except it wasn't. There was one live bullet.

They reached home, and Riley put on a coffeepot. He'd been practicin' fast drawing six-guns for years. Butch had just got started on it and bought himself a gun, but he didn't like his gun as much as he liked Riley's. So Riley give it to him, and he used Butch's. They were standin' right in front of the cookstove, fast drawing on each other. No more than two or three feet apart, just enough to clear the guns. No tellin' how many times Butch drew on Riley with that live round in there and either uncocked it or skipped it. Set the hammer back down on it instead of snappin' it.

Did it for a while, and then they switched guns.

Riley was crossin' the living room floor when Butch yelled, Now!

Riley turned, drew fast, and pulled the trigger. Gun finally found that bullet been spinnin' around in there. Butch was shot just above the heart. Riley threw his gun on the couch and caught Butch 'fore he fell. Daryl was there in a second. Butch was dead weight real quick. They got him stretched out and called the law and an ambulance. Butch was dead on arrival at the hospital. Law questioned Riley for a while and then put him in jail. Long, hard night in the lockup for a kid just out of his teens that had killed his best friend by accident.

Way Riley tells it, Daryl backed him. Even Butch's parents believed it was an accident, but the law wanted him up for murder. Law brung Riley to a room and told him they didn't think he'd done it on purpose, but, if he didn't go along with what they said, they'd indict him for murder. They asked if he remembered four years before when the schoolhouse was burglarized. He did. Even knew the two kids who done it.

Law said, Wheeler County won't be happy if we just turn you loose. You're gonna plead guilty to that burglary, and you're gonna get five years probation.

That's what happened. Two days later, he went back to work, haulin' bales of cotton to Shamrock. When he reached Shamrock with his full load, two highway patrol cars were waitin' for him. They followed him down toward the water tower and pulled him over.

Officer come over and says, Looks like you already fouled up, Riley. You're operatin' a commercial vehicle without a commercial license. We're gonna have to revoke your probation.

Just about everyone in those days operated trucks with only an operator's license. Law assumed Riley was doing the same, but a feller he worked for had once stopped off with him to get a commercial license. Riley flashed that license to the highway patrol officer and escaped prison. But he knew then that the law was after him. That's when he decided he had to go cowboy on remote ranches for a spell to avoid anymore traps. That's what he done, and he met Roy B., Tints, and Toots. Started out at Patch Creek Ranch in Roberts County. Ol' boy who was sheriff there wouldn't go along with them others who wanted to get Riley.

Said, The kid is workin' hard up there. Ain't botherin' no one. Leave him be.

So the law got two deputies out of Ochiltree County to come down to Patch Creek and harass him regular. Just a pokin' at him, askin' if he seen Sam Hill lately, been to this town or that town, or knew about this theft or that theft. Weren't even in their jurisdiction. Riley had enough of it after a while. When they come to pay their calls, they had to stop off at the yard gate. Riley's a big man.

These days, he has a white beard and a shock of disheveled salt-and-pepper hair when he ain't wearin' his trademark ten-gallon black hat. Annnnnnnyway, one time, he stuck a six-gun in his belt and marched out there to the yard gate when they come.

Both them deputies seen him comin', grabbed a handful of air, and said, We just come to talk. We just come to talk.

Riley says, Well then, get your talkin' over with, and leave. And don't ever come back.

They knew they were out of their jurisdiction, so they left and never come back. He made it through the five years of probation, but all that after Butch's shooting established a pattern between Riley and the law. Says he could hardly live with himself after the shooting, tryin' to get all that straight in his mind as a kid. Sometimes thought his head would just flat-out explode. And all the while, everywhere he turned, someone was tryin' to lock him up. Said for a spell he took baths all the time, just tryin' to wash that feeling of terrible guilt off him.

Later, he was livin' with a gal for a time. Only dime he was makin' then was either on a tractor or a horse. But his lady friend's mother worked at a department store and had the computer set up somehow so it wouldn't record all the dresses shipped in. According to Riley, she and her mother would go sell them extra dresses that weren't being recorded. Riley says he also found out later she was runnin' drugs up into the Panhandle from Dallas. Sheriff and the FBI raided his place, thinkin' he was involved. The only thing they found was a syringe as big as a caulking tube with a needle as long as a car antenna. They accused him of shootin' up with it. But it still had some penicillin in it from the last horse he used it on, and the law left empty-handcuffed.

Riley had another run-in with the law when he was workin' with BJ Ritter for TC Harvey up in Gruver. Got a call in the office sayin' a Harvey steer, a stray, been picked up on the adjacent ranch. Caller said they'd stuck the cow in one of the pens by the railroad yard. Come get him anytime. Said there were some other strays, calves, there with him. Riley stuck his horse in a trailer and left the feedlot, headin' for town. BJ went off in a water truck in another direction, but then circled around and met Riley at the railroad yard. Said he was worried Riley wouldn't be able to cut out that steer on his own. They done it. Cut that steer out from the calves, put him in the truck, and left.

Ain't but a few days and they had Riley up for rustlin' all of them strays that were in the pen with the steer. Someone who didn't own them calves come along after Riley, loaded them onto a trailer, and disappeared. The law questioned Riley about it once, twice, three times. It gone on for quite a few days. Everyone seen Riley leave the feed lot alone. No one knew BJ been there with him at the pens by the railroad yard, and Riley didn't say nothin' about him being there. Kind of the code. Didn't want to drag BJ into something he didn't belong in. Well, he and BJ turned out a bunch of cutter bulls north of Gruver on wheat. Too weak to turn into steers when they were first born. BJ and Riley was prowlin' them bulls, ropin' a couple at a time and cuttin' them. They had one stretched out on the ground, cuttin' him, when the law showed up. Texas Rangers, county sheriff, and deputy all come drivin' in, right there on the wheat field. Riley gets off the bull and walks over.

Sheriff says, Well, we got you, Riley. Today's the day. We're gonna arrest you. We know you did it.

Ol' BJ was hearin' all this, and he got off the bull and come over. He says, Hey, I was there, and I'm gonna tell you what went on.

BJ's father was a county commissioner, and BJ was a feller

who told it like it was. When he was done tellin' the law what had happened, they left, hangdog. Thought they could close the books on that one, but it weren't Riley done it. He'd escaped their clutches once again.

Ain't just the law. Riley has had his share of trouble with women over the years, too. One time, not long after he was married, it was a Sunday, and he was supposed to meet a feller who wanted to sell him a horse. Bradstreet and bride come out to the home place. Riley's dad and his sister were there, and they was fixin' to have a big dinner together. Riley figured his wife ought to stay around and help while he was off to that horse trade because there was things said at them horse trades that maybe a woman shouldn't be hearin'. Start off talkin' about the horse. Then it seems the fellers involved get to talkin' about each other's shortfalls. Then they talk about each other's ancestry in unpleasant terms. Things get said, you know. If a wife is there, maybe a husband suddenly has to defend her honor. So Riley told his wife she best stay put.

She said, No, I'm going with you.

He said, No, you don't need to go to this deal.

She says, I'm a goin'.

The home place had a circular drive that went all around the house 'fore it headed out to the road. Riley's truck was parked so he had to circle all around that drive 'fore headin' out. Well, he got in his truck, and she followed him and got in. He didn't drive more than twenty feet 'fore he stopped and again explained about honor, cussin', and horse tradin'. She wouldn't get out. He come around to the passenger door and put her out. He started 'round that driveway some more, and now she's lopin' alongside and got her foot up on the runnin' board. Opened that door on the fly and dove in. The Outlaw stopped the truck, and now he's cussin' her while explainin' about honor, horse trades, and cussin', but she ain't going nowhere except to that horse trade. He come around the truck, put her out again, and locked the door this time.

He started up again, but he was still only about halfway around that circular drive. The family was startin' to gather and line the route. His wife starts runnin' along beside the pickup, and she jumps in the truck bed. Riley starts poundin' on the back window, tellin' her to stay and help with dinner and warnin' of the corruptin' vice that surrounds most horse tradin'. By now, the entire extended family going back several generations is holdin' a reunion all around the circular drive. Riley stops the truck and puts her out.

He starts forward again. He's about three-quarters of the way around the drive now and picks up a little speed so his wife won't try nothin'. But she only run faster, and now she dives into the truck bed and rolls to a stop against the side wall. Riley is fit to be tied, which gave him an idea. He glanced up and seen a piggin' string hangin' off the rearview mirror. He jams on the brakes and runs her out of that truck bed. Flanked her, and wrestled her down. Got her arms together, brung her knees up, and tied that piggin' string around her wrists and legs at the knee. Left her on the ground by the driveway and drove off to his horse trade. Hog-tied his own wife is what he done. When he got back it was a rather quiet meal filled with dark stares, but he got a good deal on the horse.

Riley cowboyed until about ten years ago. Was always interested in raisin' horses, but he was more interested in riding them while he could, which is why cowpunchin' won out all them years as his main job. Just got too old for that now. Started breedin' quarter horses. Does a lotta other things, too. Hauls scrap iron.

Manages someone else's cattle ranch. And he has a company named Outlaw's Roost Equipment that sells backhoes, 'dozers, and farm tractors.

The Outlaw's becomin' downright respectable.

The Iconoclast

Stanley wanted a couple monkeys. Pets? Maybe. But that's thinking too conventionally. This is Stanley Marsh 3, so the whim factor is high. Basically, Stanley just wanted a couple of tame monkeys. Attaching some sort of functionality to the idea, like 'pets,' is pretty much beside the point. So he put a pair of them on a small island in the middle of a pond in the backyard behind Toad Hall, the house where he lives on Frying Pan Ranch, one of the most celebrated ranches in Texas history.

Annnnnnnyway, the monkeys didn't last long. Two bad dogs came onto the ranch, swam out to the island, and dispatched the critters. Grandkids were upset. Stanley decided to give them a proper funeral. But then he had another idea. He was down at the mall and saw a display in the window of a sporting goods store. Snorkel gear. Mannequins dressed up in masks, flippers, snorkels, and flowered swimwear. They were taking down the display just then, and Stanley decided to buy all the stuff.

Have to take a timeout here and tell you about fishing down this way. Lake Meredith is a man-made reservoir about fifty miles north of Amarillo. Huge dammed canyon with a lot of fingers off it. Some of those inlets are reserved for water skiing and others for fishermen who run trotlines. Stanley doesn't look kindly on them. Calls them meat fishermen. Those trotlines are as long as a city block, with a hook every six feet or so. The fishermen fix the hooks with shrimp and stink bait, wear miner's goggles, and work the trotline by moonlight.

So Stanley and one of his young artist friends, Michael, got the monkeys, which they'd put on ice and stored in a Styrofoam cooler, and drove up to Lake Meredith with a blowup two-man dinghy they'd bought. It was the middle of a hot summer day. No fishermen were around. They dressed the monkeys in the snorkel gear and flowered swimwear. They loaded up the dinghy, rowed out to the middle of a trotline, lifted it out of the water, attached the monkeys to adjacent hooks, and rowed away.

Never went back. Never heard in the papers or elsewhere what happened, but Stanley figures that, when the fishermen found those dead snorkel monkeys in flowered swimwear hooked on their trotline, they likely quit drinking, found God, or both.

Winston Churchill called the Soviet Union a riddle, wrapped in a mystery inside an enigma, but he could just as well have been describing Stanley Marsh 3. Not III. 3. III is pretentious. He's not easy to pigeonhole. Businessman, artist, prankster, eccentric, and philanthropist. But all that doesn't begin to capture him. His father was one of three partners in an oil and gas business that made all three among the richest men in Texas back in the day. Stanley was born, raised, and lived almost his whole life in Amarillo, except for a spell in California as a kid and going to college in Philadelphia. He married Wendy Bush O'Brien Marsh, one of two primary heirs to the Frying Pan Ranch. Stanley is seventy-two now and retired, but owned and ran a string of top-rated TV stations in Texas. But all that is backstory, as they say. Stanley is mostly known for his art and his pranks, although there's no separating the two most of the time. In 1974, he collaborated with a California art group called Ant Farm and buried ten tail-finned Caddies nose-first, at an angle and in a row, on open prairie west of town. Called it the Cadillac Ranch. Caught people's eye and their fancy, and made Stanley famous.

His office, which takes up the twelfth floor of a high-rise in Amarillo, isn't like any office you've ever laid eyes on. Stepping off the elevator is like stepping through Alice's looking glass. Instead of a receptionist, a young man with floppy hair, as skinny as a rock star, comes out of a floor-to-ceiling glass enclosure that runs the length of the building on one side. This is Michael, who is half-artist, half-office assistant, half-merry prankster. I know that's too many halves, but I told you, we're in an alternate universe now. The studio houses desks for a half-dozen artist-office assistants. Not sure a lot of art has been made there recently. Junk is everywhere, piled high. Old everything. Looks like yard sale remains. Old TV, old sewing machine, old microwave, old couch, crud atop every flat surface, and paint-dribbled, all-weather carpet that looks like it was used more as a canvas than a floor covering. A curbside-sized garbage can is overflowing. A grocery cart. Ladders. Stools stacked upside down atop one another, welded together and painted silver. A vacuum cleaner inexplicably duct-taped to a chair, as if being held captive. Then again, just about everything in the room is inexplicable. Most notable are the blowup, air-filled, plastic billiard balls the size of knee-high boulders that are scattered about. This is their winter home. In summer, Stanley has them placed on a large rectangle of green grass the size of a basketball court out on the Frying Pan so that, from the air, the getup looks like a gigantic pool table.

One of the occupants of the glass enclosure is LBK. Stands for Longboard Kid. But nobody calls him that anymore. Like, it's not International Business Machines these days. It's just IBM. And LBK is just LBK. He's not Longboard Kid anymore. His real name? Hell, who knows? It's been lost to history.

LBK shows me around the glass-enclosed studio, but picks through it is more like it. I ask him about three desks, each of which is occupant-less. He points. That's where Tom sits. And that's where Bill sits.

He says, They're in rehab. They'll be out in a month.

When I come back to visit a second time, Stanley walks me over to the studio. This time, there are about eight floppy-haired, tattooed skinnies smoking like James Dean. They jump to their feet when Stanley enters and scurry over like the dinner bell just rang. They step forward one at a time and shake my hand as Stanley introduces them.

Hi, I'm John.

Hi, I'm George.

I'm Paul.

I'm Ringo.

Whatever. We get to about the sixth guy, and Stanley has a quizzical look on his face. Doesn't seem to know him.

The kid pipes up, Hi, I'm Fred. I just got here from the bus station.

I wonder if there's a big sign on the wall of the bus station that says, Attention, all wayward artistic youth. Proceed directly to Stanley Marsh's office.

Or maybe Stanley just sends over Michael or LBK to meet every incoming Greyhound.

Right next to the glass enclosure is a round, brass-lined, and bookshelf-filled office modeled after Captain Nemo's library on the *Nautilus*. In it resides Stan Marsh, Stanley's adopted son, who looks like a youngish church elder. Hair neatly trimmed and combed. Clothes washed and pressed. Soft-spoken and polite. He's as straight as an arrow. The contrast with the occupants of the art colony next door couldn't be more striking. Stan looks like a thirty-five-year-old Pat Boone who just parachuted into this fun house. He manages all of the family's ranch operations.

Around the corner from him, on the way to Stanley's office, just past the round-edged, foam-filled furniture in a central open space that looks like it got lost on the way to a preschool, is another serious guy in an office. He stares at six computer screens arranged snugly in a cluster. He handles Stanley's stock trading. He doesn't smile, and his gaze doesn't detach from the screens.

Then there's Stanley's really large office. It's sprawling and full of oversized, abstract expressionist paintings. Stanley is reclining on a couch, ancient Greek ruler-style, reading a book. He reads one a day. Behind him is a print of Andy Warhol's Marilyn Monroe. Stanley adores Marilyn Monroe. The print fills the wall. Bigger than a man. Much wider than one, too. Every painting in the room is both. On another wall is a Jackson Pollock forgery. On another wall, filling it, is a Jasper Johns. There are two Franz Klines and a Kenneth Noland. But that's this week. He rotates them. He's wanted to be surrounded by big abstract, expressionist paintings ever since he used to see them at museums in Philly when he was in college. Stanley only wanted the best, but he didn't want to pay $25 million for any of them, much less each of them, so he decided to just fake them.

But these aren't your everyday forgeries. That's not how Stanley works. These are genuine, authentic forgeries. He found an artist named Tom Boberg who could copy anything. He and Stanley got every biography they could lay their hands on about abstract expressionists and any books that talked about their techniques. They studied their paintings. Like with Pollock. What paint he used, how he mixed it, how he applied it, and how he layered it. Flew Boberg off to museums around the country. Then he sent Boberg off to the glass-enclosed studio for eight years, and he turned out dozens of original forgeries: Pollock, de Kooning, and Rothko. Stanley says the forgery thing is cool, not a problem, because he's not going to profit from them. He just wants to look at them. And they won't ever leave his office. They don't fit on the elevators.

For twenty years, Phillip Periman, a friend of Stanley's, has been taking his family to a dude ranch in Wyoming. Lot of fancy folks from the East Coast go there, too, and Phil got to know a former director of the Museum of Modern Art in New York.

One year, he said to the guy, I got a friend who has forged a bunch of abstract expressionists.

Ex-MoMA guy said, No, you can't do that. You can't forge that stuff. It's impossible.

So the next time Phil went out to that dude ranch he brought along some photos of Stanley's forgeries.

Art director guy said, Holy you-know-what. If these get into the marketplace, how is anyone going to know the difference between them and the real ones in three or four hundred years?

Art isn't exactly sacred to Stanley. At a party, he once told the director of the J. Paul Getty Museum, which had recently bought Van Gogh's *Irises* for somewhere north of $50 million, that he should conduct a corporate-style raid on the painting, cut it up into little pieces, and sell each of the irises for a few million each. Make a little money on the deal.

Opposite the reclining Stanley, in his office, where he can keep a close eye on it, a computer screen is projected, again covering the whole wall to a height of twelve feet. On it are all of his stocks and tracking devices to show how the prices are fluctuating. The symmetry is perfect. There are two very distinct sides to Stanley Marsh 3. There's the prankster artist who defies conventionality, and there's the serious businessman who went to Wharton and built a media empire. The fact that the artworks and the stock-filled computer screen are virtually the same size—and both larger than life—visually capture his evenly split jumbo personality and the equal importance of both business and art in his life.

Out of college, Stanley worked for his father's oil and gas company for three days before deciding it wasn't for him. He was single and running a bookstore in Amarillo in 1967, wondering if he should move back to Philly, when someone came in and told him a TV station in town was for sale. He bought it because the business seemed to match his personality. Eventually, he bought five other TV stations, plus a radio station, and ran them his whole career. Only sold out a few years ago.

People call Stanley eccentric. Fair enough. He is. But some say it with dismissive condescension. That's not giving Stanley his due. He's a smart businessman. It wasn't like Daddy gave him the Amarillo TV station and he ran it into the ground. Just the opposite. He purchased an also-ran station with some partners. For thirty-two of the thirty-five years he owned it, the station was the ratings leader in the city. He put a lot of money into it, especially the news side, to make it number one, but then profited from the higher ad sales. Programming was his favorite part. He bought out his partners when they got tired of meeting to discuss whether Donald Duck should run before Mickey Mouse or Porky Pig before Donald Duck on Saturday mornings. But Stanley loved that part, and he was good at it. No accounting for how the rich kid/snorkel monkey/prankster son of a Texas oil and gas tycoon, husband of an heiress to one of the most famous cattle ranches in the state, and Ivy League-educated managed to locate his finger on the pulse of the common man, but Stanley pulled it off for over three decades.

Iconoclast is better than eccentric when describing Stanley.

He says there is an automatic typewriter out there that labels him Stanley Marsh 3, eccentric Texas millionaire, in every article written about him. He says he doesn't like that. Doesn't like that at all. He'd like to be known as a multimillionaire.

He likes art that has no value, as he tells it. Like the Cadillac Ranch. He calls it significant art, but you can't sell it. Indeed, for Stanley, the best art is art you can't sell. Two sides of him again. His TV empire was a commercial enterprise through and through, but he doesn't like commercialism in his art.

Stanley always liked to make things—as a boy, a young adult, and a college grad. He didn't necessarily see himself as an artist. When he stuck the Caddies in the ground, people called it art. So then, says Stanley, he was an artist, not just a guy who made things. Besides the buried Caddies, he's famous locally for his fake traffic signs. He just got tired of the real ones one day. All signs, really. Calls them bossy. Go to this church. Drink that beer. Stop. Go. Merge. His first alternate traffic sign was a reaction to 'Road Ends.' He made one that said 'Road Does Not End' and put it on the street next to his ranch. It lasted six months before the city found it and took it down. That triggered a guerilla sign war. Stanley found that the best way to avoid having the city take down his signs was to trespass and place them on private property. Most people liked them and kept them. They're not puns so much, just sayings: She'll Be Driving Six White Horses When She Comes; You'll Get Yours; and Don't Try This at Home. There are hundreds around the city. Hundreds more are stored in a pasture behind Toad Hall. Thirty years later, it looks like Stanley won the war or at least the colorful battle. The signs are everywhere in Amarillo.

LBK and another assistant, Drew, take me to Toad Hall to meet Wendy Marsh and see the place. LBK is preoccupied. He

is supposed to fly to Paris tomorrow with his girlfriend and visit
Giverny to inspect Monet's famous garden and surrounding envi-
rons. Stanley is re-creating all that in his backyard. Has a pond
and planted water lilies in it and willows all around. Even has that
bridge, which looks small in the paintings. But for the garden to
look like a Monet painting out the back window of Toad Hall,
Stanley had to make the bridge about thirteen feet long.

Annnnnnnyway, a troublesome volcano in Iceland is spewing
ash all across Europe and threatening to close Charles De Gaulle
airport. LBK fiddles with his iPhone and calls De Gaulle directly.
Then he phones his girlfriend. LBK met Stanley when he was
sixteen. He barely knew Stanley, but ended up at a party at Toad
Hall, drunk and without a ride. So he stole Stanley's truck, which
was painted like a 1960s hippie van, and drove to his cousin's
house, where he was staying. The cops had it staked out because
the cousin was a drug dealer. One look at LBK and the truck he
was driving, the cops surrounded the vehicle and dragged him
out. Cops threw LBK in jail. He called Stanley and said he didn't
really mean to steal the truck. Stanley bailed him out for $110.
LBK was so grateful that he's been working for Stanley ever since
and hasn't really been in trouble with the law that whole time.

The car we ride in to Toad Hall is a white OJ-style SUV, but
with a difference. Mounted on the roof is a stuffed fox. Its nose
points forward, like the snout of a family dog sticking out a car
window, but the fox doesn't look nearly as happy as the average
golden retriever enjoying the same breeze. His red coat is beautiful, but he's also gritting his teeth, girding himself against the
wind, the elements, and curious, haunting stares from passing
motorists. Drew says the fox looked a lot better a few weeks ago.
They change the mounted critter every once in a while. It can be
anything from a fox to a coyote, raccoon, or even a chicken. But

at highway speeds, the wind tends to pluck the chickens, and they don't last long. Besides, a naked chicken on the roof sends the wrong message. There has also been a variety of carousel animals up there, plus an enormous fiberglass parrot almost as big as the SUV. That display ended in abrupt contact with an overpass, the clearance of which was inexplicably lower than the fourteen-foot federally mandated minimum for such structures. There's also a big dent in the driver's side door where Stanley pulled into traffic and a guy on a motorcycle ran into him. Stanley operates a motor vehicle the way he lives his life, in largely random fashion, so someone usually drives him around.

The windmill along the driveway of the Frying Pan has a six-foot-long black bow tie attached to it underneath the blades. A couple of more artist-helpers, who occupy a room along the edge of the house, greet us. We linger there a moment while LBK and Drew forage for available food. Then we enter the house. Wendy Bush O'Brien Marsh is as gracious as the day is long. Her grandfather was the legendary William Henry Bush. He was a young but already successful businessman in Chicago when he married the daughter of Joseph Glidden, who had one of the first patents on barbed wire and had figured out how to manufacture it cheaply and quickly. In 1881, Glidden bought what amounted to a 250,000-acre spread in the Panhandle, jumping with both boots into the Western cattle boom of those years. Bush got a share of the ranch for helping develop it—stringing it with Glidden's wire. Years later, he eventually gained full control over it.

The ranch has a long and storied history. Men associated with the Frying Pan founded Amarillo at the intersection of two railroads on the eastern edge of the ranch in 1887. The brand is a bar and a circle. Story goes that a cowboy seeing the brand thought it looked like a frying pan, and the name stuck. William

Bush never lived on the ranch. He kept his home in Chicago, where he had a bushel full of business interests, but visited the Frying Pan frequently. He was in a happy but childless marriage for twenty-nine years when his wife expired suddenly. He remarried two years later to a twenty-eight-year-old woman. A year after that, at age fifty-nine, he had his first child, Caroline. A year later, they had a second daughter, Emeline. Wendy, the daughter of Emeline, inherited Toad Hall. Mary Eminy, the daughter of Caroline, lives on another part of the Frying Pan, which Grandfather Bush divided three ways in his will.

While Wendy and I talk in the kitchen, LBK and Drew hover in the background, watching and listening, like skinny Secret Service agents. They'd probably talk into their sleeves, except they're too busy eating Wendy's chocolate chip cookies. Stanley and Wendy first met as kids. They think it was at the Bikes for Ike rally in 1951. The kids in town dressed up their ten-speeds and rode in a parade for Eisenhower. Can only imagine what Stanley's bike looked like. They never dated in high school. Wendy would see him at junior cotillion dances, but described herself as a wallflower back then, while Stanley would come in crazy costumes. The showman in him isn't a recent development. They didn't start dating until their late twenties when Wendy was finishing law school. It says something about Stanley that, for all of his zaniness, spontaneity, and appearance of a Bohemian lifestyle, it's not like he's had a Picasso-like multitude of mistresses and marriages. He and Wendy have been together for forty-two years.

Shortly after they were married in 1970, they tore down the old ranch house. Although it had some historic value, cowboys who were more familiar with heifers than home construction built it. Wendy and Stanley used fieldstones from the original house to re-create the doorway and living room as best they could.

They raised five adopted kids in the house. It's sprawling and has bookshelves everywhere for Stanley's books. Even has a small zoo tucked in between U-shaped wings of the house. Mostly small critters, but a few peacocks. For a while, they had a bunch of monkeys. (Different from the snorkel ones.)

They once had a visitor who maybe had been up late the night before enjoying the refreshments and didn't know that the Marsh family had a live-in au pair from Paris. Her boyfriend was over early to do some work at the house, and they were chitchatting in the room next door. The visitor, hearing a murmured discussion, looked out his window and saw the monkeys in the zoo, jabbering in apparent conversation.

He shuffled into the kitchen, rearranging his bed head, and said, If this place don't beat all. You even have monkeys that speak French.

Haven't even told you about Stanley's famous annual trips with his entourage. They typically combined three factors. Stanley often chose the location on a whim. It had to be exotic. And it had to be a place none of their wives would ever want to go to. He took a trip just about every year for twenty-five years between 1970 and 1995. In 1982, Stanley decided he wanted to see Komodo dragons, the world's biggest lizards, about ten feet long. They only live on a couple of remote Indonesian Islands and are descended from dinosaurs. Even though they don't look anything like apes, they're said to be the inspiration for the King Kong story and maybe the dragons you see in Chinese art.

Annnnnnnyway, Stanley and seven or eight of his friends took about forty-three different flights from Amarillo to Taipei and then Bali. But they still weren't close to getting there. They took a small plane to another island. This one was so remote that islanders lined the runway for the twice-a-week arrival of the aircraft because it's the most noteworthy event in the life of the island. Not only were they the only white people there, but little kids would come up to touch them because they'd never seen one before ever. They still weren't where they eventually wanted to get, but they stayed on the island a couple days in what passed for a hotel, a two-story cinder block edifice that looked like a tenement and would have made the Bates Motel feel cozy and inviting.

They took jeeps over the mountains on the island to a harbor where they could catch a boat to Komodo Island. When they stepped onto the vessel, the Flores Sea rose about a foot through the bottom of the hull. One thing about Stanley, in life and in business, he's always done a good job of surrounding himself with people who complement him and his talents. So whereas Stanley is a bit crazy and spontaneous, he always brought along a couple guys with common sense and conservative behavior whose job it was to talk him out of things. They talked him out of the water-logged death ship. Instead, they commandeered an inter-island trawler anchored in the harbor and slept on the deck during the overnight trip to Komodo and for the three days they were actually on Komodo.

When they finally arrived at their destination, after about five days of travel, a Dutch priest blessed them and gave them hot cocoa. Then the villagers took them to a remote part of Komodo. They have a ritual of sacrificing a goat to the dragons so they don't eat the villagers instead. The dragons don't really attack humans much, but they've been known to gnaw on folks if they don't get a goat now and then. Anyway, the villagers tied a goat in the bottom of a ravine while Stanley and his friends watched from up top. Killed the goat and left it there. Before you knew it, those giant lizards were smelling blood and appearing out of nowhere at the edge of the jungle. They devoured the goat and weren't neighborly about it either. Biggest of them was taking huge bites out of one end of that goat. A bunch of little ones were at the other end. The big one would rake his five-foot tail across that goat. Whop! Sent the little dragons flying.

It got to be where Stanley's friends would just block out the first two weeks of June and wait to see where Stanley wanted to go that year on his National Geographic expedition. One time, it was to see mountain gorillas in Rwanda. Then there was the time he wanted to visit the farthest point up the Amazon where an oceangoing vessel could go. Turns out that spot is so far up the Amazon that it's in Peru. So Stanley and his merry pranksters flew to Iquitos in the eastern Peruvian rainforest. Must have been his Fitzcarraldo moment. That was the movie about the real-life guy who loved opera and wanted to build an opera house in Iquitos after making a fortune as a rubber baron. But the only rubber land available to him, you couldn't get to it from here, so Fitzcarraldo took a boat up the Amazon as far as it could go and then had natives haul it through the jungle and over a mountain to another river where he could cargo out the rubber. Not sure if he ever made his fortune or built the opera house, but something tells me that Stanley spotted a kindred spirit.

Here's how Stanley surprises you. So there's the Peru trip, the Amazon, and the whole Fitzcarraldo thing, but, when Stanley is there and on all of his trips, he instructs the guide to take him to where the poorest people live and where the richest people live. He figures it's a good way to learn about the culture to see the extremes of wealth and poverty. Like I've been saying, Stanley is complicated. Take his drinking. Did a bit too much of it early on. In fact, after one of his June trips, a friend was worried about it. He did some research and put together a presentation of sorts with articles from *Scientific American*. He went to Stanley and told him about alcoholic liver disease and such. Not sure if Stanley and the merry pranksters have ever been to Easter Island, but Stanley, in response to the presentation, did a pretty good job imitating one of the statues resident there. In any event, he didn't pay any mind to his friend and went on drinking like parched prairie in a thunderstorm. About seven or eight years later, this friend got a call from Stanley, who was just about hysterical. Wendy had laid down the law.

Stanley said, Wendy's gonna leave me! She's gonna leave me if I don't stop drinking!

Friend got him calmed down, and Stanley stopped drinking. And I don't mean gradually. That night and not a drop since. It's those two sides of him again. Seems like two people, disciplined and undisciplined. Successful businessman and madcap prankster. Like with his size. He got overweight over time. Then one day, just last year, he decided that was enough. Just plain stopped eating. Lost ninety pounds in a year. Folks in Amarillo were whispering he'd gotten his stomach stapled. Wasn't so. Has an iron will when he wants to.

Hard to describe Stanley the artist. He occupies a zone where art meets pranksterism. And he may be the only one occupying that ground. Sure, a famous artist like Toulouse-Lautrec used to go to parties with a frog in his mouth, open it, and startle the guests when the thing jumped in the punch bowl. But that's child's play. Doesn't measure up to Stanley's pranks. Not that Stanley can paint evocative Parisian nightclub scenes though.

Annnnnnnyway, one day, Stanley decided to build a temporary corral in the shape of a large hand on open range on the Frying Pan. It was maybe fifty feet long and half that much wide. He had a couple cowboys run a few dozen cows into the setup and lock them in. Cows were nose to tail and flank to flank, couldn't hardly move, with about a half-dozen fitting into each of the fingers. Then Stanley got himself a helicopter, hovered directly over the top, and took a picture. He named the thing 'Cowhand.' That was all. That was it. Got his picture. Made 'Cowhand' happen. Art. Prank. Ran the cows out, and took down the corral. Stanley is like Christo with cattle.

His next project is a life-sized pop-up Statue of Liberty that's going to appear some morning on a playa lake somewhere on the high plains around Amarillo, probably near a highway so people could see it. Playa lakes are shallow depressions in the prairie that fill with water after a rain, maybe two or three feet deep. The water eventually evaporates. Stanley dispatched LBK to New York harbor to check out Liberty. The plans are top secret, sort of, but the project has apparently been outsourced. Someone or some people somewhere in Amarillo are sewing together some type of expandable plastic material, like what's used for drop cloths—vinyl, plastic, or whatever—in a warehouse. It's translucent, partially see-through. The Lady of Liberty will be a scale likeness one hundred and fifty-one feet tall when full of air or smoke. Or maybe not. It could all be a bullcrap story Stanley is telling me. You never really know.

In the middle of the night, Stanley will deploy the big statue bag, hauling it out to the as-yet-to-be-identified playa, presumably a stand-in for New York harbor, and place it on some sort of raft he's going to build. Then he and wayward artist youths will gather peat moss and drench it in gas. After positioning the statue bag, they'll spark the gas-moss combo. The resulting fire will produce hot air and smoke that will fill the statue bag, causing it to slowly rise those one hundred and fifty-one feet, measured at the tip-top of the torch, over playa and plains. Folks fortunate enough to be driving by will be the only ones to see it. It's not a political statement. It's not really about anything. Stanley just wants to create a drive-by, translucent, pop-up Statue of Liberty lit by the morning sun rising over the high plains. It will be an experience. It will be art. It will be fun.

Then it will be gone. Maybe it will pop up somewhere else. Stanley says it might appear on San Francisco Bay before you know it. But maybe not. For a long time, he was talking about a one hundred and fifty-one-foot-long Statue of Liberty rag doll, but that was abandoned for various reasons. It was occasioned by the bicentennial. Yes, *that* bicentennial, in 1976. Time and timing are not pressing matters in Stanley's world. The whim factor rules.

The Horse Racer

CE Trimble is eighty-one now and been raisin', trainin', and racin' horses a long time. He's a small operator by any measure. He's won a lotta money, lost a lotta money, and spent a lotta money. If you were to chart his ups and downs, the graph would look like a silhouette of the Himalayas. But he's sure had some fun. When he came home after the Korean War, CE settled in Bovina, in the Panhandle near the New Mexico border. Tried quarter horses, but didn't have any luck with 'em. Found a trainer, Bob Arnett. The two went out to California in the early 1960s. Looked at a whole bunch of horses. Arnett kept circlin' back to a filly named Crazy Frills. He knew about the stud that sired her, Crazy Kid. Held the track record out there in California for a half-mile. Turned out the colts Crazy Kid produced were either great racers or complete duds.

Arnett says to CE, Crazy Frills will either be a good 'un, or she won't be no good. You won't waste a lotta money on her.

Crazy Woman owned her. That ain't a horse. Ain't an Indian neither. According to CE, a crazy woman owned the horse. He paid twenty-five hundred for the filly. They brought Crazy Frills back to Bovina. Trainer broke her. First time they run her was at Red Oak, south of Dallas. Trainer had gone ahead with the filly and was workin' her out at the track. He give CE a call a couple days before her first race.

He says, Trimble, git your money, and git down here. She's

gonna win.

CE gone down there. It was race day and post time, and they opened the gate. Crazy Frills decides to stay put. She don't move. Don't leave the gate. She might as well been chained to the damn thing. Well, it weren't forever, of course, but she weren't off with the rest of them neither. Was at least a couple of seconds. Annnnnnnyway, she finally got headed down the straightaway. When she come up on the first turn, she don't turn. Don't get the concept of the track being round. After she near slammed into the outer rail, the jockey briefed her on the program and got her turnin' left. By this time, she was more lengths behind the last horse than that horse was from the leader. CE, who'd bet a lotta money, was cursin' Crazy Frills, the track, the gate, the trainer, and the horse he rode in on, which, of course, was Crazy Frills. It was nuts.

But then instinct took over, and the racehorse in Crazy Frills kicked in, and she ran and ran. Passed one horse after another. She done everything wrong a horse could do in a race, and then she won by a length. She won seven races all told. About eighteen months after he bought her, a feller come up to CE and asked if he'd take sixty thousand for the horse. Remember, he'd bought her for twenty-five hundred.

CE says, No, I don't guess I would.

Feller wanted that filly. He says to CE, Would you take a hundred thousand?

CE says, You askin', or is you offerin'?

Feller was offerin', but CE wasn't sellin'. He bred her and kept the first colt, but sold a second colt for fifteen thousand down at Reynosa, a track in New Mexico, started by his Uncle George and a couple partners. The colt CE sold won a bunch of races, including the Sunland Park Derby in El Paso.

All told, Crazy Frills won about one hundred thousand, which was a lotta money back then. Best horse he ever owned. About four years after CE brung her back to Bovina, he come home from being away. His son met him at the door and said Crazy had died. Had the vet out. Did everything they could. Ate something bad, CE figures. CE had that horse insured while it was at the track, but when he brung her home, he dropped the insurance. A feller said he'd pay sixty thousand for her anytime CE wanted to sell.

Just call him, he said.

CE figured that was all the insurance he needed on her.

Crazy Frills had two or three good colts. CE bred one to Master Salls and got a mare with a crooked leg. Named her Crazy Salls. CE almost shot her, but eventually decided to keep her. She straightened up pretty good, and his trainer done a miracle with her. Crazy Salls could run. In 1992, she won eight races in one year in New Mexico.

CE started in rodeo when he was young. He roped and rode some bulls, but he was also around racehorses as a boy. His Uncle George raised them. When he got older, CE told his uncle he wanted to get some racehorses.

Uncle said, You don't want to do that. That's the worse thing you can do. You'll go broke with them damn horses.

CE never went broke, but he did get carried away now and then. He gone to Kentucky once. Was going to buy one good mare. One good mare. But he found several at reasonable prices, includin' one been bred to Northern Dancer, who won the Kentucky Derby, and another mare bred to a Storm Cat colt. CE's wife, Joy, says CE can't remember where he put his boots, but he can remember the bloodlines of dozens of horses. Annnnnnnyway, CE took a friend from California who knew horses and his son-in-law, Kenny, who hauls horses. When CE got home from Kentucky, Joy come out of the house while they were unloadin' horses and pullin' out one after another.

She says to Kenny, Which one of these is CE's?

Kenny stopped what he was doing and walked himself around behind the gate, apparently as a precautionary measure.

He says, They're all his.

Joy weren't chewed. It was just CE and his horse thing. CE had bought four for twelve thousand. It all worked out for him. Always seemed to. He bred one of them mares to a horse named Light Diffuse. Hauled the colt down to Fort Worth and sold it as a yearling for twelve thousand. Came out even on the whole Kentucky trip with just that one colt.

One time, CE got a call from a feller from New York who says, I heard you was lookin' for a stud.

CE says, I am. I want a horse by Damascus.

Damascus won the Preakness and the Belmont back in the 1960s.

Feller says, Just so happens I got one. Name of Red Anchor.

Damascus thing didn't seem like a coincidence then. Just later. New York feller had sold Red Anchor to a Texan who couldn't pay off the debt. CE done what you're never supposed to do. Bought that horse over the phone. New York feller gave him the name of a world-famous trainer for CE to call and ask about him.

CE says, I don't have to call nobody. I'll just trust you.

So the feller says, Mail me a check for five thousand. I'll call the feller in Austin that bought him and tell him to let you have the horse.

CE gone down. Red Anchor was there in an itty-bitty, old pen on a no-account ranch. CE tranquilized him, got him in the trailer, and brung him home to Bovina in a sleet storm. Deal may be lookin' a bit suspicious at that point.

Then the feller from New York calls and says, Trimble, you ain't gonna believe this, but my office burned up, and them papers of Red Anchor gone up with it.

Joy just shook her head and said, You got scammed. Lost five thousand.

New York feller says, It ain't no problem. Ain't no problem. Just send a full set of pictures of him, and fill out an application. I'll get duplicate papers.

Well, it all worked out. In two weeks, he got the papers. Red Anchor turned out to be the best stud horse that ever been in the Western Panhandle. Kept him for a long time. When he got old, kidneys shut down. Took him to the vet.

He says, Got to put him down.

But CE had taken a horse to that vet shortly before. A horse got his leg near broke plum off, and the vet give him a shot, but he never got that horse to sleep. Horse just stood there lookin' at you.

So CE, talkin' about Red Anchor, says, No, Doc, you ain't gonna put him down.

He brung Red Anchor home and led him down to the draw in the back pasture. Had his .22 Magnum with him. Hated to do it, even though that horse was a mean ol' son of a bitch. Kicked CE lots of times. He'd bite for no particular reason either. CE was walkin' down an alley one morning, leadin' a mare. Red Anchor was in a pen there. Was wintertime. CE had on one of them down jackets. Got a little close to the pen. Red Anchor stuck his head through and took a bite out of CE. Duck feathers went flyin'. CE had teeth marks on the back of his shoulder for a couple months.

Annnnnnnyway, he shot Red Anchor with the Magnum. Didn't bury him. Only buried one horse in his life, name of Jugs.

That was his granddaughter's horse, and she made him do it. Took two fellers all day to dig a hole big enough. CE won't say it, but suspect she's his favorite granddaughter. Only one likes horses. Left Red Anchor there in the pasture. Coyotes ate him. That was years ago, but CE says he was just down there a couple weeks ago and thought he saw Red Anchor's jawbone.

CE had a few run-ins with horses over the years. There was the time a friend of his from Clovis give him a mare to breed to Red Anchor. CE brung the mare up to a pasture he had west of town. She was a mean one. Had a colt at the time. CE separated her from the colt and put a limp chain on her. He was holdin' on to a lead rope when she jerked him down, run over him, and kicked him. CE ain't but a little guy, but he wasn't about to give in. Held on to that lead chain. She turned around and run over him again. He ain't sure how many times that mare kicked him. Whole day got fuzzy after that. He got himself away from the mare and stood up, but he tumbled right back over again. Noticed the lower part of his leg was pointin' west where it normal points south. He crawled to his pickup and managed to get in. Drove himself to the schoolhouse where Joy taught. Laid on his horn, but she weren't there. He gone to the house and done the same thing. She was in the house, but didn't hear him.

CE started back toward the school when he seen Slim, an older hired hand who worked out on the ranch for his Uncle George pretty much his whole life. Didn't have no family. CE inherited him. Slim stopped.

CE says, Slim, I don't know where I been or where I'm a goin', but I need to find Joy.

Slim was alarmed at the sight of CE and jumped in the pickup. When they got to the house, he run in without knockin', which ain't like Slim.

He tells Joy, CE is out here, and he's lost his mind.

Joy says, I just talked to him a half hour ago. How could he have lost it that fast?

She gone out there, and he was a sight all right. His nose was flat agin one check, and some teeth were missin'. When he reached into his boot to check his leg, his hand come out crimson. Bone was stickin' through the skin down there in that boot. So Joy starts to run him over to the hospital.

CE says, Turn around. Got to tell Slim something.

She said, We ain't turnin' around. We're going to the hospital.

CE says, No, turn around.

It was obvious to Joy that CE been kicked in the head and gone loco a bit, but he weren't to be dissuaded on this point. Joy done like he said.

When they reached Slim, CE told him, Go on down there and see if you can get that mare back in the pen with the colt. Just open the gate. Don't catch her or nothin'. Just get 'em back together so that colt'll be all right.

Just like CE. Got a broken leg, a broke nose, and plum crazy from gettin' kicked in the head, but he had to take care of the horses first. Doctors fixed him up, but he never did get that mare bred.

CE had run-ins with farm equipment, too. His hands and fingers look like the branches of an ancient tree. One time in late fall, he gone out to finish cuttin' maize with the combine, but it weren't workin'. He noticed a bunch of trash in the bin and figured leaves choked the fan. Went to rakin' them leaves off. The belt caught him and threw his hand up into the variable speed drive. He reached for a pair of pliers in his pocket, hopin' to yank out the fuel line and cut the power, but he couldn't reach it. By the time he got his hand loose, his leather glove was mangled.

Pulled it off. His thumb stayed in the glove. He put the glove back on, but it was sure a bloody mess.

Neighbors were out cuttin' maize nearby. One was comin' by in his truck, except it wasn't a him. It was the wife, and CE figured she might faint when she seen his hand, so he just turned aside and headed for his own truck. When he went to start it up, events had got him a bit excited, and he managed to flood the engine. Took him fifteen minutes to get it started, bleedin' buckets the whole time. Finally, he revved her up and drove to the nearest building on the edge of town. Happened to be his barber. Feller run, got a towel, and wrapped up the mess. Then he got CE in his car and headed to the hospital. When they was drivin', CE looked down and seen the barber going one hundred ten miles an hour in his Buick.

CE says, Emmett, you best be slowin' down, or there's gonna be a worse accident than there's already been.

When they got to the hospital, doctor says, *Now* what the hell have you done, CE?

See, long time before, CE managed to bust up a finger real bad while ropin' a calf. Got set. A splint was attached, but it didn't help much. Finger come to reside at a forty-five-degree angle. Well, CE kept bumpin' and bruisin' and twistin' that crooked finger. Then one day, he was loadin' a cow on a trailer. Had a stanchion to stick the cow's head through. So CE was pullin' on its nose, gettin' the head in there proper, when that cow swung its head and mashed that crooked finger. The doctor, same one we's talkin' about, was willin' to fix that finger again, but CE had had enough of it.

He said, No, just cut it off. So they did. Cut off the top half.

But we was talkin' about CE's thumb. They got that put back on, though it ain't a pretty sight to this day. Within a few weeks then, that doctor cut off one of CE's fingers and put another one back on.

Annnnnnnyway, racehorses were just CE's hobby. Had to make a livin'. He was a farmer and a rancher, but he found a way to get himself in trouble even when he was just farmin' and ranchin'. Had a partner, AL Nutall. They owned a combine together. The thumb-stealin' one. Raised corn and maize. Nutall had a big corn crop just outside of Clovis, right behind the Holiday Inn. CE bought one hundred fifty cows and turned them out on that corn.

One day, he says to his boy Charlie, who was about fifteen then, I need to check on them cows.

Charlie says, I need to get my pickup worked on.

So they jumped a horse in the trailer and headed out of Bovina. Clovis is down the road twenty miles, over the line in New Mexico. Charlie dropped off CE with his horse by them cows, and then he gone off to the Ford dealer. Said he'd be back when it was all done. CE rode through them cows and checked 'em. They were calving at the time. He counted his babies. When he was done and Charlie weren't back yet, he decided to just ride on over to the Ford dealer. Wasn't but a half-mile away.

When CE got there, mechanic come out from behind the truck he was workin' on. Guess he was used to seein' vehicles more than horses when he looked up from under the hood.

He says, I bet you can't ride that mare in on the show floor.

CE says, Open that door, and we'll see.

Feller opened the door. CE rode all around that show floor and them new cars in there.

Mechanic says, You win the bet, but it'll still be an hour before I'm finished with Charlie's truck.

CE says, Okay, I'll just go down to the Holiday Inn and have a beer.

CE rode down there and tied his horse to a telephone pole. This is Main street. Nothin' else there but cars. He gone into the Holiday Inn and the Red Carpet Lounge. Had a beer with Nutall and a coupla other fellers he knew.

Directly, some ol' loudmouth boy come in and says, Whose damn horse is that tied to a telephone pole out there?

CE says, She belongs to me.

Loudmouth feller says, I'll tell you what. I'll bet you a hun'erd dollars you can't ride her into this bar.

CE says, I haven't been in here long enough to consider that.

But after thirty minutes and three more beers, his thoughts had changed on the subject.

Someone in the lounge perceived the shift and says, You reckon you can ride that mare in here now?

CE says, I'll bet that hun'erd dollars I can.

So he went out there and mounted that horse. Nutall opened the door. And in he came. Before you actually get to the lounge, there is a big slate floor. This was an expensive racehorse. Belonged to CE's friend, CW Grissom, lives over there in Taiban. Just like CE to be checkin' his cows with a racehorse belongin' to someone else and then ridin' her into the Holiday Inn.

Annnnnnnyway, she just come from the track and still had on aluminum shoes. That mare got to trippin' and slippin' all over that slate floor, legs windmillin' like you seen in a Saturday mornin' cartoon. Sparks were flyin' ever'where.

They had entertainment in the Red Carpet Lounge evenings. A petite young gal from Chicago was in there that afternoon by an upright piano. When that crazy cowboy and his fire-hooved horse made it past the slate floor and hit the carpet, she jumped up on top of that piano like a chicken. Course, the horse was a bit spooked, too. That's why the locals got to callin' it the Brown Carpet Lounge for a spell after that horse come through there.

Annnnnnnyway, CE decided he best vacate the premises, but Nutall didn't get the door open in time. A stirrup hung on it. Ripped the door plum off. Then the glass above the door come shatterin' down on CE like a seven-foot basketball player just broke a backboard. CE dismounted. Ever'one come out, and they were jabberin' and lookin' at that glass and payin' off their wagers. Just then, fifteen-year-old Charlie drove up.

He says, Dad, give me that horse.

Charlie loaded the mare in the trailer and just drove off. Left CE standin' there, talkin' it through with ever'body. Wasn't the only time he got snubbed that day. After he got a ride home and explained things to Joy, he called CW Grissom and says, You got any liability insurance on that mare of yours?

CW says, Any what?

CE says, You got any liability on your horse? It just ripped the damn front door off the Holiday Inn in Clovis.

CW didn't say another word. He just hung up and drove to Bovina. Didn't even stop by the house to say hello to CE. Just backed the trailer up to the pen, loaded in his racehorse, and left.

CE knew the ol' boy who run the Holiday Inn. He called him a few days later and says, Bill, what do I owe you for that damn door?

Bill says, Owe me? Trimble, you need to do that every month. There's people comin' from ever'where to see that door you tore off. It's helped my business a bunch. You don't owe me nothin'.

Course, seems more'n a coincidence that CE didn't ride a horse into any other buildings his whole life, but he rode into two in one day. Kind of wonder who was darin' who on them deals. CW Grissom sold that horse for twenty-five thousand.

CE has a cousin named Francis, lives over near Wellington. Married a Methodist preacher's son. Her husband and father-in-law owned a ranch together. This was back when the farmers went on strike and drove their tractors to Washington. While the husband was away doing that, Francis called CE, said her mother-in-law had phoned up and said Grandpa hadn't come home that night. He's out on the ranch somewheres.

CE tells Francis, As soon as I do my chores in the morning, I'll be over and we'll go look for him.

Next mornin', CE got up, done his chores, and then got in the pickup and drove over to a small town north of Wellington called Lutie, where this ranch was, on the Oklahoma border. They'd farmed it at one point and then turned it back to grass. He got Francis, and they went out onto the ranch. Cows were grazin' around an old pickup, but Grandpa wasn't there. Then they gone down to another pasture near a creek and seen an old car there with two bales of hay on the trunk and two on the hood. They come around it. There was grandpa lying on the prairie, stiff as a board. Dead. His hair just a blowin' in the wind.

CE says, What do you want to do, Francis?

She says, He's laid out here long enough. Let's take him to town.

So they lifted him up and tried to put him in the backseat. He wouldn't fit. But he was so stiff he wouldn't bend neither. Couldn't get the door shut. So CE went around, rolled down the window, and tilted him up so his head stuck out the window. Got in the car, but the battery was dead. Jumped it and got it started. CE told Francis to drive the pickup and follow him into Wellington. CE says it was an uncomfortable sight lookin' at that sideview mirror and seein' the dead man's head stickin' out the window and his hair a blowin' in the wind, but they finally got to town.

He drove to the sheriff's office, went in, and said, I got a dead man out here.

Sheriff said, Well, we don't want him. Take him up to the hospital.

CE says, He don't need to go to the hospital. He's dead.

Sheriff says, Well, we just don't want him.

So CE took him up to the hospital. He gone in and says, I got a dead man out here.

They said, We don't want him. Take him to the sheriff.

CE says, I already been down there. They don't want him.

They said, Well, I don't know what you're gonna do. We can't take him until the sheriff's declared him dead.

CE says, Declared him dead? This feller's so stiff you could iron a shirt on him. He's dead all right.

Hospital feller says, Take him to the funeral home then.

By now, CE been drivin' around so long that there's folks startin' to line the sidewalks of Wellington, pointin' and wonderin' what that feller's doing drivin' all over town with a dead man in the backseat with his head stickin' out the window and his hair just a blowin' in the wind. Why don't he take him somewhere? CE drove up to the funeral home.

Woman says, Take him over to the hospital.

CE says, I been there. They don't want him.

She says, Well, take him on down to the sheriff then.

CE says, I been there, too. They don't want him neither.

She says, Well, I guess we'll call the doctor. Have him come over.

So the doctor come over, drew on decades of medical trainin' and experience, and declared the dead man dead.

Funeral woman says, Guess we best be unloadin' him.

CE ain't sure what happened between the field where they found him and the funeral home, but it took eight of them to get the old man out of the car. Then again, out on the ranch when they loaded him, CE had to kick on his feet to get the door closed, so maybe he got wedged in there a bit. Took some doing, but that preacher finally found his eternal rest.

CE ain't quit on the horses yet. Oh, no. Still lookin' for his next Crazy Frills. Thinks he might have a mare now near as good as she was. Horse named She Moves. Raised her himself. Came from one of them mares he got from Kentucky, the Northern Dancer line. Just a few weeks ago, he run She Moves down at Ruidosa, and she won twenty-one thousand.

Enough to buy a couple more good mares.

Lindy's Wing Man

Weldon George grew up poor in Sweetwater, Texas. His dad died when he was two, and his mother made five dollars a week as an assistant in a doctor's office.

He smiles and says, Poor people felt sorry for us.

One day when he was eleven, Weldon's older sister, who worked for Western Union, came home excited. Weldon was in the backyard playing Tarzan in a cottonwood tree.

She said, Charles Lindbergh just flew by himself across the Atlantic Ocean in thirty-three straight hours and landed safely in Paris.

Weldon was dumbfounded. He was certainly old enough to know what flying was, but he still couldn't quite comprehend the feat. Pilots were barely flying across states, much less oceans in storms. Were planes even capable of that? Or pilots?

At that moment, something clicked in Weldon. Or maybe even snapped, or at least got branded in consciousness. From that very moment on, he wanted to be a pilot and nothing else. He built an airplane out of an apple crate, a two-gallon bucket, a coat hanger, and whatever else he could find around the house and yard. He'd sit in that plane and fly it all day.

About that time, a barnstormer came through Sweetwater. He set up his operation at Weldon's uncle's farm on the outskirts of town and gave rides for two dollars each, taking off and landing in a pasture. Of course, Weldon couldn't afford to do anything but watch the spectacle. The plane developed engine trouble. The pilot didn't have the money to fix it, so he left it at Uncle Bunk's farm. In fact, it was a year before the barnstormer got the cash to come back and repair the plane and fly it away. In the meantime, Uncle Bunk let the pilot store the plane in his barn. Whenever he could, Weldon would sneak out to the farm, slip into the barn, open the doors wide, and climb into the cockpit. He'd check out the instruments and feel the stick in his hands. He would have played with the rudder pedals, too, but his legs weren't long enough for his feet to reach them. Sitting in the pilot's seat, he'd look out across that prairie, into the wild blue yonder, and dream of being sky high.

When he got old enough to take flying lessons, they were three dollars per. With his mother's salary, affording instruction was a fantasy. But he had to get in the air somehow. The military was about the only way to get free lessons. The Army Air Corps would only accept certain categories of candidates for flight school. You had to be a graduate of West Point or the naval academy. Weldon wasn't. Or you had to be a noncommissioned officer. Weldon wasn't that either. But there was a third category, others, the main requirement of which was two years of college. Weldon saw a path open before him. Nothing in the world was going to stop him from becoming an Other.

He left Sweetwater and enrolled at Texas Tech. His plan and ambition were as laser-focused as they could get. Finish two years of college so he could fly. But he was penniless. There was one four-story building in Sweetwater, and Weldon had been in it—and rode the elevator—exactly twice. But he was mechanically inclined and had carefully watched the operator and which levers he moved and how he moved them to open and close the doors and go up or down. When he got to Lubbock, there was an elevator operator job, and he applied for it. They asked if he knew how to run an elevator.

Of course I do, he said.

They checked him out. He stepped up and worked the levers with casual confidence, like he'd done it for years. The elevator went up, and it went down. The bluff worked. He got the job. He worked every day from three to eleven and put himself through two years of Tech.

He passed the army physical and was accepted to flight school. In September 1939, at the age of twenty-three, having harbored a dream to fly for twelve years without ever having gotten off the ground, he headed to Lindbergh Field in San Diego, a field named after the very man who inspired him to fly, for training. It was named for Lindy because the *Spirit of St. Louis* was built in San Diego, and he started his epic journey there. Forty students were in Weldon's class. The standards then, before the war had begun and the demand for pilots became critical, were very high. They washed him out after forty-six hours of training when they were down to twelve student pilots. The excuse they gave was that he had no inherent ability to fly. Of course, they couldn't have known when they told him that they were handing him a phrase that might get etched on his tombstone.

Weldon was bitterly disappointed. Crushed. His dream was shattered. He returned to Lubbock, sad, mad, and frustrated. But there isn't a lotta quit in Weldon.

He said, I'll show 'em.

He went to work for a surveyor, dragging a chain and laying out roads. Twenty-six dollars a week. But he got his private flying license with those forty-six hours he'd earned in the Army Air Corps. By 1942, with America fully engaged in the war, the military started the Civilian Pilot Training Program. It was meant to turn out instructors. Weldon was accepted and passed the course. He graduated with a flight instructor's rating and a commercial license.

By then, with World War Two creating an urgent need for military pilots both in Europe and the Pacific, the powers-that-be decided they needed to start employing female flyers. The idea was to get women flying non-combat missions stateside to free up male pilots to go overseas. Life has an odd way of coming full circle. Of all places, they established a WASP base in Weldon's hometown of Sweetwater, which isn't exactly a metropolis. WASP stands for Women's Airforce Service Pilot. The municipal field in Sweetwater was turned into an army airbase and named Avenger Field. Weldon was accepted to primary training school there. He passed the course. He quit the surveying job and became a civilian contractor instructing military pilots.

The first class Weldon taught happened to be a bunch of RAF cadets from England. After that, it was mostly women. Weldon chuckles at the prejudice against female pilots back then. A lot of military brass thought it was hooey wasting money trying to teach women how to fly.

Weldon says that, except for physical strength, there wasn't a thing the gals couldn't do that a male pilot could. The course qualified them on four different kinds of aircraft: a primary trainer, a basic trainer, an advanced trainer, and an advanced twin-engine trainer.

Like I said, life has an odd way of coming full circle. Wouldn't you know, they also started sending Army Air Cadets to Sweetwater for training. Weldon George, he who had 'no inherent ability to fly,' ended up training pilots in the very program they washed him out of. Sweet. Before things got started, an army major came out and gave Weldon a check ride to see if he passed muster as an instructor. When they got back on the ground, the major looked at Weldon's paperwork and started scratching his head.

He said, I see here we washed you out, but, hell, you're a better pilot than I am.

Weldon said, Does that mean I'm hired?

The major said, It sure does.

When the last class of women came through and they were about to shut down the program in Sweetwater, Weldon wasn't anywhere near ready to give up flying. He called a friend at Chance-Vought aircraft in Bridgeport, Connecticut. They made the famous F4U Corsair fighter plane. They told Weldon to come on up. He became a test pilot, an honor reserved for only the most qualified and deserving aviators. It was a long way from no inherent ability to fly. He spent the rest of the war there, basically taking planes coming off the factory line in Stratford skyward on their maiden flight.

Three companies were building fighter planes in southwestern Connecticut during the war. Besides the Corsair, Republic was building the P-47 and Grumman the Hellcat. Over a thousand planes a month were coming off those assembly lines, keeping eighteen test pilots busy, so the skies got a bit crowded. Checkout flights were restricted to specific airspace. But Weldon and his test pilot friends would ignore all that and head out into the blue sky, looking for some elbow room. They'd fly around the Statue of Liberty sometimes, but their favorite destination was Atlantic City. They'd drop down low and slow along the coast, just above the ocean, paralleling the surf line and the beach while trying to spy bathing beauties.

One time, he was up flying and saw another plane in the distance. He'd finished his test run. When you saw someone aloft, oftentimes, you'd join him and fly in formation for a while just for fun. Of course, you don't ever sneak up on a pilot. Weldon eased over and could tell the pilot saw him, but the Texan couldn't see the other pilot's face. When they drew close, the other pilot turned and waved. It was Charles Lindbergh. Weldon could have done a hundred barrel rolls and not felt as lightheaded as he did at that moment. The man who inspired him to be a pilot, who caused him as an eleven year old to build a plane out of a milk crate, who he thought of when he sat in that barnstormer's plane in a barn in a small town in Texas, and who may have been the first global celebrity, was in the air right next to him. Weldon thought about the pain of wanting to fly as a teen and not getting the chance. Thought of washing out of the Army Air Corps and then the triumph of becoming an instructor and a test pilot. The two men flew in formation for about ten minutes. Their wingtips were four feet apart. Weldon couldn't manage to get his mouth to stop smiling. It was like getting called up to the big leagues in baseball and being put in the same lineup with Babe Ruth.

Lindbergh was living in Westport, Connecticut, at the time. The War Department was having trouble with fighter planes escorting bombers on runs over Germany from their bases in England. The bombers had a long range, enough fuel to get to their targets and return, but the fighters didn't. The fighters would accompany the bombers partway and then have to turn home for lack of fuel, leaving the B-27s vulnerable. Lindbergh was no flying dilettante. He knew planes and aeronautics. The War Department hired him to do fuel consumption testing. He was looking at everything from power, prop, and manifold pressure settings to optimum gear up and gear down, anything that would extend the range of the fighters.

Weldon saw Lindbergh a few times after that over the next

month, including in a locker room they had for pilots. Lindbergh
told a group of test pilots firsthand the story of the famous flight.
All night in the air, very cold aloft, thirty-three hours without
sleep, dodging thunderstorms, and primitive instruments. When
he reached the coast of Ireland, he was only two miles away from
his checkpoint. It was both a consummate act of bravery and a
remarkable feat of flying. Weldon said you could have heard a
pin drop in that room when Lindy was telling the story. It was an
extraordinary experience, reliving the historic event with Lindbergh himself.

When the war ended, Weldon returned to Lubbock and
became the first crop duster in the area. A migrant worker, he
called himself. In the early days, there weren't any planes specifically built for ag work that could get in and out of tight places
and carry a big load. So pilots like Weldon had to modify the
planes they did have and push them a bit. Sometimes too far.
Weldon bought a J-5 Cub up in Kansas. He was flying it back
to Lubbock. The engine quit on him southeast of Amarillo. The
Llano Estacado is one of the flattest stretches of ground in the
United States. It's a high and very broad plateau. A few million
square miles are all one great big grass airfield. The exception is
Palo Duro Canyon on the edge of the Llano, beautiful, rugged
country that's been turned into a national monument. Think of
it as a miniature Grand Canyon. Of all the places for his engine
to die, the J-5 quit over Palo Duro. But he spied a flat piece of
ground, ran roughshod over a few hundred feet of mesquite while
landing, and then rolled out safely. The area was so tight and
the ground so rough that he couldn't have taken off even after
repairing the engine, so he disassembled the plane in order to get
it out of there.

That plane was jinxed. When Weldon got it back to the

shop, he figured he needed more power and upgraded to a larger engine. The mechanic who did the conversion put in a rubber heater hose instead of an asbestos one. Asbestos was a must because the hose connected directly to the red-hot exhaust manifold. The manifold was positioned at the pilot's feet, behind a firewall, and helped keep the cockpit warm. The hose itself ran right between the pilot's feet. On the maiden flight with that new engine, it caught fire. Weldon isn't one to make a big deal out of your average death-defying crisis, but trying to land a plane with fire flaming up between your knees and dense smoke filling the cockpit and obscuring your vision is never a walk in the park. He made an emergency landing south of the airport in a field. He got out and walked away with fire raging and smoke billowing behind him. He only had a scratch. The plane burned to ashes. Weldon had a sharp monologue with the mechanic who put in the wrong hose, but he didn't report him. The guy had a wife and three kids.

Another time he was crop dusting, telephone wires were at the end of the field. He had to fly under the wires after making a run and only then gain altitude and circle back around for another pass. The wires were no more than twenty feet off the ground, but the plane was only two or three feet above the field when he was spraying for weeds or bugs. So it was no big deal slipping under the wires at the end of each run. There was clearance. But on one pass, he either came in too high or started to ascend too quickly. His tail clipped the wire. It tore off the top third of it. Weldon limped back to the airport and landed safely.

The mechanic came running over and said, The farmer's after you. He's on the phone.

Weldon went into the shack they had there at the airport. The farmer was on the phone.

He was angry and said, How come you didn't finish my field?

Weldon had cheated the grim reaper once again and was lucky to be alive—lucky the plane hadn't cartwheeled into the ground. But he didn't say anything about that.

He just said, Didn't you see the top part of my rudder get torn off?

The farmer said, Yeah. But I thought you were just marking your place.

Weldon had a heart attack in 1961. The doctor later told him there was no trace of it on the EKG, so Weldon kept flying for a while, but no longer professionally. He was a successful stock-broker for many years before retiring in 1985.

His first wife, who he was married to for twenty-five years, died of cancer. His second wife, who he has been married to for forty-two years, is dying of cancer. Going through some things a second time doesn't make them one bit easier. Weldon is ninety-three now. He hasn't flown since he was seventy-eight. He lives in a house on what once was a cotton field, one he used to crop dust.

Yes, life has an odd way of coming full circle.

The Spur Maker

Jerry Cates was a cowpuncher long before he became maybe the best spur maker in Texas. After he cowboyed a while, Jerry ended up at the Amarillo Livestock Company. Some colorful characters at the sale barn in them days. At the time, it was the largest cattle auction in the country. Leonard Zielke was an auctioneer there for a few years, startin' in 1951, but, for decades after, he was a cattle buyer and seller. One time, Leonard's checkbook slipped out of his back pocket. Lost it in a feller's pickup truck, except he didn't know that. Few weeks gone by without him findin' it. Leonard figured it was lost for good. But it weren't. Some of his closest friends got together and found them a black lady who walked the streets on the blue side of town. Tall, striking woman, especially in them clothes she wore. One day, she come into the sale barn. It's round with seating to match. Leonard used to sit up around the top row with his hat pulled low. This woman come up the incline and walked into the arena and right over to the auctioneer. First and last time anyone ever remembers a sale being halted like that.

She says to the auctioneer, but in a loud voice so everyone can hear, Is there a gentleman named Zielke here?

Auctioneer points up toward Leonard and says, Yeah, that's him right there.

Well, ain't hardly any women at the sale barn. Ain't hardly any black folks neither. And there ain't *never* any black hookers dressed for business like that. Everything in the place come to a pin-drop dead stop. Ever'thing. Cows, people, even the ventilation fan. Every eye in the arena is followin' her as she climbs up them bleachers to Leonard.

When she reaches him, she holds up his checkbook and says to him, but loud enough so everyone in the state can hear, Thought you might like this back, Leonard. You left it at my place last night.

Leonard damn near had a thrombosis. He's a talker and a storyteller. It was the first time any of them cattlemen seen him at a loss for words.

Those ol' boys at the auction barn were an ornery bunch. Just about ever'one of 'em smoked back then. Cloud was so bad most days you could hardly see across the ring. Couple of times, if a cattle buyer been readin' the newspaper but was also busy talkin' to a feller on his right, the feller on his left would excuse himself, but, before he departed, he'd touch the end of his lit cigarette to the bottom of the paper. By the time the miscreant got himself clear of the scene and the other feller quit talkin' and noticed the crisis brewin' between his hands, that newspaper would look like a pep rally bonfire. He'd a jump up, be hollerin', throwin' down the paper, and doing a jig on it.

Annnnnnnyway, wanted to tell you about Jerry Cates. He cowboyed on the LX Ranch, which starts just north of Amarillo and runs almost twenty miles to the Canadian River. He done some gunsmithing when he was young and was known for repairin' spurs, but a cowboy come to him years ago and asked if Jerry would make him a pair. He'd never done it before. Those boys knew how handy he was and saw his drawings. Knew he had artist in him. For that first order, Jerry went to his cousin and bought a pair of plain spurs he'd got from an outfit in San Angelo.

Then Jerry remembered an old washtub layin' on its side in the pasture near the bunkhouse at ranch headquarters. It had a pure copper bottom to help heat the tub water. It was soft enough that Jerry was able to cut off a section of that copper with a pocket-knife and then carve a set of longhorns out of it and overlay it on the spurs, along with the feller's initials. That first pair was a hit. Made those forty years ago. Now, without a word of advertising, he's sittin' on seven hundred back orders.

Growin' up, Jerry liked guns and liked to tinker. As a kid, he made a cannon out of a heavy piece of pipe and some old wheels used for oil and gas drillin'. Contraption looked like something out of the Civil War, but smaller. He'd pack it with powder from firecrackers and roll a steel ball down the barrel. His father had a shop behind the house. Jerry once set the cannon up on top of the storm cellar doors and fired it off. Not sure where he was aimin', but the cannonball shot plum through the shop. Bored a perfect hole in one wall, crossed the shop on the fly, and exited out the back wall. Livened up the conversation at dinner that night.

Shortly after Jerry got out of the service, he took that job on the LX. Married Perky, who he'd known growin' up in Foard County. She come up and run a cookhouse on the LX all them years he was there, cookin' for the cowboys. The ranch was so big and the headquarters so far from town that Perky would buy groceries by the month. Jerry cowboyed for nine years, workin' with some of the best hands in the Panhandle in them years. But he don't miss it. He remembers subzero mornings in January when a two-man team would be up at dawn and headin' out to feed seven or eight hun'erd head of yearlings. One feller would drive the wagon. Tie his horse on to one of the mules. Other feller would be an outrider. He'd steer off into the pastures and sing out to them yearlings. They'd come a runnin' for breakfast. Snow on the ground. After spreadin' the feed, they'd pull out an old Prince Albert tobacco can with a snap lid. Kept the matches in there. Had a gallon can of gas and firewood in a box in the wagon. Build a fire and put a pot of coffee on—if it weren't too cold to strike a match. Wasn't a bad life, except when it was five below.

One time, only time he ever seen it, they were north of the Canadian River, neighborin'. Plan was to pen some yearlings after dinner, but that's never a wise idea. Most times of the year, it's hot in the Panhandle. After dinner is the heat of the day. Try to get most of your work done in the mornin'. Annnnnnnyway, they crossed the Canadian and drove all the cattle out of the draws along the river and up onto the flat. Thunderheads were off to the northwest, except plural don't capture the visual. It was just one big mass, dark as night. You could tell that storm was gonna be a dandy. The pens was still too far off to reach.

Jerry says, We better turn these cattle lose and get back under the hill.

Neighbor says, No, we can bring 'em.

Feller had leased a ranch to gain weight on some yearlings, but he was basically a farmer. Didn't know anything about cattle to speak of. Jerry knew they were gonna get wet, if not lightning struck. But when you're neighborin', it ain't polite to question the neighbor's orders. So they crowded up the cattle—it helped get them to move faster. They began rubbin' agin one another. With all that electricity in the air, a blue glow started comin' off the back and horns of them cattle. St. Elmo's Fire is what they call it. Jerry ain't never seen that 'fore or since.

Course, the storm hit and scattered the cattle. Cowboys was soaked through and through 'fore they could get back to the trucks. At least no one was lightning struck. Didn't lose any cows neither.

Foreman at the time was a funny feller. Once, he was out with Jerry and a couple of other hands when they were mammyin' up the herd after branding. When you drag the calves to the fire for branding, you're separatin' them from their mommas, maybe for the first time. After they're released, the two don't necessarily find each other right away. Well, on roundup mornin', cowboys get up around four and work pretty hard all forenoon. Have dinner. Then they got to mammy up them calves. Don't take much. Just herd 'em all together and let nature take its course. Mommas are lookin' around. Calves are bawlin'. Can take a few hours, but they usually find each other. If they don't, cowboys nudge out the pairs that have found each other and lower the odds for the ones that haven't. But for the most part, it's just a bunch of cowboys settin' in their saddles for hours, holdin' them cattle, gettin' drowsy, rollin' Bull Durhams, and smokin' 'em. Just sit there and sit there. Time doesn't mean much to a cowboy. Finally, the foreman just rides off. Doesn't say a word. Not a word. Just rides off. That means your day is done, too.

Annnnnnnyway, after that first cowboy come to him in 1969 and asked Jerry to make him a pair of spurs, business took off. It was right around the time that he joined the Amarillo Livestock Company. Things were going good there. They were payin' out bonuses regular. Jerry used his to slowly outfit a shop with the tools he needed to work on spurs and bits. He did both jobs for ten years, but the bit and spur makin' business just kept growin'. Folks kept a comin' to him. Name got known. In 1979, so many orders were comin' in that he couldn't handle them part-time. He either had to stop takin' orders or quit his day job. After a family conference, Jerry left his job at the sale barn and went into the spur makin' business full time and on his own. Used to be about three-quarters spurs and one-quarter bits, but, these days, it's almost all spurs.

In the 1980s, the whole collectibles market kicked in. The first spur show in Amarillo was 1984. Jerry's still ridin' that wave. But he never got fancy with his designs. See, there are three kinds of spurs, mostly just two now. There's Texas, California, and Northern Plains. Jerry does Texas style. It's old school—workin' spurs. Others do ornamental spurs you wouldn't dream of puttin' on boots. Jerry sometimes gives his spurs to Dave Lane, a cowboy I'll tell you about next. Dave wears them spurs around until Jerry wants 'em back. When Dave is done breakin' 'em in, they don't just look like authentic workin' spurs. They *are* authentic workin' spurs. Like, a couple months ago, Dave was dehornin' cattle while wearin' a pair of expensive Cates spurs. Heck, you could buy a nice little used car for what Dave was spillin' cow blood all over.

California style is ornamental, jewelry-like. Northern Plains is pretty much a mixture of the two, but you're not seein' much of it anymore. California style is scrollwork, normally cut into the metal instead of overlaid. Jerry will do any kind of design, like a longhorn, initials, flowers, or wheat strawing. Overlays on the steel boot cuff are made mostly of copper or silver nickel. One pair of his spurs brought forty thousand. Wasn't the material really. Wasn't jewel-encrusted or nothin'. Just hours and hours of work. Typical pair runs more like two or three thousand. Jerry won't say, or don't want me to say who, but a former president owns a pair of his spurs and quite a few actors whose names you'd recognize.

He don't advertise. Don't have a Web site neither. Just word of mouth. He still goes to shows though. Was in Abilene recent. Took spurs he'd made for someone else, but hadn't delivered yet.

If someone wants to order a pair, he's happy to take their name and specifications, but they're sometimes discouraged when he tells them he has seven legal pads full of names of people who've placed orders. Figures there are about seven hundred names on them pads. He used to make a pair of spurs a day when he was younger and earnin' a full-time livin' at it. He'd work twelve- and fourteen-hour days, depending on how long it took to finish a pair. Just had that goal—pair a day. Did what it took to get 'em made. But he's seventy-two now and happy with makin' one pair a week. That multiplies out to a waiting list of almost fifteen years.

He got a call recent from a feller who mentioned he'd put his name in six years ago. Wasn't mad. Just wonderin' how things were comin' along.

Jerry said, Doggone it, mister, I apologize. If it's been six years and you're not put out about it, I'll make you a pair.

Next week, he ignored his list and made the feller a pair.

Six hundred and ninety-nine to go.

The Straw Boss

Lot of ranching families see their sons drift off into other professions. Maybe they leave for the city or, if they stay local, work in oil and gas. Reverse of that for Dave Lane. His family moved from Oklahoma in the 1930s. Father worked for Phillips Petroleum near Borger, northeast of Amarillo. Old-fashioned company town called Phillips. Had a bad explosion at the refinery years ago, and they did away with the town. Dave's father was killed in a trucking accident when the boy was five. Family was friends with some people who owned the Crutch Ranch east of Borger. Growin' up, Dave started to spend time out there. Pretty soon, he was spendin' more time there than he was at home, sleepin' over most nights. Just about everyone who lived around there went to work for Phillips when they graduated from high school. The company had jobs waitin' for 'em. In fact, they called Dave when he graduated and told him where to report. He told them he wasn't gonna report. He was gonna be a cowboy. The four 6s hired him for ten days to work cattle. After ten days, they didn't tell him to leave, so he stayed for thirty-three years.

He met Coon Jeffers there. Best cowboy Dave ever knew. Coon was runnin' the 6s when Dave started there. Worked for him for sixteen years. Coon was a great roper. Loved to rope. Nowadays, you go buy a rope for ropin' cattle, and it's all tied for you. All stretched out and worked in. Back then, stores had one big spool of cord. Cut yourself thirty-five foot of rope and tie it yourself. Most fellers would use a pickup and wire stretchers to break in them ropes. Not Coon. He had a bay named Jeep. He'd pick a bull and line old Jeep out, lasso an ornery bull, and let him run to the end of it. Stretch his rope that way. Coon just knew horses, cattle, and cowboys. Knew how to run a ranch. He could multitask 'fore they had a word for it. Like if there was cattle spread around in a few different traps, maybe a couple of hun'erd head in each, and they needed countin'. Coon could count cattle while he was barkin' orders to a couple of hands and carryin' on a conversation with another.

Coon cowboyed all his life, mostly on the Matador Ranch, one of the oldest and biggest in Texas. Coon's father, Claude Jeffers, was a wagon boss at Matador. That was back in the day when they camped out near year-round. Claude was famous among sure enough cowboys. They said he mighta broke more horses than anyone ever. Literal. Even got ranch records to prove it. Course, back then, they were breakin' so many horses that they'd ride one three times and call it broke. There was a feller worked with Claude back then, name of Piloute Vivian. He'd been there forever. Part Indian. Them two had a disagreement and didn't talk to each other no more. Never. Decades. But they worked pretty close so they used sign language all them years to communicate. When Claude died, a buncha ranch hands was horseback, going to the funeral. They passed Piloute's house. He was settin' out in the yard under a tree, eatin' a pie. They stopped to talk to him. Asked if he was going to the service for Claude.

He said, Hell, no. Some buck ain't comin' to mine.

Usually a story behind a cowboy's nickname. A morral is a nosebag and slips over the muzzle of a horse or a mule. Grain in there to feed 'em. Keeps stock from spillin' and hoggin' each other's feed. One morning 'fore sun up, when Coon was a young cowpuncher, he was puttin' morrals on mules in the barn. Pitch-black. Them morrals was preloaded with feed the night before. Unbeknownst to Jeffers, a raccoon had stowed away overnight in one of them bags. It was still unbeknownst to Coon when he slid the hanger over the head of a Jenny. The coon took a bite outta her snout. Despite being in the dark in more ways than one, it was readily apparent to Coon that there was a problem of imme-diate consequence when that mule went plum loco, kickin' and hee-hawin' like to raise the dead. It was loud. I mean Fourth of July loud. Lights come on in the bunkhouse, and cowboys come runnin' over in their union suits, wonderin' if they was bearin' witness to the end of civilization as we know it. That mule 'bout deconstructed the barn 'fore Jeffers figured out a critter was in that morral. When things had calmed down and them cowpunchers had quit laughin', he was Coon before breakfast been served and was known by that name 'til the day he died.

Annnnnnnyway, supposed to be tellin' you about Dave. One time on the four 6s, he had a bad wreck. Had rained overnight. In the mornin' they gone out to gather cattle. Bit of a wild bunch, these partic'lar cows. Cowboys threw 'em up in a corner and held them for quite a while. Then Dave and another feller gone out in front of the herd. Were gonna drive 'em a couple miles to a new pasture. They went through a gate, come off a creek, and gone up a hill. Cattle splattered on 'em at that point. Ground was rotten from the rain. Dave's horse, Hattie, got in a hole. Dave couldn't get away, and the horse rolled on top of him. The herd split and went around him. His son, Ron, was behind the herd and later said all he saw was the sun reflectin' off Hattie's horseshoes when she rolled over.

When they all reached him, Dave was in a bad way. Said he thought he'd broke his shoulder. Them cowboys is all the same.

They start talkin' about who's gonna get his spurs and who's gonna get his saddle. Like Dave's about to die and they's dividin' up his stuff.

They gone up and got the crew cab, which was a couple miles away, and brung it over. But every time they sat him up, Dave gone to throwin' up. They decided they best get an ambulance. Big Ron Cromer was cowboyin' with them that day, and he called headquarters on the two-way radio.

Shari, Dave's wife, answered.

Big Ron says, Shari, could you do me a favor? Could you call and get an ambulance?

She didn't say nothing for a minute. Then she says, Who's hurt?

Big Ron says, Now, he's not hurt very bad.

Who's hurt, she says.

He says, Well, Lane.

She says, Where are y'all at? I'm comin' over there.

He says, You can't get here. It's too muddy. Tell the ambulance we'll meet them at the little pasture gate.

Big Ron gone down to meet the ambulance, but the creek was runnin' from that rain. Them boys drivin' the thing weren't gonna cross the creek.

Big Ron says to them, You got two choices. You cross the creek now, or I'm gonna whip your ass, and then you'll cross the creek.

So they crossed over easy enough and loaded Dave on a board. Got him in the ambulance. At the local hospital, they couldn't find nothin' wrong with him except some bruised vertebrae. They sent him home. Rough weekend tryin' to sleep, but, on Monday mornin', he got up, showered, and got ready for work. Shari come in the bathroom and asked what he was doing. He was stickin' pins in his arm.

He says, I can move my arm, but I can't feel nothin'.

That's it, she says. We're going to Amarillo.

They laid him down in the hospital and did tests. When they figured out what the real problem was, acted sudden like he'd turned into nitroglycerine.

Nobody move. Don't touch him. Stand back.

He'd broken his neck.

They said just a little bit of wrong movement, and it might be the last move you ever make.

Put him in traction for a couple days. Carved some bone out of his hip. Put in some screws and a plate. Had a neck brace for three months and didn't ride for six. Cowpunchin' ain't a stroll on the beach.

Dave's son, Ron, is named after Ron Cromer, so there's Little Ron and Big Ron. Big Ron Cromer is fill-a-doorway big. About six-foot-four, maybe two hun'erd seventy-five pounds. Big Ron and Dave grew up together in Phillips. When Big Ron was thirteen, a feller by the name of Jim Jordan decided to drive a buffalo herd from Woodward, Oklahoma, which is near the northeast corner of the Panhandle, to Clayton, New Mexico. Had a wild animal park and curios shop he'd built for tourists. Had to get the buffalo there. Friend of Big Ron's family heard about the two-week buffalo drive and got him involved. Quite a menagerie. Jordan had a bear on a chain ridin' in one of the wagons. A couple of monkeys were swingin' around the hoodlum wagon. Probably thirty-five buffalo and about twenty-five Brahma bulls. Think he had them bulls because they was payin' the bills. Followed the Santa Fe Trail part of the way.

Big Ron says you don't drive them buffalo so much as herd them. They're ornery critters, much more powerful than a cow and with a mind of their own, so you had to treat them different, show them some respect. It was hard work, long hours in the saddle, hot, and dusty. And if you ventured too close to the hood wagon, one of them monkeys would leap onto your shoulder, bite your ear, jump back on the wagon, and squeal at you. Jordan's lucky there ain't trees out there, or one or both of them monkeys woulda been strung up.

Jordan was a showman, so it wasn't a quiet little buffalo drive. Every night when they stopped and camped, they'd have a barbeque. Sell tickets. Folks from the small towns they were passin' through would come out and see the buffalo and the bear and get bitten by the monkeys. This was 1953, long 'fore the number of buffalo begun to build back up after the slaughter in the 1870s.

Course, in 1953, there was hardly any open range left, so Jordan got permission to cross a bunch of ranches. But one old boy, prissy feller, wouldn't let them cross his land. They drove them buffalo and cattle down his fence line. He was parallelin' them on the other side of the fence, watchin', sittin' in a fancy English saddle and ridin' a Tennessee walkin' horse.

They camped next to fancy saddle's ranch that night. In the mornin' a newscaster Jordan had arranged for come to film the buffalo drive. Reporter was out of Amarillo, feller by the name of Cotton John. He was as big a showman as Jordan. He got to callin' the Panhandle the Golden Spread. Them TV people is funny. Settin' at their typewriters, inventin' funny names, and hoping ever'one will start using them funny names.

It's a beautiful mornin' on the Golden Spread, he'd say.

He drove up in a paneled jeep with a cameraman and film camera big as a refrigerator. Course, TV hadn't hardly even got going in 1953.

Cotton John had previous asked Jordan if he could arrange a stampede for the camera. It wasn't the kind of request Jim Jordan refused. They happened to be near a little peak out there on the high plains. Close to Boise City. Flat all around, but a good little rise was there. Jordan wasn't in camp that mornin' but the rest of the hands herded all them buffalo and cattle up near the top of the peak. Harder than it sounds. Cecil B. DeMille woulda had trouble stagin' that whole deal. Like I said, buffalo ain't exactly the most agreeable critters. But they done it, buffalo and cattle near the top of the peak. Cotton John was sittin' in that paneled World War Two surplus Willy's jeep below. Cameraman stood on the roof of the jeep with that big ol' camera on a tripod.

One of the cowhands fired his .45 in the air. All of them boys got to whoopin' and hollerin' and wavin' their slickers. Them buffalo and Brahma bulls took off, and it weren't at a leisurely pace. It's pretty much for sure that none of them boys ever started a buffalo stampede in his life. This was new ground they was breakin', and they broke it good. All that noise from the shootin' and hollerin', combined with the momentum they picked up on the downslope of that peak, them buffalo worked themselves into a near panic. They couldn't have moved any faster if Comanches were chasin' 'em. They come down that slope and headed straight for the jeep like a runaway freight train. Just a thunderin' like apocalpyse on the hoof.

Sittin' in that jeep, Cotton's eyes got as big as a harvest moon. Forget the Golden Spread. He saw the Golden Beyond. The cameraman was tryin' to keep his eye on the lens, but the ground under the jeep starts shakin'. The jeep itself starts shakin'. The camera starts shakin', and the cameraman starts shakin'. The herd was outta control and hurtling forward. If them buffalo hit the jeep, they'd flip it like a tiddlywink. Just as the lead buffalo was about to ram the Willy's head-on, herd split and run down both sides of the vehicle. But they were tightly packed, shank to shank, and nudgin' and pushin'. Some of them buffalo was bangin' against the sides of the paneled jeep. The cameraman hit the deck and held on to both edges of the roof to keep from fallin' amongst them churnin' hooves. Cotton was inside, prayin' at high decibel—really high—apparently convinced volume and the effectiveness of his spiritual entreaties was directly linked. The TV camera tumbled off the truck and was crushed beneath the stampedin' beasts. To make matters worse, them buffalo kept right on going, right over the fence owned by the prissy feller with the English saddle.

Took most of the mornin' to round up the herd—and Lord knows how much money from Jordan to make good with that rancher.

Annnnnnnyway, I was tellin' you about Dave. He was a real good hand. After a time, they made him straw boss at the 6s. That's the cowboy boss. Straw boss pretty much runs the cattle operation on a ranch. Tells the cowhands what to do. Dave credits Coon Jeffers with showin' him how it was done proper. Dave had a motley crew workin' for him. Like Kevin Burns. Ever'body likes Kevin, but his work ethic is notorious for not being real hard. Cowboy crew would get through with something about nine o'clock in the mornin' and Burns would say, Boss, it's too late to start anything else now, ain't it? We gonna quit for the day?

Dave says Kevin might be one of the best bit and spur makers around, along with Jerry Cates, but he don't look ahead much. Dave says if it cost him one dollar a day to live, he'd be happy with ninety-nine cents.

One time, Dave says to him, I'm gonna go to work for you.

Burns says, Do what?

Dave says, I'm gonna go to work for you, but I'm gonna be your boss. You're gonna come in the shop every mornin' at seven o'clock, and we're gonna work eight hours a day.

Back then, Burns was probably gettin' three hun'erd dollars for a pair of spurs.

Dave says, I'm gonna sit by the door so you can't come out. You're gonna build a pair of spurs, and your wife is gonna get one hun'erd dollars. I'm gonna get one hun'erd, and you're gonna get one hun'erd.

Kevin looked like he seen a ghost. Not 'cause of the way the money been split, just the idea of workin' solid every day.

He said, Boss, I can't do that. Just can't do that.

Few years ago, Kevin's bit and spur makin' shop burned down. All them folks up in Stinnett, where he lives, like Kevin. The town got together and built him a new shop. They say he had mixed feelings about the gesture. See, some folks think he burned it down himself so he wouldn't have to work.

One time, Little Ron had ordered spurs from Burns for his father's birthday. It was July. Little Ron had just graduated from high school. About two o'clock in the morning, he knocked on Dave's bedroom door. He come in and presented him with his spurs.

Happy birthday, he said.

Dave said he appreciated the gesture, but wondered if it couldn't have waited until mornin.

Little Ron said he'd just gotten 'em. Said he went over after supper to get the spurs, but Kevin only had one done. Little Ron sat there and made him build the other one. Took until one in the mornin'.

Yeah, Burns always got an angle. One fall, Dave called Kevin to do some day work on the 6s. They was short-handed, and

Kevin had hired out for Dave before. Ranch run cattle solid three or four months, yearlings, and I mean a lot of 'em. They'd get in three to five hundred head of calves every day in the fall. They'd vaccinate 'em and then have to keep pushin' them calves away from headquarters as more come in. They'd end up with maybe fourteen thousand head.

Kevin said, What about horses? I just got two horses now.

Dave says, Yeah, bring 'em. And we got some extra ranch horses you can ride.

So Kevin came over and he had a small sorrel got crippled, and it was new to the herd, so some of them older horses was pickin' on him—bitin' and kickin'. Dave says, Kevin, why don't you take that little ol' horse home and turn him out? He'll get all right.

Yeah, I'll do that.

So they come back late one evening from doctorin' and movin' cattle. Two or three days later. They was unloadin' horses and Kevin says, Boss, can I get a bale of hay for my old sorrel?

Dave says sure. He went off to his office on the northwest side of the big house at ranch headquarters, fixed himself a drink, and raised the blind. Could see down the road where it joined the highway. When Burns left a bit later, it was with the dangedest load of hay you ever seen. Looked like an Okie movin' to California during the Dust Bowl with an overloaded truck, except, instead of that Model T being humped over with everything you could ever fit in a house, it was full to tippin' with hay.

Another cowhand knocked on Dave's door, comin' in to get his mail. Dave invited him to sit down and share a toddy. Dave asks the feller if he helped Kevin get his bale of hay. Feller got to grinnin' like a cat and looked over. Seen that blind was up.

He says, You see him leave?

Dave said, Yeah. How much did he have?

Feller says, I don't know. Fifty or sixty bales.

Dave's just a real good cowboy. He done rodeo and done real well at it. But he's just as good a range cowboy. Like judgin' the weight of cattle. He had some cattle on wheat last winter for a feller don't live in the country all the time. He was back to sell 'em. Was gonna load them on a truck and bring them into town to weigh 'em, but there were ninety head of heifers and seventy head of steers, so movin' them was gonna be a chore. Dave tells him to sell the steers at seven twenty-five and the heifers at seven hun'erd. Wasn't easy to judge. Tough winter. Them cows should have been fifty pounds more each. And they was all mixed together on that wheat, steers and heifers. But the feller did like Dave said. When they did finally get weighed, them seventy steers averaged seven twenty-six, and the ninety heifers averaged six ninety-four.

Dave worked with another feller I talk about in this book, but I ain't gonna say his name. Feller was tough on stuff. Legendary tough on stuff. Shari used to do the billing for the ranch. Dave would come in after supper.

She'd say, Go sign the bills.

Well, he'd hardly look at 'em if she done all the work. Just signed 'em.

But one time, she says, Has so-and-so had a lotta flats?

Dave says, Hell, I don't know. I guess I heard him say something about going to town to get a flat fixed.

She said, He had forty-two flats last month.

Dave looked at her like she said a million. Finally, he says, Did you just say forty-two?

She nodded. Got the receipts from the service station.

One or two flats be normal for a month.

So-and-so had a dual wheel pickup, two tires in front but four in back for haulin' heavy trailers.

He calls one mornin' and says, I got a flat, and I don't have a spare.

Dave was a long way from him. No one else was close. Everyone was feedin' cattle.

Dave says, Jack that dual wheel pickup and take one off the back.

Feller says, I already had a flat, and I don't have a spare.

Dave says, I think what we got here is a failure to communicate. Just jack up the back and take off another one of them duals.

So-and-so was silent for a minute and then finally says, I already had three flats this mornin' and already used the spare and two tires off the back. Now I got a fourth flat.

Thirty-eight to go.

Dave never did figure out how that feller could get forty-two flats in one month, although four in one day is a good start. The straw boss wasn't sure he himself could get forty-two flats in a month if he went lookin' for sharp objects to drive over.

One time, there was a grass fire on the ranch. Ever'one come around, includin' so-and-so. They got the fire put out easy. Ever'one was standin' around, chewin' the fat. Suddenly, kaboom! There was an explosion. Ever'body looks around. The noise come from so-and-so's truck. A spare he had in back had blown out. No cause. Wasn't fire-related. Wasn't heat. Wasn't no pressure on it. Just kaboom! Ever'one knew about this feller and flat tires. They all looked at each other wide-eyed. Ever'one was thinkin' the same thing—there's somethin' supernatural about so-and-so and tires.

But that ain't half of it. One winter, it snowed like hell. Drifts higher than barns. Well, maybe not that high, but high enough.

All the pickups is four-wheel drive on the ranch, but they weren't doing the job in them big drifts. Feller by the name of George, lived in west camp, put chains on all four tires of his truck. He was braggin' on the two-way radio the next day, sayin', This son of a gun is just like a tank. I can go anywhere I want.

So-and-so was livin' in east camp. He was snowed in there, and he heard that braggin' on the radio. He gone down to the barn after supper and put chains on all four of his truck tires. There was a big snowdrift just past the barn. So-and-so drove his truck through there, but it don't make it. Got stuck.

He called on the telephone for George in west camp. It's about ten or twelve miles across there. Asks him to come pull him out. By then, it was about ten at night with the wind and snow still blowin'. George says he ain't comin' over.

So-and-so says he don't want Dave to know he's stuck. But his truck weren't the only thing not budgin'. George wouldn't come. Feller remembered a little old Ford tractor there in east camp. He managed to use it to pull that flatbed out of the drift.

Dave was over the next mornin'. The feller says, There's something wrong with the bed of my truck. The rack is rubbin' against the cab.

Dave looks at that truck, and it ain't right. Whole thing is bent where it should be straight. If that truck were a horse, he woulda put it down. Dave gets on his belly in the snow and looks up. Frame was broke on both sides. Them forty-two flats was flashin' through Dave's brain, but he ain't puttin' two and two together. Sends so-and-so into town to get it fixed. And it weren't gonna be cheap.

Next day, Dave gone over where the truck had been in that snowdrift. He sees tracks ever'where. Examines the situation. Turns out the feller had hooked that tractor on to the front end and yanked the truck from side to side like a dog on a meaty bone. Then he done the same on the back end. Got the truck out, but broke it in two, too.

Feller might have been hell on equipment, but he's the nicest some buck in the world. Dave says he's the only cowboy who ever shook his hand after he fired him and told him he'd enjoyed workin' for him.

Dave's wife Shari died of cancer two years ago April. They were married near forty-five years. He had her home all but the last four days. They just had the one son, Ron. No grandkids.

When Ron was only about three years old, Dave come home one night. Little Ron met him on the front porch. Had his boots switched. Had the right boot on the left foot and the left on the right. Dave says, Cowboy, you got your boots on the wrong feet.

Ron looked down at them boots and then looked up at his father. Scrunched up his face a bit and says, But, Dad, these are the only feet I got!

Dave retired to Groom where Little Ron has a horse place so he could help him manage it. But a year later, Little Ron got a job offer to run the Pitchfork Ranch, down in Guthrie. It's another famous ranch in Texas history. Founded in 1883. It's right next to the four 6s. Dave stayed at the place near Groom.

He used to rodeo. Little Ron still does, but he's mostly too busy workin'. Dave did team ropin'. He was a header. Amarillo has a big rodeo every Fourth of July. The Will Rogers Range Riders Rodeo. Dave won it twice. Beat out maybe two or three hun'erd other teams. Little Ron has come in second twice. His ambition has always been to win it. Win a Range Riders belt buckle like his father.

Dave ribs him and says, You're gonna get your two Range Riders buckles.

Ron says, Dangit, I know it, but I want to win 'em, not inherit 'em.

Dave won them belt buckles in 1992 and 1996. When he won that second one, he was fifty-four years old. Beat a bunch of twenty-year-olds. Course, that puts Dave's age near seventy now. Hasn't rodeoed since 1997, but he just bought a few ropin' steers three weeks ago. Hasn't roped them yet. But he's got an arena across the street from his house. And he's got a good ropin' horse these days.

Someone might want to tell the young bucks to cinch up. Don't look like the straw boss is done yet.

The Stone

Bill O'Brien and I are driving four-wheelers near the southwest corner of his sixty thousand-acre LIT—short for Littlefield—Ranch in the Texas Panhandle. We're going to look for some stones. The Frying Pan Ranch is probably the most famous in the Central Panhandle, but the LIT is a storied ranch as well. The old Frying Pan is a long north-to-south rectangle that presses up against Amarillo on the city's northwest side and stretches from below Interstate 40 up to the southern bank of the Canadian River. The southern boundary of the LIT runs along the northern bank of the Canadian River and stretches north from there. If the river didn't exist, the southeast corner of the LIT and northwest corner of the Frying Pan would just about touch.

The dirt road we're cruising down turns to asphalt. We slow as we enter Boy's Ranch, a town and school rolled into one. More than a century ago, this was the site of the Wild West town of Tascosa. It was known as the Cowboy Capital of the Plains. There wasn't much more to it than bars and brothels in the 1880s. The town started out as a plaza, founded by sheepherders pushing down the Canadian River valley out of New Mexico territory about the time Comanche dominance was beginning to wane. By the late 1870s, with cattlemen moving into the Panhandle in a big way, Tascosa became the southern terminus, the gathering point, of a cattle trail to Dodge City. The New Mexicans were squeezed out. There are stone ruins of a shepherd's camp on the LIT.

Billy the Kid frequented Tascosa. They say he ran stolen horses out of New Mexico, tethered them in a draw along the northern side of the Canadian River east of town, also on the LIT, and then doubled back to Tascosa. He'd round up cowboys in the bars, bring them out to the shady spot, and sell them the horses at bargain prices. The site is an acre-big oasis, full of cottonwoods. It hugs the river near towering rock outcroppings. Round holes, six inches deep, formerly used by Indians to grind corn, punctuate the top of the formation. One can imagine Native Americans at work here, enjoying the commanding view of the valley across the river.

Legend has it that a bunch of ranchers hired Pat Garrett, who eventually killed Billy the Kid, and his boys to run the Mexican sheepherders out of the territory. With the ranchers' range-land secured, Tascosa thrived as the first and largest city in the Panhandle. All the cowboys from the surrounding ranches gathered there to get watered down. There was plenty of brawling, gambling, and gunfighting. Its Boothill Cemetery is famous.

A rancher by the name of Lee owned a big spread south of the river, across from Tascosa. At the time, the railroad was deciding where to locate a right-of-way through the area. Every time the town fathers sponsored a civic improvement, they raised Lee's taxes, sometimes exorbitantly. Lee complained about the practice, but his protests fell on deaf ears. Proud to be the biggest, and as they saw it, best town in the Panhandle, the Tascosans played hardball with the railroad, demanding a high fee for a right-of-way through town. Lee, seeing an opportunity for revenge, offered the railroad free passage on his land south of the river. The railroad accepted the offer it couldn't refuse, and Tascosa immediately began a long, slow decline into obsolescence. The last resident left the same year the town was reborn as the first boys ranch in the country in 1939. There's certainly some irony there, a reform school on the site of the wildest of Old West towns.

Bill O'Brien's grandfather, Will, first came out to the Panhandle as a nineteen year old and worked on the XIT ranch as a cowboy. That was about 1890. I keep telling you about famous Texas ranches, but the XIT may be the most famous. That's debatable, of course, but not the fact that it was the largest of all Texas ranches. The XIT was a three-million acre land grant that a Chicago-based syndicate got in 1882 in exchange for building the new statehouse in Austin. Three million acres is a couple of Delawares.

Annnnnnnyway, Will O'Brien had been working for the XIT for a few years when a caravan of wagons arrived one day, loaded down with barbed wire. Remember I mentioned William Bush was one of the first to fence the range in Texas on Joseph Glidden's Frying Pan Ranch, using Glidden's newly patented barbed wire. The rest of the big spreads started doing the same. Will knew instantly that it was only a matter of time before he'd be turning in his spurs for a pair of pliers and leaving behind cowboying to build fence the rest of his life. Instead, he bought a homestead down in Lamb County. He later moved up to Deaf Smith County, due west of Amarillo on the New Mexico border.

Bill and I turn and follow a dirt road along the Canadian River. We pass under a highway bridge. We're leaving the LIT and crossing onto the Bivens Ranch. One of the first cattlemen to graze stock in the Texas Panhandle was George Littlefield. He was essentially a cattle trader. He bought big herds in south Texas, drove them north to the railhead in Dodge City, and sold them for huge profits. But he discovered he could make even more money if he wintered his herds in the Panhandle, along the Canadian River breaks, and got his cows to Dodge in spring. Supply and demand. Annual cattle drives originating in south Texas were only getting underway in spring. So without much supply, cattle prices at Dodge City that time of year were high. By the late 1870s, homesteaders were moving in. Littlefield was getting nervous about the future of his operation. He didn't own much of the land, but that didn't stop him from selling his two hundred forty thousand-acre ranch, which was basically his cattle and squatters rights, to a Scottish outfit called the Prairie Cattle Company in 1881. About that time, the first surveyors for the state arrived in the area and went to work.

The romance of the West is not solely a latter-day occurrence. It infected plenty of people and companies, including Europeans, even as the Old West was an ongoing reality. That explains in part why Scottish and English companies bought land in Texas in the 1880s and set up cattle operations. They didn't know much about cows, couldn't find experienced managers, and couldn't get a handle on their vast holdings. Perhaps most crucially, they had no historical perspective on the vagaries of weather. A combination of winter blizzards and summer drought in the mid-1880s combined to decimate Panhandle cattle herds and caused the overseas companies to sell out. A cattleman named Lee Bivens bought out a lot of the foreigners and put together a five hundred thousand-acre ranch, which originally included the LIT. Although heirs parceled up and sold much of the Bivens Ranch over the years, Bill and I pass through a gate onto a substantial remnant of the original Bivens' place.

Bill was raised in Amarillo, next door to Stanley Marsh, not on a ranch. His dad owned an eighty-five thousand-acre spread outside of Roswell, New Mexico. Every summer, the day after school let out, he put Bill on a Greyhound bus and sent him down to Roswell. It was all but desert. The land could only sustain a thousand cows, one per eighty-five acres. The Panhandle isn't exactly the garden of Eden, but the stocking rate is more like one cow for fifteen or twenty acres. Bill would rise at four thirty every summer morning, saddle up, and ride the range all day long, checking on cattle, or just try to find some. By the time he graduated from high school, if not before, he knew he wanted to be a rancher—just not in New Mexico.

The Panhandle is the beef capital of the country. When Bill got out of college, feedyards were just starting to get concentrated in and around Amarillo. Eventually, a large percentage of all feedlot capacity in the country was located in the Panhandle. But back then, there weren't enough slaughterhouses in the region for all of the fat calves coming out of the feedlots. Bill partnered with an older guy who had contacts at a number of small processing plants in Alabama and Mississippi. The older man needed a junior partner to do the actual buying of cattle, which took a lot of legwork and hustle. For about three years, Bill made a lot of money acting as a middleman, buying feedlot fat cattle and shipping them to various beef plants in the South where he and his partner had contracts. Those were the days when small-time plants killed two to three hundred cows a day. Once big processing factories that kill five thousand head a day started to locate in the Panhandle, the heydays were over for Bill, but, by then, he had already shifted his focus and bought his own feedlot. He partnered with Stanley Marsh's brother, Tom.

Bill later bought the sixty thousand-acre LIT ranch and turned it into a modern cattle operation. He doesn't do any breeding. He buys calves at about six months of age, grows them out for another six months, sends them to feedlots (he still owns a few) for several more months, and then ships the cattle to market.

As he got more and more familiar with his ranch and its boundaries, he became curious about the early surveying. He obtained records from the Texas Land Office that included the original surveyor's report and field notes. He did the same thing for the neighboring Bivens Ranch, part of which was originally XIT land. The XIT Ranch, shaped like a modern-day gerrymandered congressional district, did have one straight edge. It ran half the length of the north-south Texas-New Mexico border, starting at the Oklahoma line and stretching down to the same latitude as Lubbock. The XIT was first surveyed in Spanish leagues, about forty-four hundred acres to a league. At each corner of a league, the surveyor placed a marker. Many of the markers were a standing stone with XIT carved in it. Other times, the markers were mounds of stones or a metal pipe.

Prior to 1875, surveying in Texas was dangerous work. Crews were easy prey for roving bands of Comanches. The surveyors would usually employ local cowboys to carry their measuring chains, and they'd pay them in whiskey instead of cash. The thinking went that the ground surveyed by cowboys in the morning was probably accurately done, but, when they did surveying in the afternoon and had a little hooch in them, well, perhaps the measurements lacked a.m. precision.

As a project, Bill decided to find as many surveying markers on the LIT as he could. He says it's like a crossword puzzle. The original 1880s surveyor records are all in Spanish *varas*. A *vara* is 33.3 inches. And each league is five thousand square *varas*. So he converted all those to the American system of measurement. Then he went on his computer and created theoretical plot points on Google Earth. He then made notations of the supposed coordinates and, using GPS, went out looking for the surveyor's markers. In his research, Bill found that seven different surveyors surveyed his LIT Ranch and submitted reports to the Texas Land Office. Some of the surveying teams were excellent. Some weren't. It took a lot of false starts and recoordinating, but Bill eventually found scores of markers on his land.

Because Bill has scoured his own ranch, today, we're heading out to find 1880s surveyor stones on virgin ground on the Bivens' place. Our goal is to find league corners that were originally part of the old XIT. Armed with theoretical coordinates Bill has developed from the original surveyor's notes overlaid on Google Earth and a Garmin GPS finder, we set out on our treasure hunt with stone slabs as our hopefully not buried treasure.

As I swallow dust kicked up by his four-wheeler, I recall another Bill I met the day before, Bill Breeding, a veterinarian who lives in Miami. Not everyone in the Panhandle is a successful cowboy or rancher like Bill O'Brien and the others I'm telling you about. One time, there was a guy there in Miami who got mad at the family dog, the kids' pet, when it got into the chicken house and killed a bunch of egg layers. One day when his wife was out and the kids were in school, the guy took the dog, a rifle, and a shovel out to the back of the pasture and shot the dog. He dug a shallow grave and threw some dirt over the carcass.

That night, the kids were pretty distraught when they learned their dog had run off. Big family meeting to console them and assure them the dog was no doubt safe and would return home soon. When the kids were asleep and the husband and wife were going to bed, a dog could be heard howling way off somewhere. It was muffled and distant, but carried in the clear night air. Not that unusual to hear dogs and critters at night, but the wife thought it was their dog and wanted her husband to go investigate. Because the husband knew the dog was dead, he wasn't of a mind to go investigating dog ghosts, and he wasn't the superstitious sort—didn't think that dead dog had come back to haunt him. He told his wife to roll over and go to sleep.

Two days later, Bill Breeding, the vet, got a call from the husband.

He said, Wonder if I can bring my dog in. Think he's been shot.

Bill could hear the guy's wife in the background yelling at him.

She said, You son of a bitch, you *know* he's been shot!

They came into the clinic, and the guy didn't say much. He was sheepish. His wife was hopping mad. He repeated his comment about thinking the dog had been shot, but he didn't say much more than that.

She said, He was howling for two days. That's how long it took him to dig out of that hole and come home.

Took Bill a while to figure it out, but turns out the husband mostly missed when he shot the dog. The bullet grazed the side of the dog's head, which was enough to knock him out, but it hit a vein in its ear, which gushed blood. So between the gushing blood and the unconsciousness, the guy figured he killed the hound and went ahead and buried him in the shallow grave.

When they brought him in, the dog was in decent shape, considering. Had a flesh wound on its head. The ear was messed up, his coat was covered in dirt, and he was dehydrated. But the dog was downright perky by the time Bill got done with him and they were leaving. Of course, the dog seemed to favor the wife for company. As they headed out the door and down the walk, the wife started yelling at her husband.

She said, I don't want to hear anymore how you *think* he got shot. You *know* he got shot because you're the son of a bitch who shot him!

They sold their ranch a short time later. Moved downstate a bit. He went back to college. He's a lawyer now. Think they're still married. Not sure how the dog has fared.

Annnnnnnyway, back on the Bivens Ranch, Bill O'Brien points, and we leave the narrow track on our four-wheelers. We dodge mesquite bushes, sagebrush, and maneuver around small cactus and tufts of bear grass, a kind of yucca plant, at relatively high speed. Then we slow as Bill checks the GPS. We're still rolling but homing in. He signals, and we stop, kill the engines, and start scouring the underbrush, prowling for an unnatural-looking stone. It's spring, but we can feel the Texas sun. Bill puts away the GPS for the time being. Once you get to where the old records and the GPS says the marker ought to be, your eyes and boots, used for kicking away vegetation, have to take over.

Old West surveyors would carry stones non-native to an area as markers because they could be more easily spotted in the future. Many of the stones, a foot or so tall, were set in an upright position, like a tombstone. Again, for easy identification. But over more than a century's time, most of those stones have fallen, brushed up against by cattle or toppled by erosion. The fact that the stones are fairly large and non-native helps our search effort, but the likelihood they are lying flat and probably obscured by sage or covered with windblown soil hinders our prospecting.

I look up. No other humans or man-made objects are visible to the horizon in all directions. Low hills are nearby, so my perspective isn't exactly an unimpeded ocean-like view to the brink of earth's curvature. Nevertheless, the landscape is barren, lonely, stark, rugged, and remote. Only the deep blue sky, which fills more than half my vision, softens the tableau. I imagine the surveying team, out here for weeks in the 1880s. To some extent, it was still the untamed West then, even though the days of the explorers, frontiersmen, and soldiers—Fremont, Kit Carson, and Ranald Mackenzie—had long passed and the Comanche had quit for Oklahoma. The surveyors were the last of the tamers, along with the ranchers who strung wire along their surveyed lines. There may have been little glory in surveying, but they were pioneers in their way.

Bill calls out excitedly, and I race over. He's raising a two-inch-wide stone slab, a foot high, roughly shaped, but looking a bit like a triangle. There's no question that it's a surveyor's stone. There are no carved numeric markings on the back, but it's non-native stone. The dead giveaway is the strand of barbed wire wrapped around it, the sole purpose of which is to identify it as a survey marker.

I hold it and lift it. It's just a stone, a league corner marker for the famous XIT Ranch, but the feeling is profound. It's a connection with history. History in the wild. History that can be touched. Cattle have roamed here for over one hundred thirty years. A cowboy or two may have chanced by this precise spot during that century-plus, but, as remote as this location is, probably not. In all likelihood, the stone hasn't been handled or even seen since it was set in place in the 1880s. Bill is looking at me and smiling.

We carefully lay the stone back down in the impression it has rested in for many moons. We high-five and nearly break into a run getting back to the four-wheelers. There are a half-dozen other markers on our list to find.

The Veteran

There's a feller I want you to meet who lives way out on the northwestern edge of the Llano Estacado, on the flat, wind-whipped high plains of Panhandle Texas, not far from the New Mexico border. The country here spreads like the sea in all directions to the ruler-straight, encircling horizon. The sky ain't up there somewhere. It reaches down and blends into the earth. The clouds are low and vaguely oppressive. There's nothin' but fence posts and wire, telephone poles, and a few cattle. A couple of grain elevators miles away. Otherwise, nothin' but grass. For a dozen miles, three hundred sixty degrees, less than fifty trees all told, just about the lot of them planted as wind breaks 'round houses too far away to make out clear.

Jack Patterson is eighty-nine now. Been livin' here near sixty years. Sixteen miles west of Friona on asphalt and then another three on a red dirt road to his place. Farmed the whole time. Some folks live lives marked by a buncha job or career changes or a buncha marriages, or maybe they're restless and move all the time. Then there are guys like Jack. Might say he lived a routine life once he got to Texas. Things don't change much out here. But if his life wasn't defined by a rash of job changes or marriages, it was defined all right in a few months maybe more eventful than all the changes in a normal three score-and-ten combined. Havin' a bunch of Nazis shootin' at you tends to create a lasting impression.

Jack was the eleventh of nineteen children, born on a hard-scrabble farm in Hell's Hollow deep in the southern Appalachian mountains of northern Georgia. Grew up in the Depression, but, when there's twenty-one mouths to feed and your father owns an eighty-acre farm, most of which is timber with only a few patches of tillable ground you work with one mule, a plow, and a bunch of kids with hoes, it's a might hard to tell the Depression from any other decade. His dad worked at a sawmill now and then, after the crops were planted. He'd make a few bucks that way, but they mostly lived in a cashless world. Grew or shot what they ate. Made what they wore. They had sheep. His mother had a spinnin' wheel. Ate a lotta sauerkraut they made and beans they canned. Sometimes, four kids to a bed.

None of the kids had shoes until the winter 'fore they started school. But even the kids with shoes had to put them away come May. No reason to be wearin' 'em out in the warm weather months. No different for Jack. He run around barefoot until age six, winter and summer. One February day, six months 'fore he started school, Jack's grandparents come to visit. When they left, Jack run alongside their wagon a spell, kickin' up mud and ice. A neighbor couple in another wagon come up behind them on the track, gainin' steady. The couple been watchin' Jack's barefoot dash. When they got close, husband reined the horses to a stop, and the wife hollered for Jack to come over. Did as he was told.

When he got there, the wife reaches out, holdin' a one-dollar bill, and says, Jack, have your mother get you a pair of shoes with this here dollar.

Jack thanked the woman and flew home over that snowy road. He might be shoeless, but he sure knew what they were and wanted a pair real bad. But there was a problem. Nearest town was a dozen miles away, and weren't no way his father was gonna hitch up the mules and wagon and drive twenty-four miles just to fetch a pair of shoes. But just about every family back then had a Sears Roebuck catalogue, so they fixed on mail-orderin' Jack's shoes. Got another problem though. The order form asked for his shoe size. Family had no idea what size shoe Jack wore or how to measure such a thing. So they got two straight sticks and laid Jack on the floor on his back. Placed the end of one stick at the bottom of his heel and stood it vertical against the underside of his foot. Clipped off that stick where it reached the top of his tallest toe. Then they stretched the second stick the width of his foot and clipped it, too. Stuck them two sticks in an envelope, along with the order form and the dollar bill, and sent it to Sears Roebuck. Jack still remembers when the package come back from Atlanta and the way his very first pair of shoes felt. No socks, of course.

Jack was a crack shot 'fore he ever been in the army. Got good with an M-1. They rated the soldiers as shooters, and the best in a division, about one hundred fifty men, generally shot only a point or two better than the second-best man. But Jack was practically born with a gun in his hand. In his outfit, he was not only best, only one feller ever shot within four points of him. He could hit a target a couple of foot across at four hundred yards. He remembers the time his father give him the shotgun and let him go out huntin' on his own for the first time. He was eleven. It was fall. Squirrels were feedin' on hickory nuts. He shot two. Skinned 'em. His mother boiled 'em to get 'em tender. Made a milk gravy. They dipped them chunks of squirrel in that gravy and ate like kings. He got good at huntin' all right. Had to. If his aim was off and he hit a hare in the body instead of the head, why, he'd have a whole houseful of kids and parents beratin' him for the buckshot in their rabbit stew.

When he turned eighteen in 1939, he quit high school and joined the Civilian Conservation Corps, buildin' roads in the Blue Ridge mountains. Made thirty dollars a month. Kept eight and sent twenty-two home so his brothers and sisters could get some shoes. He knocked around Florida and Tennessee, but always come back to Georgia for visits. Reason for that. When he was sixteen, he'd met a gal who was fourteen. He was visiting his cousin once, and she said she wanted Jack to meet her friend, Ona. Ona and the cousin would fetch water from the same spring, so, one day, the cousin, Ona, and Jack went for a walk together up to that spring. Jack picked some flowers for Ona that day, and they were friends ever after. They married in September 1942 when he was twenty-one. Uncle Sam got him three months later.

Did his trainin' in Salina, Kansas. Because he was married, he didn't go into town carousin' with the other GIs on weekends. Instead, he hung back in camp and volunteered to drive the officers around in a jeep while they scouted sites for the upcoming week of trainin'. Got to know the officers. They appreciated his help. He got one furlough in spring and went back to Georgia to see Ona and his family. But Ona was pregnant. When she give birth to their first daughter in July, Jack wasn't allowed to go. Fact, by the fall, he still hadn't seen his three-month-old daughter. His unit come out of Kansas and ended up doing maneuvers in Tennessee, east of Nashville. One time, they had to run an errand down to Chattanooga. That's practically Jack's hometown. It was killin' him. Hell's Hollow and his wife and baby girl he'd never seen were less than an hour away. But there was a war on, and he wasn't about to complain or ask if he could go see them.

The officer he was with said, Jack, ain't you from around here?

Jack said, Yes, I lived about forty miles away.

Officer said, Why don't we go for a little ride?

And they did. Took that jeep over the mountain. Jack saw his wife, held his baby girl for the first time, and visited with all his kinfolk.

Weren't the only time Jack's friendship with them officers paid off. After Kansas, but before they shipped out for Europe, they finished up trainin' in Mississippi. It was orienteerin' mostly. Platoon that got from point A to point B quickest over a three-day period won a weekend pass. Well, with Jack's backwoods experience, his platoon won. He got the weekend pass, but couldn't find an officer to give him an extra day so he could make it all the way home. Decided to go any way. When he got back to Georgia, he was just so comfortable and tired of the army that, come Sunday, he plain old didn't leave. Went over the hill. When he finally did leave, he told his wife and family that, when he next wrote, he wouldn't be no private first class any more. Just be a plain ol' private again. They'd bust him for sure. Won't shoot me, he said. But they'll take away my rank, maybe some of my money. Give me extra duty.

Supposed to be back in Mississippi on Monday at reveille, but didn't make it until Wednesday morning. Thursday, the captain sent for him. Went past the first sergeant's desk. Feller could only shake his head at the fate that awaited Jack. Captain told him to be at ease. Then lit into him. What in the hell happened? They could have told me any other man in this outfit gone over the hill and I'd believe it, but not you.

Jack was known in the outfit for being an honest man, but it seemed an appropriate time to fib a bit. Jack had told stories about Hell's Hollow and the moonshine got made back up in them hills. Everyone had heard the tales, so he tells the captain he's sorry, but some of his friends had got excited about him a being there.

They said, Ol' Jack is gonna win this war for us, so let's celebrate.

Well, Jack hadn't drunk a thing on the trip. Just wanted to visit with his wife, daughter, and folks. But he told the captain he and his buddies got into the shine more than a bit.

He said, Sir, I woke up a coupla days later and realized I was away from my outfit, and I hurried on back here.

The captain didn't say much more. Just looked at him a lot and then dismissed him. Jack stopped by the first sergeant's desk. The feller already had a pencil in hand, fixin' to write down whatever punishment the captain give him.

Sergeant says, So what did he give you?

Jack says, I don't know, but I bet it'll be a plenty.

Sergeant scratched his head and says, If he didn't tell you nothin', then he ain't givin' you nothin'.

Friday afternoon, the ratings went up on a bulletin board in the HQ building, and Jack had been promoted to corporal. Over the hill on Wednesday. Promoted on Friday. One of Jack's buddies been over the hill and had to peel potatoes for a month. When he seen Jack's name with corporal next to it, he come back to the barracks and cursed him out the better part of the afternoon. Finally, he says, Hell, if you'd gone over the hill a week instead of a coupla days, they woulda made you general.

Jack left New York Harbor for the war on August 6, 1944, aboard the *Queen Elizabeth*. It was built as a passenger liner, the largest in the world at the time, and would be for over a half-century, but, before she become an ocean liner, she begun life as a troop ship. Twenty-two thousand GIs were crammed on board with Jack. They crossed the Atlantic without an escort. Told the troops it took the German U-boats 'bout ten minutes to line up their torpedoes, so, the ship zigzagged every seven minutes. Don't imagine it was a lazy, carefree crossin'.

Jack was awarded the Bronze Star for what he done in a small town in Germany in February 1945. When he and his outfit landed in Normandy in September, the Germans been beaten back from the coast. Jack was a member of the 94th Infantry Division. In particular, he was part of a reconnaissance group. Supposed to be the eyes and ears of the division, which means they were in the lead, square in the middle of harm's way. Went right to the front and pushed across France, but then the Germans counterattacked in the Battle of the Bulge. After that, the 94th was moved south around the Mosel River. Jack and his outfit were fixin' to take the town of Thorn, Germany.

Winter of 1944–1945 was one of the worst they'd had in Europe in years. Jack remembers the only time he took off his boots or clothes the entire winter. Rain had come and melted a lotta the snow. Mosel had overflowed its banks and was runnin' along the base of a railroad grade as it come into town. Jack was on point in the middle of the night, leadin' a recon team along the tracks and the river and checkin' defensive positions around Thorn. The Germans had set up a machine gun nest up river where it curved. Must've detected some movement. They launched a flare and then opened up on Jack's position. He was out ahead of his three buddies a stretch. The others were able to dive and take cover at water's edge, but Jack was exposed. He could see tracer bullets start to strike the embankment above him. Only place for him to go was in the river, full of ice, so he jumped in up to his helmet. Only his eyes were exposed with his helmet bobbin' on the surface. Germans rained fire on them a while, with Jack poppin' up a few inches now and then to get air, but otherwise hunkerin' down in that freezin' river. Says he didn't feel a thing. Says havin' bullets whiz past your ear has a way of takin' your mind off the cold.

Annnnnnnyway, when the flare burned out, he and his men made it out of there and back safely to where they was bivouacked in the basement of a bombed-out building. His men got him out of his freezin' clothes, warmed him up, and put him in a spare uniform. He was fine. But it was the only time he changed clothes or took off his boots in four or five months.

Two days later, they moved in to take the town. Fightin' was light at first, and tanks backed them up, but, after takin' the town, the Germans began shellin' it. Eventually, the Americans suffered sixty-three percent casualties, killed or wounded. But it weren't over. Germans counterattacked. Jack got himself positioned in a building on the edge of town. When the counterattack come, he picked off the lead man, an officer. Remember that he was a crack shot. Another ten Germans surrendered to him instant, like it was part of a script. Jack figures them soldiers seen the writin' on the wall. With their leader dead, decided it was time to retire from the war. That's what won him the Bronze Star. But Jack's not so sure that's what really won him the Bronze Star. Earlier, in the middle of the battle for the town, Jack seen a German come up out of the basement of a castle they'd surrounded. He was about to toss a grenade at a lieutenant in Jack's outfit, the platoon leader. Jack shot him 'fore he threw it. German fell back into the basement where the grenade exploded. Lieutenant looked over and made eye contact with Jack. Knew Jack had saved his life. So that Bronze Star medal was for capturin' ten Germans single-handed, but the officer who wrote up the citation is the same one whose life Jack saved, so Jack figures that other episode was mixed in there somewhere.

Jack saw a lotta action in his eight months of fightin'. His recon group punched through the famous Siegfried line, which Hitler said was impen'trable. Ended up a dozen miles behind German lines. Surrounded a small town filled with seven hundred fifty German artillery troops, but them troops figured they was safely behind their own lines. Didn't know quite what was happening until they was walkin' outta town with their hands on their heads. Americans numbered 'bout one hundred fifty. The GIs didn't know what to do with the prisoners so they destroyed all of their artillery and radios and ordered the German officers to march their men toward the Allied lines. Jack says he don't know if they done that or not because the Americans took off east. Had a river to get to. In fact, Jack was one of the first American soldiers to reach the Rhine. Figures he was the fourth.

All that fightin' and Jack was never touched the whole time. Irony of life and war. Jack had two brothers who was also in uniform during the war, but neither one left the States. Jack didn't get discharged and back to Georgia until late September 1945. After penetratin' enemy lines, gettin' shot at, near froze to death in a river, but comin' out almost without a scratch, his brother and his young son, while ridin' in their car, were killed by a train one week to the day after he got home. And just before Christmas, his father died.

For two years, Jack worked odd jobs until he rented a little one-horse farm not far from where he'd grown up. They had six acres of corn, five acres of cotton, and a big vegetable garden. Farmed it for two years, 1947 and 1948. He done well and won a contest for most cotton grown per acre. But one day, he and Ona was out pickin' cotton, which ain't work anybody chooses to do. Haul a sack and just about bust your back the first hour of the day. Their oldest daughter was five. She was there pickin' with them. Pickin' more daisies than cotton, but she was out there.

The youngest was two, and she was in a playpen in the back of the pickup.

Jack raised up, rubbed his back, stared off to the west a spell, and said, Ona, I do believe there is a better place in the world to make a livin' than here. And I'll thank the Lord to find it if you're game.

Ona raised up, put her hands on her hips, looked at him, and said, You start lookin'.

They sold everything, includin' the wild hogs Jack had trapped in the mountains. Sold all the canned vegetables and the furniture. Everything was turned into cash by Christmas 1948. After January 1, Jack headed west with two of Ona's brothers in one of their cars, a 1939 Ford. Didn't know more than a goose about where he was headed or where he'd land. Stopped to see some relatives in New Mexico, and they ended up convincin' him to stay. He found a farm job back over the line in Texas, about two miles from where he later bought a farm himself. Ona and the girls come out on a train to Amarillo. Arrived at their new home in the dark. When Ona got up and saw no trees and that barren plain stretchin' to the horizon in all directions, took some wind outta her. They didn't get back to Georgia for three years. Ona was terrible homesick, but, when they did get back, things had changed, and people had changed. When they come back to Texas, Ona knew it was home.

Jack farmed with his father as a boy and always liked it, but done it with a mule. By the time he got out to Texas, about ten years after he'd last farmed, he'd driven a car, a pickup, a jeep, an armored car, a half-track, and a light tank. But not a tractor. When he got on a tractor for the first time and watched that dirt flyin' out behind it, he fell in love with farming. Took Jack a long spell, until 1975, before he could afford to buy his own place of four hundred forty acres. Raised the girls. They moved off to Amarillo and California. Ona passed just a couple years ago after sixty-four years of marriage. Jack stopped plantin' in 1997. But he still remembers those early years in Texas when he would plough all day, come in for dinner with Ona and the girls, and then go back out after dark and ride that diesel tractor some more across the Texas high plains, livin' a routine life and lovin' every minute of it.

The Special Texas Ranger

Ol' boy was stealin' cattle out of Arkansas. Lived down there, but he was thievin' cows in five states. Texas was his favorite. Got close to five thousand head over five years. October through April, he done his work when the cattle was off the range and ranchers were feedin' 'em. He'd leave Arkansas with a brand-new truck and a new twenty-foot stock trailer. Had some spots in mind he'd scouted out beforehand. Usually, they looked the same. Be a remote road and a pen near a gate. He'd park that rig by the gate, round up the nearby cattle, get them into the pen with a little feed, and then load them on the truck and drive on back to Arkansas. Sometimes, he'd cut a fence, but, most times, he found gates weren't locked. When they caught him, he said he never went near the well-kept, well-fenced places. Those fellers knew every ol' cow they had. But the places rundown a bit, heck, he went back to them two, three times. Not sure the rancher ever knew the first buncha cows gone missin' by the time he come back to steal a second bunch or a third. He'd be out several nights a week, every week, rustlin' cattle, and he never did go back to Arkansas without a full trailer.

Chumpy Cates was born in Foard County. His folks owned a section, both cropland and grass. Chumpy grew up farmin' and runnin' cattle. He was the oldest. When he was in the army, he'd tell his buddies there were five boys in the family and we all got a sister.

They'd say, You mean there's ten kids?

Chumpy would smile. No, that'd be six total.

One brother was Jerry, the famous spur maker I told you about. No tellin' on Chumpy's name. Thinks his mother give it to him. Maybe a brother. Can't remember. Just always been. Out of high school, he worked on several of them big ranches they got down there around Crowell. For four years. When he come back from the military in 1959, he went to work as a Foard County deputy sheriff. Done that near five years 'fore he joined the Texas Southwestern Cattle Raisers Association. Formed in 1877 when they was movin' all them trail herds north to the railroads in Kansas. Association inspected cattle headin' outta state. Chumpy was commissioned as a Special Texas Ranger in charge of investigatin' cattle rustlin' and other ranch thefts. After a few years, they transferred him up to Canadian in the Panhandle. Served as a Special Texas Ranger for the association for forty years 'fore retirin' in 2004.

Annnnnnnyway, them cattle thefts got to be a regular thing on the ranches around Canadian, Chumpy's territory. There were three thefts in a row, each on a Wednesday night a month apart. Chumpy knew the same feller done 'em. Places he picked. Timing. The law set up a network all across the Panhandle, western Oklahoma, and up into Kansas on a Wednesday night the next month. Had a lawman on every main road from Amarillo to Oklahoma City and points north and south. But the weather moved in that night. Got to snowin'. Visibility was poor. When mornin' come, they got a report of some stolen cattle out of Beckham County, Oklahoma. Twenty-one head. Called all them jurisdictions together and had a meeting. Asked if anyone seen anything. A deputy seen a brand-new truck and brand-new trailer at a motel in the area the night before. Looked out of place somehow.

See, this feller from Arkansas always had a new rig 'cause, if he ever broke down with a load of stolen cattle and had to get help, he'd been found out. So he always had new everything as a precaution against breakdowns. And he'd usually rent a motel room, lay low, and do his thievin' in the middle of the night. Like I said, one of the deputies down there in Beckham seen a new rig parked at a small motel. Thought it looked out of place, but not enough to investigate. Well, wasn't a hard thing to go to the motel and figure out which guest owned the rig. They got the name, but it was a black guy from Dallas. The feller the motel clerk seen was white.

No one ever said these rustlers was geniuses. He weren't no hillbilly from Arkansas, but he weren't no mastermind neither. As an alias, he used the name of a black rodeo calf roper, a friend of his who helped him sell the stolen cattle. The thief was a rodeo calf roper himself. The black guy was well enough known that one of the big car companies give him a new truck every six months. When the six months was up, he could do whatever he wanted with it, so he sold it to the thief.

All of this happened after Chumpy been a Special Texas Ranger for a lotta years.

When they gone to the black guy to find out who he sold the truck to, Chumpy says to his fellow lawmen, It's gonna be one of three fellers.

And he listed off the names. They were all rodeo ropers or former ropers who run together. Chumpy knew they weren't makin' as much from ropin' calves as they was spendin'. One of the names Chumpy mentioned was Stogie Stevens. That ain't his real name, but I ain't tellin' you his real name.

Stogie had rustled cattle maybe twenty-five years before and been put away for three years up in Kansas. Apparently learned his lesson, at least for a couple of decades, but then got back into it. Black calf roper coughed up Stevens' name. When they gone to pick up Stogie, he confessed easy enough. Rig was there. Bunch of spare tires, too, that he rotated so his tracks didn't look the same one theft to the next. And a whole mess of cattle that weren't his.

Stogie just had a thing for thievin'. Got in his blood. Wasn't like he needed the money. Wasn't broke. Didn't have no gambling debts or nothin'. Didn't drink. Didn't smoke. Heck, he almost went to nationals one year as a calf roper. When they arrested him after that five-year rustlin' spree, they found sixty thousand cash in a cigar box at his house. Was the thrill of it.

Chumpy ended up escortin' Stogie to about all five of them states where there were court cases against him. One time, Stogie and Chumpy were comin' back from a trial, Oklahoma or somewhere. Wasn't like Stogie had handcuffs on or nothin'. Fact, Chumpy would let that ol' rustler drive the pickup while Chumpy napped. Annnnnnnyway, they once didn't leave court until the end of the day, so they were on the road really late.

All of a sudden, Stogie was thumpin' Chumpy in the ribs with his elbow and sayin' real excited, Wake up, Chumpy! It's two in the morning. Time to steal something!

'Bout then, Chumpy realized he'd gotten himself attached to a habitual criminal.

The big trailer rig was only one way Stogie stole cows. He had a pickup with an old camper shell. When he wasn't doing long-haul thievin', he'd steal two or three baby calves at a time. Local jobs. All the time. Every week. He once told Chumpy that, if Chumpy started countin', it would take him a year to get to a number equal to how many baby calves he'd stolen over the years.

Once, Chumpy was with Stogie in a court in Arkansas. One of them things where they run thirty or forty defendants a day in front of the judge. All plea bargain deals. Some words is said, and then it's on to the next case. So the judge don't know what or who is comin' next. Stogie steps up before the judge, and the judge brightens up. Knows him. Chumpy figures it's from a previous case, but that weren't it.

Judge says, Mr. Stevens, what brings you to my courtroom today?

Stogie says, Well, stealin' cattle, Your Honor.

Blood drains from the judge's face. He stammers and stops and has to collect himself a moment 'fore he can go on. In the car after, Chumpy asked Stogie why the judge reacted so strange after Stogie said what he said.

Stogie says, One of them good Hereford bulls I stole up in Kansas, I sold to that judge a while back.

Chumpy sure got a laugh outta that. Meant his Honor was receivin' stolen property.

One feller Chumpy chased for a while was a saddle thief. Probably stole more saddles than anyone ever stole in Texas. Ranch barns and feedlots, anywhere you'd find saddles. He was a big feller, over six foot, but wide like a football player. He'd hire out at a place, a ranch or feedlot. Get to know it, get to know people's movements, and get to know where the saddles were. Then he'd steal every saddle they had and disappear. Changed names some. He was from Oklahoma and ended up in California in jail, but he worked the Panhandle a bunch because of the feedlots. More feedlots in the Panhandle than anywhere else by far. He was actually a good cowboy, and them feedlots was always needin' good hands. So he'd get hired, steal their saddles, and move on to the next feedlot. You could get close to a thousand dollars for them shop-made saddles. He was businesslike about it, too. Get him a load, rent a truck, and haul them saddles to the East Coast to sell. Or he'd drive out to California.

He had a deal he done every time, which was how Chumpy finally caught him. He'd never park his rig near the spot where the saddles were. He'd park a ways away to be safe, sometimes a half-mile. And then he carried the saddles over to his truck. Them things are heavy, but, like I said, he was a big ol' boy.

Chumpy got a report of a theft at the Hitch feedlot near Guymon, just over the border in Oklahoma. Poor Guymon. If the Dust Bowl of the 1930s had an epicenter, it was Guymon. But that was decades ago. Annnnnnnyway, thief cleared out the saddles. Chumpy gone out there with the sheriff, who'd already visited the crime scene. Sheriff is pointin' and explainin' and says, Feller pulled up right here next to the saddle house.

Chumpy don't say much. He's just lookin' around. He knew right away it was the same feller who parked a long way away. Chumpy seen a back door. While the sheriff talkin', Chumpy slips out that back door. There's an alley there, a lane between stock pens you move cattle through. Chumpy heads down that alley. This was a sortin' alley, run about a quarter-mile straight north. 'Bout a hun'erd yards up, the fence got low. Over it, he seen where the grass was smashed down. The feller had tempo-rary dropped the saddles there. And then Chumpy could see the direction he'd gone through that tall grass.

Meanwhile, the sheriff and a coupla fellers from the feedlot come 'round in a pickup.

They says, Chumpy, what are you doing out here?

Chumpy says, That ol' boy carried them saddles up through here. I'm followin' his tracks.

They look at each other like Chumpy thinks he's starring

in *CSI: Texas*. But then they seen that smashed grass. By then, Chumpy was in the truck.

He says, Go that way.

They gone out the main gate of the feedlot and headed north a quarter-mile. Chumpy remembered that, when they come in, the road crossed a low bridge over a dry creekbed.

As they come up on it now, Chumpy says, Go down in that culvert.

Them boys was rollin' their eyes. *CSI: Texas* was takin' them on a wild goose chase. When they got down in the culvert, they all seen a saddle right away. Thief decided it was too old or not in good enough condition to take, so he just left it there. Eye-rollin' stopped at that point. Chumpy seen some tracks headin' down alongside a maize field. They followed them a couple hundred yards. Where the tracks showed he stopped, they found a kid's saddle in the field. Another one he decided he couldn't get much for and left behind. But he did get away with three top-grade saddles.

Sheriff was scratchin' his head and says, How did you figure all that out, Chumpy?

Chumpy says, How? I can tell you who. It's Lester Lumpkin. That ain't his real name neither.

One of the feedlot fellers says, Lester Lumpkin? He used to work here.

Chumpy knew that. Knew it 'fore he ever got to the feedlot.

Well, Chumpy mighta known it was Lester, but it went on the longest time. They couldn't never find him, make a case against him, or get a prosecutor interested.

Few years later, a friend of Chumpy's called him and says, You know Lester Lumpkin is workin' at the feedlot here in Canadian? He's stayin' down at that old Riverside Court.

Chumpy meandered down there one night and seen Lester's old pickup parked outside a room. Knocked on the door. By this time, Chumpy knew Lester, and Lester knew Chumpy. Weren't exactly Al Capone and Eliot Ness, but they knew each other well enough. They exchanged pleasantries, and Lester told him he'd got a crippled leg from the last feedlot he worked at. Was waitin' on a settlement. Horse threw him, but caught his leg in a stirrup and drug him down an alley. Way Lester told it, woulda killed a lesser man.

Chumpy says, We've been dealin' with each other for fifteen or twenty years now, Lester, and I'm advisin' you friendly. When it comes time and you quit that feedlot, leave behind the saddles, horses, and anything else that ain't tied down. That way, if anything gone missin', I'll know it wasn't you that took it.

Lester laughed and said, I'm through with all that. I've changed my ways.

Chumpy says, The statute of limitations almost run out on most of these deals, so I'm just wonderin' for my own information. I know you took them saddles from the Hitch feedlot. Where'd you sell them?

Lester smiled a crooked smile. He knew Chumpy couldn't make a case against him.

He says, They gone a long way from here. Sold them in North Carolina.

They talked a while. Chumpy proceeded to close the books, so to speak, on a half-dozen other cases and determined where a lotta them other saddles been fenced.

Coupla months later, Chumpy's informant called again to say Lester was movin' on. Chumpy gone down to the motel and seen him packin' up.

He says, Well, Lester, I understand you're quittin' you another job.

Lester says, Yeah, I'm going to see my mother in Oklahoma for a few days.

When he left, Chumpy followed him at a distance down to Shamrock and the interstate. Oklahoma and his mother were east. Lester went west. He never was a good son.

Finally got Lester when he was picked up on a charge in California. They brought him back to Texas. Prosecuted him in Carson County, and he went to jail.

Chumpy was a very good ranger all right. Best cowboys just know cattle and horses. Chumpy just knows cattle and cattle thieves. Got to where he could think like 'em. One time, he and Stogie was on one of their road trips to a court hearing somewhere. Chumpy was lookin' out the window. Middle of nowhere and been drivin' for hours. He says, Way the road is laid out here and the gate and the pen and it being isolated and all, looks like a place you mighta hit before, Stogie. You ever steal cattle here?

Stogie says, Oh, yeah, right here.

Then he told the story of the theft, giving dates and details and verifyin' he done rustlin' there. Chumpy and Stogie are friends of sorts now. Chumpy calls him every Christmas, wishes him well, and checks on his conduct.

The Carny

Lowell Stapf is a showman. Not the way PT Barnum was a showman. Isn't a huckster. Lowell is honest to a fault. But the lights, color, noise, action, and fun of the midway got in his blood early and never got out. He was in the carnival business for fifty years all told, forty on the road.

Talking to Lowell, you get the feeling he's spent his whole life just trying to get people's pulse rate to quicken a bit. Shock them, get their eyes to widen in delight, make them feel fear and the wind in their hair on a ride, make them laugh, giggle uncontrollably, barf cotton candy and popcorn, ooh and aah.

Lowell's dad, a barnstorming pilot, was a showman in the air. Lowell just did it on the ground. Went to work as a machinist out of high school at a shop in Denver after World War One. Barnstormers would hangar their planes in Denver during the winter and have them worked on. Lowell's father got to know both the engines and the pilots. They taught him how to fly. He was named Lowell, too. When a couple of the flying circuses happened to come together in the same area, they would often set up big pylons and have races. Once when that happened in Denver, the pilots all gathered at a restaurant afterward. Someone called out the name Lowell. Lowell's father looked up, but so did another guy, Lowell Yerex. A friendship was born and then a partnership. The two Lowells wound up buying a flying circus in 1921.

During those years, especially before about 1925, people had barely seen a plane in some of the smaller towns. When the flying circus blew in, half the population turned out just to watch them land. Of course, they landed in a field. No airports in those days. Usually on the weekdays leading up to the weekend show, Lowell's dad and Yerex would take people up for rides. Made half their living just doing that. In 1923 or 1924, they bought a Ford Trimotor that held fourteen people, but had some standing room, too. Charged three dollars for a seat or two dollars to stand.

The weekend shows were something. All sorts of aerobatic maneuvers. They'd toss fireworks out of those open cockpit planes. There would be wing walkers. Also had a skydiver jump out with two parachutes. The first opened, but then released and blew away. When it did, things got interesting, but the timing had to be perfect. First, the in-cahoots announcer on the ground would panic at the sight of the freefalling skydiver. The crowd would gasp in horror as the unfortunate daredevil plunged toward terra firma. Lowell's mother and Mrs. Yerex would be the first to scream, which would ignite the primed audience. And there would be a deal with the local emergency service. They would already have the motor running on the ambulance parked by the side of the field. When the first parachute blew away like an oversized hankie, they would squeal away toward the drop zone with lights flashing and siren blaring. With announcer distraught, crowd horrified, and ambulance screaming, the jumper would deploy his second chute mere seconds and feet prior to experiencing Sudden Skydiver Death Syndrome. Of course, in some of those towns, itchy ambulance drivers would start racing forward and turn on the lights and siren before the skydiver even jumped. Just ruined the whole thing.

That Lowell Yerex was interesting. He was originally from

New Zealand, but, during World War One, he'd flown for the British and got shot down over France. Spent time in a prisoner of war camp. After Lowell's father sold out to him, Yerex kept the business for a couple years, but flying circuses were losing their appeal with audiences. So Yerex sold out, too, and apparently used the money to buy a heavy equipment business in Arizona, New Mexico, or somewhere, but that went under. He managed to hold on to the Ford Trimotor the whole time and started working for Wrigley, the big chewing gum feller. Chicle is the main ingredient in gum, and there's a mess of it in Guatemala. Yerex used that Trimotor to fly chicle to America for Wrigley. There was a revolution of some sort down there. They didn't want the gringos messing with the chicle, so they shot at Yerex and hit his plane. Injured him somehow, but he recovered. Ended up turning into a big shot himself. Got to know that area and founded TACA airlines in 1931. Ran that for quite a while and then started two other airlines, too.

Not hard to see how Lowell the Younger became a showman. When your father is a daredevil pilot and your mother helps support the family business by screaming at the top of her lungs, you're probably not going to become an accountant. And being on the road was in Lowell's gene pool, too. Even though his mother and father's barnstorming days were over before he was born, they both traveled nonstop when they owned the flying circus. Lowell's mother and Mrs. Yerex would go ahead a couple days and do the advance work, selling tickets and getting the town talking.

Lowell's parents finally settled down in Amarillo. It was a boomtown in those days. Lowell Sr. bought a machine shop and added a foundry. As far back as he could remember, Lowell hung around his father's shop. Whether it was in him or learned, Lowell was mechanically minded. Always good at building things. He once built a set of stocks from scratch, like the colonials used to punish criminals, with the holes for arms and legs that kept the perp locked in. Not only did he build it, he banged on it some, sandblasted it, and made it look ancient. Someone eventually bought it. He later discovered his creation had been sold to a museum and had a whole history attached to it.

When he came of age after World War Two, the writing was on the wall about the machine shop business. Times were changing. Lowell was looking around for a career. When the traveling carnivals came to town, the ride superintendent would find the local machine shop because there were always repairs to be made. Lowell got to know all of them. As an apprentice, he got to know the machine parts. The ride superintendents would always give him free tickets. He'd take his girlfriend out to the fair and ride the rides for hours, but he'd also slip underneath them and check out the mechanics. He saw how simple they were, and he saw all those people lined up to buy tickets.

He bought an amusement ride called the Caterpillar from a big operator named Floyd Gooding out of Ohio. At one point, Gooding had something like thirteen different crews hauling rides to fairs all over the country. Lowell went on the road with Gooding in 1955, operating his Caterpillar alongside Gooding's rides. Gooding also had a ride called the Hurricane, a big monstrous hydraulic thing with cars at the end of arms. It would spin around, and the cars would rise up on the arms. It was hard to maintain. It would break down a lot and spew oil on people. So he gave it to Lowell.

Around this time, Lowell met his longtime business partner, Duane Steck. Duane took the Caterpillar on the road. For a couple of those early years, Lowell went out on the road, too, but then he

got busy with a manufacturing business he started in Amarillo.
He built carnival rides in a warehouse just south of town. Lowell
would buy the rights to manufacture a ride. Sometimes, it was a
fancy design. Other times, it was just a rough sketch. He'd build
a prototype, test it, and then start taking orders. Those carnys in
the off-season didn't have much to do. Sometimes, they'd come to
Amarillo for weeks and just watch Lowell build their ride. Unfor-
tunately, they watched more than they paid, and the company
went bankrupt. When it did, Lowell wrote letters to each of his
creditors and told them he'd eventually pay off his debt dollar for
dollar. He did, too. Later got a letter from a well-known paint
company. They said he had unlimited credit in any of their stores
worldwide. Said they hadn't seen honesty like Lowell had shown,
and they intended to reward it.

All of that might have been the best thing could have
happened because it freed Lowell to go on the road, hauling his
rides to different carnivals and fairs he booked. Always had a
team of able-bodied young men come with him. The work wasn't
easy. Everywhere they stopped, they had to put the rides together
and then tear them back down a few days or a week later. And
just driving twelve to twenty hours at a stretch in the summer
heat with no air-conditioning and no interstates was a grind. Jack
Sisemore went on the road with Lowell. So did Robert Witherspoon. They called him T-Spoon. And Royce Mitchell. Lowell
would start on the road in early February, sort of a test run. Do
a few stock shows around Texas. Then they'd play San Angelo,
the Fiesta on the streets of San Antonio, and then Corpus Christi
for Buccaneer Days. They'd come back to the shop and tweak
the rides before heading out for all the state fairs: Illinois, Ohio,
and Michigan. They'd get up into Canada and New England.
Had a regular route every year. At the peak, he and Duane had

eight or nine rides, which translates to twenty-six or twenty-seven different trucks, semis and bobtails, some with generators mounted on them.

They'd always go to the Canadian National Exhibition in Toronto. Patty Conklin, who was big time, owned it. Biggest in Canada. Had parks all over. Patty loved Lowell. Two birds of a feather. First visit, Patty told Lowell he had an old German fun house in a warehouse nearby. He said, Nobody knows how to put it together. It's been sitting there for several years. Why don't you take it and get it running? If it starts making money, why, send me whatever you think it's worth.

That's how it worked back then. Big fraternity. People trusted each other. And there weren't a lot of regulations and government types checking on you. To make sure the rides were safe, the owners would use their employees as guinea pigs. Like the Flying Coaster. Lowell had a problem with his. Inside the ride, the cars climbed a ramp to the ceiling, crested, and dropped down. When that happened, people's heads were snapping forward, and they were losing teeth on the metal safety bar that rested horizontally in front of them. Had to fix it, of course.

Lowell told T-Spoon, Get in there, and ride that thing.

They cranked it up, and T-Spoon climbed aboard. The train disappeared inside the shed. When it came out, T-Spoon was holding his mouth. He said, Guess what?

Lowell said, What? T-Spoon said, It knocked my tooth out. Lowell said, How did it happen? When did it happen? Why did it happen?

Not that Lowell didn't care about T-Spoon's tooth. He took him to the dentist later, but he really wanted to know how to fix that darn ride. All about safety, you see. He quizzed him for ten minutes while T-Spoon tried to talk and staunch the flow of blood at the same time. Lowell finally figured out the problem. He changed the angle of that crossbar. Never had an issue again. And T-Spoon got a cap on his tooth.

They ended up putting together the fun house one winter in Lansing, Michigan. They were taking it on the road. Another carny Lowell knew, Rob Link, let them stay at his winter quarters for free. Took three trucks to hold all the parts of the fun house. They got it set up at a park in Springfield, Massachusetts. T-Spoon was the operator. He was maybe seventeen at the time, skinny as a rail. Probably didn't weigh much more than a hundred pounds. At a certain point when the cars came through, T-Spoon would push a button. A burst of air would blow up the dress of any female passenger. He said some girls would come through time and again to show themselves off, but others would get mad, or their boyfriends would. Wasn't a secret when it happened that the operator had pushed a button and shot that jet of air.

One boyfriend yelled over at T-Spoon, If you do that again, I'm gonna come over there and kick your ass.

So, of course, T-Spoon hit his girlfriend again. Sure enough, feller popped a cork. But he couldn't get to T-Spoon right away. Had to finish the ride and come around. T-Spoon could see the whole thing developing. When it was clear trouble was imminent, he hopped up on the wagon, went to the end, slipped behind a curtain, and disappeared into the cab of the semi parked right next to the ride.

The offended boyfriend had no clue where T-Spoon had gone, but the ornery rascal sat down at the controls and started to punch the air jet button and blow up the dresses of other gals. Apparently, it was fun as long as it wasn't your girlfriend.

Pretty soon, Lowell came through the back door.

What in tarnation is going on here?

Chased the kid off. T-Spoon came out when it was clear. One reason T-Spoon was ornery himself in that case was he knew he had backup. Those carnys stuck together. At age seventeen and a hundred pounds, T-Spoon didn't exactly strike fear into the hearts of troublesome fairgoers, but some of those carnys were tough some bucks. Mostly, though, it was their numbers. If one of them was challenged, there was a thing they did.

They'd holler, Hey, Rube.

When any of them did that, all the other carnys would come running from nearby rides. Even the toughest townies would find their lost temper when a dozen carnival constabularies, most of whom had seen their share of brawls, surrounded them. T-Spoon said it was funny. Could be something been building up between a couple carnys over a summer or a few years, and maybe they even hated one another. But if one of them got in trouble, the other was there in a second, shoulder to shoulder or back to back, fighting the drunk if they had to. It was the code. And then, as soon as it was over, the two carnys went back to hating each other.

Of course, it didn't help their macho image with the local toughs that Lowell made the ride operators wear lederhosen when they ran the German fun house. But there were ways of dealing with hard guys other than fighting with them. Once when Royce was operating the Hurricane, a guy trying to impress his girlfriend ordered him to keep it going extra long. He didn't say it nice either. Remember, the Hurricane has cars at the end of spokes, and the center axis spins. Think the deal was the girl was supposed to get a little sick, and the guy would look good by not getting sick. And maybe he'd get a chance to nurse her a bit, too, you see.

Annnnnnnyway, about halfway through the ride, neither the guy's face nor his body language could hide the fact that he was getting sick. So Royce turned that Hurricane into a category five. It spun and spun and spun some more. Guy tried to signal him, but Royce had a ride to operate and didn't really see him. Royce was also trying to stand clear. Operator on that ride is right in the line of fire when people's stomachs turn into cannons. If you're a carny, you have to learn to protect yourself. Before Royce stopped the thing, the guy had spun more than a broken dryer. When he got off and stumbled away, he barfed from here to there across the midway. Think his girlfriend was on to him. She laughed the whole way.

Lowell was a prankster, too. When he was in his early twenties, before he went on the road, he bought a pawnshop, back when they were respectable. He kept it for a long spell, well after he was spending most of his time on the road. The guy who ran the pawnshop for him was named Bill Wofford. Straitlaced, he was always dressed in a suit, pressed shirt, and tie, but that didn't stop Lowell from roping him into some prankstering.

One time, an electrician came in. Lowell was in the back room, but saw the guy through an interior window. He started flicking a switch on and off really fast, which made a light out on the shop floor flicker on and off just as quick.

Wofford started to help the electrician. Then he said, Excuse me. He cursed under his breath, walked over, reached up, and slapped the light a couple times. It stopped flickering and stayed on. Deal wasn't planned or anything. The normally proper Wofford was just riffing off Lowell.

The electrician said, Does it do that all the time?

Wofford didn't even look up. He was busying himself with some papers on the counter, but, a bit exasperated, he said, Yeah, just gotta hit it. Comes right back on.

Electrician said, Well, I never seen anything like that before.

You either blow a circuit breaker or maybe the bulb blows, but …

You could see the wires in his electrician's brain starting to get crossed. He said, That don't make no sense at all. Mind if I take a look?

Wofford wasn't hardly paying a mind. Yeah, sure. Take a look.

Guy got a ladder and climbed up there. Took things apart, shook a few things, poked a few things, and twisted a few things. Then he shook his own head and said, Everything's working good. I can't understand this.

So he put it back together. After Bill rang him up and wished him a good day, the light started to flicker again. Wofford reached up and hit it like he was swatting at the same fly been bugging him all day. Light stayed on, and Wofford turned to another task.

That poor electrician just walked away, shoulders slumped. He glanced back at the light a few times as he went out, his faith in his electrical prowess shaken, questioning the validity of his entire life and career. Cruel, but funny.

Course, Wofford didn't escape Lowell's joking either. Wofford had a magnifying monocle eyepiece he used to examine jewelry. Lowell would come in early in the morning and depress the rim of the monocle in an inkpad. Wofford would put it up against his eye, and it would leave a black circle there without him knowing it. First customer came in after that would ask why he was looking like a one-eyed raccoon. Wofford got wise to it after it worked more times than it should have, so Lowell started pressing the telephone earpiece into the inkpad instead. Wofford would walk around all day looking like he'd used his ear as a coaster.

Annnnnnnyway, Lowell was always thinking, always looking for the next ride, or trying to make one he had better. Like with the fun house. There was a big room inside the ride after the part where they blew up the girls' dresses. Well, it doesn't take

genius insight into the teenage male mind to figure out the boys
would congregate there to watch the dresses fly rather than keep
moving through the fun house. Lowell saw a thing somewhere
and decided to build one like it in that big room. Combination
of contraptions. You walked into a spinning flat-ways barrel.
Either you made it out the other side on your feet, or you got
knocked down. It was painted in a corkscrew pattern just to mess
up your mind along with your balance. But before that, you had
to cross a moving platform. There were swinging small barrels,
like whiskey barrels, hanging down from ropes over the platform
trying to knock you over as you moved forward.

Wasn't like today where everything is made in China and
put on a boat. They had to build stuff themselves. They headed
down to the nearest lumber store in Lowell's black Fleetwood
Cadillac. He took three cars on the road, along with all the
trucks. Lowell had names for everything. The black Fleetwood
Caddy was named Sinbad. One of the two Lincolns he brought
along was called Lincoln. The other was Abraham. The kids
would drive the cars. Lowell would always be in the lead, driving
a semi hauling the German fun house. Annnnnnnyway, they got
nowhere else to put the plywood and the two-by-fours except on
the roof of Sinbad, so that's what they did. They tied it on the
best they could and then headed back to the fairgrounds with one
of Lowell's boys hanging out one window while trying to keep
the load steady. A kid on the other side was also trying to keep the
plywood from becoming roadkill. Then they built it. Just built it
from scratch: wood, metal, gears, and hydraulics.

First place they set up the barrel in the fun house was Detroit.
Thing was a huge success. Kept three separate ticket booths busy.
But it broke down that first day. They didn't figure on the load.
Thought people would pop through that barrel pretty quickly.

Maybe get knocked down once, but then get out. Lowell, who could think like a teenager, shoulda known. The kids would get in with their friends, and it would be like playing inside a cement mixer. They'd get floored a dozen times, bang into each other, fall over each other, get their shirts ripped, and get footprints on their faces and bloody noses. Thought it was the greatest ride ever. They'd finally tumble out the back, knotted over laughing.

By the middle of the first Saturday, a guy came storming over from the first aid station and asked what in blazes they were doing. He said, Are you operating a ride or a war over here? I got casualties lined up out the door of the trailer. Said they were rolling around in some kind of barrel yonder.

While the presence of blood might be expected to signal carnival failure of some sort, blood combined with smiles and laughter pretty much spoke of success for Lowell. Nevertheless, they cooled it after that. Just let one kid through at a time.

One reason Lowell did so well in the business and lasted so long is, he's honest. He was about doing the right thing. Spoke his mind, too. Sometimes, those two elements came together and not always harmoniously. Like when they wintered one year in San Antonio. Lowell never married, so he didn't have a reason to come back to Amarillo. He'd sometimes spend the cold weather months in Florida—Tampa, or Jacksonville—or somewhere else in the South. Usually set up shop in a warehouse owned by a showman friend, repair the rides, or maybe build a new one.

The winter they stayed in San Antonio, they headquartered in a Quonset hut owned by another friend of Lowell's in a bad part of town. Right behind the Quonset, a woman was living with a passel of kids in a handmade tin hut. Looked like something from another country. One time, Lowell and three of the young guys working for him were driving back to the Quonset in

Sinbad when a police car passed in front of them, lights flashing, siren blaring, going *backwards* through an intersection. Lowell didn't care what the emergency was. Not even sure there was one. Never found out if the cops were having some fun, making good on a bet, or what. But Lowell thought it violated their sacred trust as law enforcement officers, or maybe offended truth, justice, and the American way. Who knows.

But he jumped out of Sinbad, shook his fist, and started yelling at the cops, You're not allowed to do that. You shouldn't be doing that.

Boys in the car started yelling at Lowell, telling him to hush up even as they sank down in their seats. They didn't want any trouble from the cops or anyone else in that neighborhood. Lowell didn't even hear them, just kept on with his righteous anger. Sure enough, no sooner had that backwards-headed cop car disappeared around a corner and a building, then it was suddenly going forward and coming right at them. Pretty quickly, they were all out of the Fleetwood with their hands on the hood and spread eagle, getting patted down. But Lowell wouldn't quit. Kept after those cops. Said he was going to call their captain and tell him they were riding around town backwards in their squad car with their lights flashing and siren blaring. That was when the tide turned on that whole operation. Cops started looking a little sheepish, knowing they done wrong. They invited Lowell to step over across the way with them, out of earshot of the boys.

This is the thing about Lowell. Everyone liked him because he was straight with everyone and he liked them. Next thing you know, the cops were apologizing to Lowell, the citizens of San Antonio, the Fraternal Brotherhood of Policemen, and anyone else they could think of. All was forgiven, and the three of them came back over to Sinbad, all smiles. Not only were Lowell and the boys free to go, but the cops were invited over for coffee and donuts the next morning. Even gave them a frontwards escort to the Quonset. The two cops ended up coming over almost every morning that winter and providing protection in the neighborhood.

Life on the road was fun but seldom easy. One time, after he was old enough to drive a truck, T-Spoon remembers working seventy-two straight hours. They worked the last night of a carnival, spent the rest of the night and part of the next day tearing it down, and then drove a whole day to the next fair. Took nearly a day to set it back up. By then, the fair opened, and they worked all the first evening and night. T-spoon said they were hallucinating zombies at that point. When the fair closed, they just laid down on the grass next to the ride and slept all night. One thing for an eighteen-year-old to work like that, but Lowell was right there alongside them the whole time.

Lowell was in the business to give people a good time. Jack remembers a couple times where a little boy would be standing by a ride, looking up at it, half in awe and half hangdog. It was clear the kid didn't have a dime in the world.

Lowell would say, Have any money?

No.

You want to make some money? You want some tickets?

Real serious and kind of shy, the kid would say, Yes, sir.

Lowell would say, Go on over to the Ferris wheel and ask the guy running it if you could borrow a bucket of steam.

Kid would run off over to the Ferris wheel. The operator would listen to him, then look over yonder at Lowell, get it, and tell the kid he didn't have any, but they might have some steam to borrow over by the merry-go-round. Go on like that a spell. Then the kid would run back, out of breath and earnestly bothered he couldn't fulfill the assigned task.

He'd say, I'm sorry. Everyone is plum out of steam, mister.

Lowell would say, Important thing is you worked hard and you tried.

He'd hand the kid a fistful of tickets. That little face would light up like a hundred-watt bulb.

Duane Steck, Lowell's longtime business partner, died just three years ago. He was setting up a Ladybugs ride at the San Angelo Stock Show and Rodeo and just dropped over dead from a heart attack. Lowell himself is eighty and retired now. Never married. Got close three times, but never quite found a woman who fully embraced his lifestyle of being away from home eight or nine months a year. That is to say, he never found a woman who wanted to make the road home. His barnstorming father settled down in Amarillo when he was twenty-seven. Lowell only settled down in Amarillo five years ago, when he was seventy-five.

He still has the warehouse that served as home base for forty-five years. It's in an old part of town. When they wintered in Amarillo, the rigs would be parked in the lot outside with the rides disassembled on flatbeds. They'd bring in parts to do maintenance and paint. The painting was eternal—the framework and the scenery on the front of the rides. The day I was there, a partner who used to travel with Lowell as a teenager and who took over some operations when Lowell retired, was in a side room banging on part of a famous sixty-six-horse carousel built in 1923, which he runs for the Texas State Fair. His college-aged daughter was working beside him, painting the scenery.

Lowell's antique cars take up most of the space in the warehouse. He has a 1921 fire engine, 1929 Chevrolet, 1936 Ford, 1937 and 1941 Chryslers, and a 1970 Corvette, bought new. He also has other side rooms filled with ancient mechanical devices:

a seventy-five-year-old jukebox, a fortune-telling machine of similar vintage, a 1915 phonograph, and a 1906 Dewey slot machine, all in working condition. There's nothing in his warehouse that doesn't work. If there were, Lowell would fix it. He loves history and collects everything. When they shuttered the Paramount Theater downtown years ago, he bought the huge neon marquee that hung out front, along with the massive chandelier in the lobby. Thirty years later, when they were restoring downtown and that building, Lowell donated them back.

Out in the cavernous main room of the warehouse, next to the antique cars, is an ancient calliope, ornately carved and painted in all the colors of the rainbow, with a motor that was originally built in 1915 and rebuilt in 1926. Lowell plugs it in, and the warehouse fills with the sound of a raucous band. It's a music roll playing "Beer Barrel Polka" on a military band organ that uses pipes to simulate the sounds of a trumpet, trombone, clarinet, and piccolo. There are also chimes, snare and bass drums, and cymbals.

Instead of letting it play for only a few seconds, Lowell closes his eyes and listens to the whole song. Clearly, he is back on the road. Maybe driving his semi down the highway, hauling the German fun house in pieces on his flatbed trailer, a few fairs of summer behind him, adventure ahead.

Slamming percussion from the calliope continues to echo through the warehouse. The aging carny may no longer be on the road, but he'll never quite be off it either.

Waiting on the Big Score

It don't pay to be a cowboy. And makin' it as a rancher ain't easy neither if you don't inherit a dozen sections or more. Boom, bust, or break even—whether it's land, cattle, or oil prices—ain't nothin' steady in Texas. Prices buck like a wild bronc. Not even the smart ones can predict drought and disease or war and revolution across the water. And then there's splittin' the family ranch between all the kids. A place that could barely make it runnin' cattle when it was whole has no chance when it's in pieces. Or a ranch don't get divvied up, but a dozen cousins all think they're foreman of the thing.

Still, there's plenty out here who start with not much and keep scrapin' and scratchin' and clawin', not lettin' the busts kill 'em or the booms swell their heads, and find a way to make a livin' off the land. Bob Conatser is one of 'em. He got lucky, got unlucky, missed some opportunities, took advantage of others, got his timin' right, and got his timin' wrong. And now maybe he's sittin' pretty for the big score. Maybe.

His grandfather come into the country on horseback in the early 1880s, out of Tennessee, when he was still a teenager. Bob was young when his grandfather died in 1940, but he still remembers two stories his father passed down. First happened pretty quickly after his grandfather was hired on at the Laurel Leaf Ranch south of the Canadian River. He begun as a cowboy, a real cowboy—no fences or pens in them days. But cooks got paid better, so he switched and run the chuck wagon. Could stash away some money that way and eventually buy his own land.

One night, they put out the cook fire and went to bed, but later heard horses comin'. It was a band of Indians, about a half-dozen headin' north. Remember, most of the remainin' Comanches had been driven out of Texas after the battle of Palo Duro Canyon in 1874, but not all of the warriors gone right to the reservation – or stayed there. Annnnnnnyway, these Indians weren't the murderin' sort, but they did make Bob's grandfather get up and make them some dinner.

When they moved on, Bob's grandfather said, That might be the last time we ever see Indians in this country.

And it was.

Did what he set out to do and put away enough of his cook's salary to buy some ground. Worked it, and kept adding. By 1905, he'd gotten pretty big, at least by the standards of them days. Patched together ten sections and called it the Big Bull Ranch. Had another seven sections upriver a stretch. The Big Bull was on the north side of the Canadian River, about eighteen miles downstream from the town of Canadian. Nowadays in a car, you cross the river on the big, wide highway bridge and cover that whole distance in twenty minutes. But in them days, before cars, before the bridge, and before the dam upstream, the river was a mile wide. You come to town in a horse-drawn wagon. One day in 1905, Bob's grandfather gone into Canadian for groceries, a trip that took all day, there and back. Bob's dad and uncle come along. The boys were about five and six years old.

It was winter. On the way back, storm kicked up out of nowhere. There was only a bearskin to wrap them boys in. Snow got deep in a hurry, and Bob's grandfather barely made it back to the house. Boys were in a bad way, but he got them in front of a fire, and they recovered. He was so mad at himself for riskin' those boys' lives that he sold the Big Bull Ranch. Had everything paid off by then, the ranch and his cattle, and forty thousand in the bank. Moved to California and bought a prune orchard. Went all right for a while, but then some sort of bug deal wiped out the grapes, and he busted.

Bob's grandfather brought the family back to Texas in 1912, and they settled on the seven sections of land he hadn't sold. The rest of his life he talked about how he would've had it made if he'd just kept the Big Bull. The family's regret only got worse decades later when oil and gas was discovered on the Big Bull. Wasn't too long ago the current owner was gettin' a hun'erd thirty thousand a month in payments from an oil company.

Bob's father Tom and his granddad leased the Lockhart Ranch in 1928. Four-year deal. Bought a thousand cows. Tom wanted to get big in a hurry. But weren't no time 'fore prices started to drop. Tom wanted to wait it out, but Bob's grandfather, who'd seen it all, says, Tom, you get on your horse, and you cut two hun'erd fifty of them cows and sell 'em.

Meanin', cut out two hun'erd fifty head from the herd of one thousand and sell 'em at a loss. Almost all Herefords in them days. So Bob's dad cut out the dries and some others, sold them, and used the money to pay off a note they had on the ranch. When they finally sold the rest of the herd years later, they lost forty-five dollars a head. Had to sell. Depression just wouldn't quit. One deal, forty-five thousand-dollar loss. In them days, when cash was scarce as water, that was a lot of money. Took Tom eighteen years to pay back the money. If he hadn't sold them two hun'erd fifty head when he did, couldn't have paid the mortgage all them years and would've lost the ranch.

There was a time, think it was the late 1940s or maybe the

1950s, when Tom had a chance to buy the Persimmon Creek Ranch west of their seven sections. But Grandmother was still alive, and she said, Tom, just ain't the time to buy.

The Depression had scared her to death. It wasn't like Tom didn't remember eatin' Hoover hogs night after night neither. That's what they called jackrabbits. A feller from the federal land bank even come by the ranch and offered to lend Tom the money. Said he'd checked Tom out, and they was willin' to give him the loan. But Tom wouldn't do it. Grandma in his ear. Decades later, oil and gas wells was all over the Persimmon Creek Ranch.

By the last half of his workin' life, Tom had added ground and was up to ten sections, which was just enough to get by in them days as a full-time rancher. He talked to Bob once about the life. He said, At first, you like the horses and ridin'. Then you get interested in cattle and the business. But last … last you appreciate the land.

Bob cowboyed on the family ranch when he was a kid and loved the life. It's all he ever wanted to do, all he ever talked about. But when he graduated from Texas Tech, the family ranch wasn't big enough for him to join his dad and both of them to make a livin' off it. And day work punchin' cows paid a hun'erd and a quarter a month. So he went to work for an oil company for six and a half years. Hated every day of it. Went to work for another oil company for almost three years. It was worse. Only thing saved him was gettin' weekends off to rope. Kept horses at the family ranch. Had an arena there. Trained horses and did some rodeo. No money in rodeo then, but he done pretty good at it. Done even better sellin' horses to rodeo cowboys.

In 1969, about when his dad turned seventy, Tom told Bob it was time to come home. Said he was sellin' his cows for cash and would lease the ranch to him. Bob jumped on the deal, even though he didn't have no money to start a herd. But luck or timin' or both were with him then. It was summer. His father wanted one-third of the lease payment up front, another one-third with the New Year, and the other third whenever Bob could get it. Bob had to borrow big to cover the first lease payment and get some cattle. Remember, you can't hardly make a livin' off cattle on ten sections unless you own the land outright. Even if you ate bacon and beans every night for years and didn't go to town, owing on the land is a deal breaker.

Didn't stop Bob. Cattle were cheap at the time. He started buyin' yearling heifers. Some at auction and some direct from ranchers. Didn't stop until he'd spent ninety-two thousand of borrowed money, near about two hun'erd seventy-five head. Granddad thought he was starin' at 1928 all over again. That was in February. By midsummer, the price of cattle had nearly doubled. Bob sold the calves from those heifers in the fall, and they paid for what he'd bought all of them cattle for less than a year before. Didn't keep all the heifers, but he kept enough. The next fall, when they calved, he got $1,022 per pair after payin' $325 for each of those yearlings two years before.

All of that was enough to pay off the lease on his father's ranch. When he first took out the ten-year loan on the lease, told the bankers he'd have it paid off in two years. Them at the bank said, We ain't never seen it done.

When he gone in to pay up after two years, a few jaws dropped, but Bob didn't gloat. He knew it was just lady luck takin' his side that time.

After he paid off all his debts and banked some cash, he only had about twenty-five cows left. Prices dropped back below what they'd been two years before. So he sat on them two dozen cows for four or five years. One of the fellers he bought cows low from, only to sell high a few months later, 'fore prices turned and tumbled again, was Ollie Scott.

Every time Bob saw Ollie in town after that, Ollie just shook his head and said, You're the luckiest some buck ever walked the planet.

Bob knew all the legendary cowboys out that way, like Toots South. Bob worked his own ground rather than hirin' out, so he only really been around them fellers while neighborin'. Told you about Toots. He was a great hand with horses. A rich rancher lived north of Canadian. Oil money. Kind of a prickly feller. Thought he was smart rather than lucky. Backed out on a coupla oil deals when he got a better offer later. That ain't how it's done. One time, he brought a colt for Toots to break to ride. Toots done it and delivered the horse back. Feller called one evenin'. He don't know nothin' about horses. He says, That horse you trained won't stop.

Toots says, What do you mean he won't stop? Feller says, You didn't hardly break him. You didn't take him out to a pasture, go get a crazy ten-year-old cow, and try to pen her, did you?

Well, Toots had ridden more horses and roped more cows than there are stars in the sky.

He says, You just bring him on back here, and, if he won't stop, I'll fix him for nothin'.

Feller come over with his wife, and Toots saddled the horse and loped on down a flat, rocky road. He reined up sudden and just made the ground roar. Stopped that chestnut on a bottle cap. Toots rides him on back. He hands over the reins and says, I don't see no problem.

Feller's wife says to her husband, Why don't I take the horse home and you stay here with Toots?

Meanin', maybe it's you needs trainin', not the horse.

Was another rich family. This one in Miami. Had more money than sense and more ego than money. Feller called Toots one day and says, We got a horse got a problem with.

Toots says, What's the problem?

Feller says, He don't buck us or run off or nothin'. We just can't get on him. Haul him out to the pasture in the trailer, and unload him, and he won't let you on.

Toots says, I can get on. Bring him over.

Think this feller and a friend he brought along knew Toots well enough, but, when they come by, they was lookin' Toots over. He was in his seventies then, had a bad knee, and had trouble gettin' around. Feller had about twenty-five years on Toots. He don't come right out and say he was younger and healthier, but he did mouth off a bit when Toots hobbled over to meet him. He says, If we can't get on him, don't see how you will.

Toots don't answer. Just helps them unload the horse out the trailer. Puts on the bridle and saddle. All he done was gone back over to the trailer and loop the right rein over one of the horizontal bars there on the back. Sucked the horse's head up into that trailer. While that steed was thinkin' about his head being at a funny angle and the slight strain in his neck, Toots stepped up on him like he was gettin' into his pickup. He loosened the rein and did a lap around the pasture. Didn't really say much when he got back and handed over the horse. And neither did that rich feller or his friend.

Toots did a certain thing for twenty years when breakin' horses, but first time Bob seen it, he says, What in tarnation, Toots?

Toots made a dummy out of paper sacks, mounted it in the saddle, and tied it on. He explained to Bob that, nine times out of ten, a colt bucked 'cause it was scared. With the dummy on board, he could simulate a human and let that fear drain out of him over a few days or weeks. Toots would use a long pair of lines, like for drivin' a wagon team. He'd stand behind the horse with that mounted dummy and get the colt to stoppin' and turnin'. They'd buck plenty, but it wasn't Toots they was tryin' to throw off, and the tied-on sack dummy never left the saddle. After drivin' a colt for two weeks like that, when Toots mounted up for the first time, horse was pretty much full broke.

Toots was a funny feller. Bill Breeding, the vet in Miami I told you about, knew him, too. Them old cowboys like Toots were more at home on the range than in town. One time, Bill was comin' into Miami. From a long way off, he seen a pickup parked in front of the café. Miami ain't even a one stoplight town. It's a one flashing yellow light town. When you park by the café, you pull in at an angle. This truck Bill seen had a one-horse trailer on it, and that trailer was juttin' halfway across the highway. It was out so far that westbound traffic had to curve around it into the eastbound lane. Toots always hauled a one-horse trailer after he retired, but kept doing day work. He'd load in his horse and go wherever he needed to go. Bill got closer and seen it was Toots's rig all right. He parked and went in the café. Toots was in there, just finishin' up his dessert.

Bills says, Toots, you forget you got a trailer on when you parked out there?

Toots about gagged on that last bite of cherry pie, dropped his fork on his plate, said Oh, goddamn, and rushed out the door.

Bob won't brag on himself, but he was a fair horse trainer himself. Trained ropin' horses for rodeo riders. Did it for twenty-five years. Sold them to four world champions. He shakes his head at the ropers these days. Says they're amazing athletes, but can't do nothin' with horses. They just burn 'em up. Horses are like humans. They run outta air. But these fellers don't know or can't tell when they're tired. They'll go through twenty or thirty horses when they could get by with six if they knew something about the animals.

Annnnnnnyway, cattle prices didn't stay low forever, and Bob was able to scrape by in the 1970s. He traded cattle some and trained horses some. Competed at the big rodeo in Cheyenne for twenty years, steer ropin' and trippin'. Placed seven times. Won third in 1969. But like I said, there was no money in rodeo in them days.

Bob's father, Tom, had a brother and two sisters. One of the sisters didn't have any kids, and she ended up givin' her quarter share of the family ranch to Bob and his brother. Bob was forever tryin' to hold the ranch together. He had a cousin who lived in California, and part of the ranch was left to him. But he'd never been back to Texas to see it. Didn't know the value of it. For ten years, Bob kept talkin' him out of sellin', but the feller finally hired a realtor. Bob couldn't afford to buy it. Cousin called Bob and asked his opinion.

Bob said, Don't do it. You're plannin' on sellin' it way too cheap.

Cousin says, You just don't know what it's worth.

Bob says, Maybe I don't, but it's gone up.

Cousin called later and said, Got it sold.

Bob said, Land is bringin' between seven hun'erd fifty and twelve hun'erd an acre.

At the time, Bob didn't know Salem Abraham had just paid fifteen hun'erd an acre for the Payne place south of the Canadian River. Only difference is Bob's ranch was north of the river. Prettier place, but there were more breaks along the north bank, so maybe it wasn't quite as good ranch land.

His cousin says, I got four seventy-five per acre.

Bob says, You just gave it away. You got your britches taken off.

Bob was about sick to his stomach. But that's the way it goes. If there's one rule out here, it's this. Your cousin in California don't know nothin'.

Bob's other aunt, who owned the last quarter of the ranch, had one child. Lived in Midland. Got to listenin' to some stockbroker and wanted to cash out of the ranch. Only child. Her husband was smart. He went broke about four times, but finally built up an oil business and sold out to the Japanese. Got filthy rich. Just before the first oil boom. Run the company for them for about five years before it went bankrupt. But he already had about thirty million in the bank from sellin' out.

Annnnnnnyway, this was 1996, and Bob didn't have no money to buy out his cousin in Midland. Frustratin' deal. Like I been tellin' you, cattle don't make money unless you're already big and own the ground. But Bob went to a bank anyway and asked if they'd lend him money to buy out his cousin. They said yes, but at 11 percent. Cattle would earn the equivalent of two percent. Numbers just didn't work.

So they sold the family ranch. Surface anyway. Kept the minerals. When it was all said and done, Bob owned the mineral rights on about two thousand acres. The rest was divvied up among the cousins or sold off. For the next ten years, Bob couldn't get anyone to lease the oil and gas rights on his ground. Couldn't even get fifty dollars an acre. One boy said that, if Bob would give him a section option, he'd drill. Dependin' on what they found, they'd lease the other sections. But even that fell through.

Things changed about three years ago. That same feller, a friend, called Bob and said, Be careful. They're comin' after you.

A company out of Colorado called, and they agreed to two hun'erd fifty bucks per acre for one section. Bob kept gettin' calls but held off, then leased his two other sections for three twenty-five per acre. But they never drilled because gas prices went down.

The lease ran out this past April. They hit gas on the next ranch over, so there's plenty of interest in the ground Bob got mineral rights on. Another company out of Denver sent him a lease contract in the mail, three fifty per acre. All three sections. Six years. But Bob wanted three years and a three-sixteenths override. Meanin' the owner of the mineral rights gets nearly 20 percent of the output. Pretty standard these days. Well, another company got wind of that deal and called Bob. Offered him four hun'erd an acre, three years, and the override he wanted. Took that deal and thought he was smart. But just last month, in July, he got another call. The paperwork on the deal Bob had signed hadn't gone public yet, so this new company that come callin' didn't know about it. Bob told the feller he was leased out, but asked him, just being curious, how much they woulda paid.

Feller said, Five hundred per acre.

A coupla weeks before I visited with Bob, a well east of Wheeler hit, maybe twenty-five miles from Bob's ground. Besides the gas, it was pumpin' thirty-five hundred barrels of oil a day. Remember, aside from the lease rights, rancher typically gets three-sixteenths of the output. At eighty dollars per barrel, that means the rancher's puttin' fifty thousand a day in his saddlebags. Before you could snap your fingers, all the land nearby had leased for three thousand an acre.

Bob and his wife spent twenty-six years on the family ranch from 1969 to 1996 before he had to sell it. Moved to Amarillo. He misses his cows most. If he had it to do all over again, he'd just be a rancher with cattle. But he's still managing the minerals.

He can't help but think about the prune orchard deal that just about busted his grandad in 1912 and the cattle deal that near broke his father in 1928. Wonders if the family is on the verge of wipin' out those memories forever. Maybe the oil company will hit a thirty-five hundred-barrel-a-day well on his land. That ain't likely. That's like winnin' the lottery. Except your chances of winnin' the lottery are one in a million. If you own the minerals on two thousand acres of ranch land in oil and gas country, and producing wells surround those acres, and someone thinks your land is worth leasin' for five hundred an acre—maybe your chances of hittin' it big are more like one in a few.

Maybe.

The County Agent

I suppose growin' up in a small town in Texas ain't no different than growin' up in a small town anywhere else, except Texas is bigger and more expansive than anywhere else, so the chances of gettin' in trouble are bigger and more expansive than anywhere else.

Blackie Johnson kept Don Reeves in trouble all their growin' up life in Hedley. They got school turned out one day. Blackie could imitate voices. There was a weatherman on the radio in Amarillo, HC Windermere, and Blackie could talk just like him. Ever'one in the Panhandle listened to Windermere and knew his deep voice. In the spring, country would get its share of tornados. Fact, couple of towns been blown away a few weeks before. Don and Blackie was across the street from the school in a Laundromat, and they called up the superintendent.

Talkin' like HC Windermere in a low, gravelly voice, Blackie says, Mr. Davis, this is HC Windermere in the weather bureau in Amarillo. There's a tornado southwest of Hedley. I'd recommend you turn school out and get the children home.

Weren't a cloud in the sky. Prettiest day God ever created. Didn't matter. Them two boys was watchin' from the laundry. It wasn't ten minutes 'fore it looked like a red ant invasion in front of that school. Mommas in cars zigzaggin' in, pickin' up their little ones, and transportin' them to safety. Hustle and bustle ever'where. School busses come in, loaded up, and were gone.

Don and Blackie thought it was safe to go back across the street. They seen this old feller who'd been workin' on a big clock in the school come runnin' out. He says, You boys get on home! Big twister is coming!

And he run right past them by the Laundromat, holdin' his hat on against the wind that weren't, his tools janglin' in his little black bag.

Don and Blackie were about halfway across the street when Mr. Davis, who was directin' cars, mommas, and school buses, looked up. Don still remembers seein' the light go off in his brain. The superintendent lifted his chin to that cloudless sky and then looked back at them boys. Put the pieces together right quick. The trial was over 'fore it started or even an arrest been made. The executioner come at them while slippin' his belt outta his trousers. Left them cars and busses and wailin' mommas behind and met them boys in the middle of Main Street.

Whipped the tar out of them. Just wailed on 'em. Right there by the double yellow line. Not sure what happened first, if justice got served or his arm got plum wore out. But that was it. Bad news was there was no chance for the defense to make its case before the verdict was rendered and punishment applied. But good news was, once the sentence was carried out, it was a done deal. No detention and no cleanin' blackboards after school. Just your basic ass whuppin' in the middle of Main Street.

Blackie and Don were heroes in school when word of their triumph got around next day. And they kept right on being heroes until that Saturday when all the kids had to go to school to make up for the lost day. Their teachers weren't real happy about it neither.

One night, three of them got kidnapped. It was Don, Blackie, and Turdy Bailey. Don't ask about Turdy's name. A schoolteacher they knew drove the boys down to Memphis. But when it come time to go home, they didn't have a ride. They seen two girls lived there in Memphis that Blackie knew, and he explained that a truck driver had kidnapped them and brung 'em against their free will to Memphis. Now they needed a ride home.

We're in a bind, he said.

Story had some credibility, although just the barest. A grocery store in town been robbed two nights before. Not something happened a lot in them parts, so ever'one was on edge. Girls told them three to climb in, but they'd have to go ask their mother 'fore they could take them all the way back to Hedley. It was about ten o'clock at night. Mom was already in bed. They woke her up and explained that Blackie, Don, and Turdy been kidnapped, had survived the ordeal, but now needed a ride home.

She was horrified, but not especially. Left the girls home, and drove them boys home herself. They had to stick with that story all the way to Hedley. Blackie gone on and on as the endless road to Hedley gone on and on, explainin' how the feller got them in the truck and menaced them with a weapon and why he dropped them off in Memphis. She just nodded her head, intrigued.

In the backseat, Turdy was elbowin' Don, whisperin', Tell Blackie to shut up. We've taken this story as far as she'll go.

Don says, I can't do nothin' with him now.

For years after, decades even, every time the woman's husband seen him, he asked, You been kidnapped lately, Blackie?

One time when Don wasn't with him, Blackie got shot at. It was him and two other fellers, Stanley and Jack. There was a place south of Hedley where the highway crossed a culvert. Built like a little tunnel. Let cattle pass under the road. They got one of Blackie's mother's old purses, tied a string to it, and set it down on the highway, right above that culvert. When a car come by, it

would almost always stop, and a feller would come back lookin'
for that purse. Well, between the time the car passed and the feller
stopped, put the car in reverse, stopped again, and got out to look
for that purse, Blackie and them would yank on that purse. It
would drop down into their hands, and they'd hide in the culvert.
Feller would be up above them on the highway, turnin' circles,
scratchin' his head, and wonderin' if he's gone crazy. Swear he'd
seen a purse right there by the side of the road. Blackie and them
would hear the feller talkin' to himself and cussin'.

One time they done it, it was gettin' dark. Summer night.
Past nine. Bait was out. A feller stopped, but, when they pulled
the string, the purse got caught on something. Wouldn't move no
more. They knew that if the empty purse got grabbed, the game
would be over, so Stanley run up the side of the bank. But his
timin' weren't the best, and he and the driver that stopped met by
the purse at the same time.

Stanley didn't know what to do, so he lowers his voice and
says, This is a holdup.

Well, like to scare that feller to death. In the near dark, he
don't know if an effeminate desperado is about to shoot him or
what. He run like mad, got back in his car, and left.

Course, Blackie and his friends was just teens, didn't have
enough sense to fill half a thimble, so they kept right on playin'
their game. Wasn't twenty minutes 'fore it looked like a platoon
of Texas Rangers was rollin' down Highway 287, comin' to get
'em. The line of veh'cles woulda made a dead man proud if it'd
been his funeral cortege. It was the police, plus regular citizens
formed a posse. And the driver who'd been scared to death. Jack
climbed up the embankment to see what all the fuss was about.
By the time he slid back down and told them other boys it looked
like the army was invadin' and they all had guns, they was pinned

down in the culvert.

Stanley started crawlin' away in the grass. Next thing you know, they was shootin' at him! For real. Dust was flyin' up all 'round him where bullets was hittin'. Found out later it was the deputy sheriff's father, not even a lawman, firin' a rifle he'd taken off a Japanese soldier during the war. That's how accidents can happen. Blackie wasn't sure if Stanley was hit, but he weren't waitin' 'round to see if he was next in line for a dose of World War Two nostalgia. Took off out of that culvert. Run the other way. He gone down by the creek where the rusted-out hulk of an old Ford been beached for years. Hid inside. When he finally snuck a peek, it was all lit up on the highway. Jack and Stanley was standin' there with their arms reachin' for the sky.

The police got to hollerin', Come out! We know you're down there. If you don't come out, we're gonna shoot you out.

Blackie was scared to death and hunkered down. Bullets started sailin' over the top of the car and rippin' through the leaves nearby.

Blackie says, Hold the farm! I'm comin' out.

Blackie got up to the road. The sheriff was there, and so was the driver they scared. Oh, was he mad. He was cussin'. He had a gun, and he was wavin' it around.

Blackie knew the sheriff. He says, Raymond, we was just playin' around. You best take that gun from him.

Well, they finally got the driver calmed down and let the boys go home, but they charged them later with attempted robbery. Sheriff come over to school one day and called Blackie outta class. Come on, you're going before the grand jury this afternoon.

Blackie got there. Jack and Stanley were there, too. They thought for sure they was going to Alcatraz. Ever'one who gone up before that grand jury ahead of 'em that day got hauled off to jail. When it was their turn, the judge chewed out the boys pretty good and said how dangerous what they did was.

Blackie thought, Dangerous? Purse thing was dangerous? We're the ones been *shot* at.

In the end, grand jury didn't bill 'em.

Believe it or not, Blackie was a constable for fourteen years when he got older. One time, Don's elderly Aunt Myrtle was drivin' down to Memphis, the next town down Highway 287 from Hedley, and run right off the road. Flipped upside down and landed at the bottom of an embankment. Blackie, as constable, got there quick and seen Myrtle in the car, suspended upside down and snug in her shoulder belt. He busted the back windshield, crawled in there, and got up close to the eighty-five year old. Tryin' to figure out if she was okay, he says, Do you know who I am, Myrtle?

Myrtle was spittin' mad. Mad she'd run off that road. Mad she was late for gettin' her hair done. Mad she was stuck upside down in a car in a ditch. She says, Of course I know who you are, Blackie. I changed your damn diapers when you was a baby. Now get me outta here!

Blackie sawed through her seat belt. She went kerplunk right on her head. But the old gal was fine.

Don done a few things without Blackie. One Saturday night, he slipped under the gate of his father's lumberyard and got a twenty-foot log chain. Local sheriff in Hedley was named Ben Speers. A telephone pole was near the Sinclair station, right in front of the drugstore. Ben used to back his car right up to that pole so he could get a runnin' start on any kids racin' their cars down Main Street. When Ben gone in the drugstore, Don and his friend Red Leeper hooked one end of that chain to the rear axle of the squad car and wrapped the other end around the telephone pole.

When Ben come out of the drugstore, Don and Red, in the darkness, floored the accelerator of Red's dad's nearby old car. Tires squealed, and they roared out of town. Ben spilled his coffee on himself, jumped into his squad car, and stomped on the gas pedal. Tires spun and rubber smoked. That car got up about as much speed as could possibly be developed in nineteen feet. Then that heavy chain did what chains do. Ben took a nosedive into the steerin' wheel when he hit the end of them links.

Boys were out of town and didn't actually see the wreck as it happened. They let things cool down, circled around, and come back into town about a half hour later. Squad car was dismembered. Ben was standin' there yet. A tow truck driver was alongside, scratchin' his head. Axle was a few feet behind the back bumper. It was the only time Don ever seen a police car looked like a stretch limo.

Ben, what happened?

He turned around slow and said, I don't guess one of you boys wants to claim a log chain, do you?

Sheriff never could pin it on them, but he knew, like the sun rises every mornin', who done it.

Years later, Red Leeper became the superintendent of schools.

The same year that squad car got de-axled, Don's Uncle Billy died. About June. He was an old pioneer, much beloved. Had the town barber, Fat Reed, sit up with the body at the funeral home. It was a thing done back then. One after another, different fellers would just set there for a few hours as other folks come in and paid their respects. Don gone in to see Uncle Billy one evenin'. No light but a little ol' forty-watt bulb hangin' down by a cord from the ceilin'. Flowers ever'where. Fat settin' over in the corner, readin' the paper. Had steel horn-rimmed glasses on. He'd peek over the top of that paper when he was talkin' to you.

He says, What you doing here?

Don says, Daddy sent me over to set up with Uncle Billy.

Fat says, Well, we got to stay here until nine o'clock.

Miss Mabel Jones, the postmistress in town, turned from the sidewalk and come up the path. Always dressed pretty. Nicest woman you ever knew.

To this day, Don says he don't know why he done it. But he gone behind the flowers and hid there in the dark. Miss Mabel Jones come in, dipped her head and bonnet at Fat, and gone over to the open casket to pay her respects to Uncle Billy. When she got close, she kind of peeked over the edge the way you do to see the face.

When she did, in a deep voice, Don says from his hidin' place, How ya doin', Mabel?

She pivoted on her high heels, hit the screen door, and flew outta there like a quail flushed by a hound dog. Never looked back. And never came back.

When Mabel was well cleared out, Fat looked over the top of that newspaper and said, I'm tellin' your daddy.

Don begged him not to, all the way until nine o'clock. Musta worked 'cause his dad never come after him for it.

Don's father was a lumberman, but his grandfather, who done a lotta things, was a cattleman first and foremost. He went to New Mexico as a teen. His family's house was burned down in Georgia or somewhere during the Civil War so he joined another family movin' west to escape the carpetbaggers. As a child, Don's grandmother crossed the plains in an ox wagon the year Custer was killed. Her family settled in Arizona territory, but, after a few years, they moved east into New Mexico, where she met her husband. Together, they moved east to Texas, which was not the general direction most immigrants arrived from in those days. They kept movin', always lookin' for decent schools. Ended up in Newlin, then along Whitefish Creek, north of Hedley, and then Hedley itself. Don first started workin' cattle as a boy on his grandfather's ranch.

In them days, the local ranchers sold their cattle through a commission company. Shipped them to the stockyards in Kansas City. Don remembers being eleven and gettin' out of school in the fall when they loaded yearlings on the train. Three or four ranches would come together and ship their cattle by truck down to Memphis, where the railroad comes through and they had stock pens. They'd fill forty cars full of cattle. Ranchers would ride with the cows to Kansas City in an extra caboose and sell their stock there. Annnnnnnyway, the call would go up that they needed thirty head to fill the next rail car. Cowboys would cut out the thirty. It was Don's job to drive them up the chute into the car. His horse would start to follow that last cow in. He'd go so far as to stick the horse's nose in. Then Don would back him out and go get the next load. Felt like a real cowboy.

Last time he done it, his grandfather said, Maybe your mother will let you go to Kansas City with us.

Don asked, but she said, You're a little short in the britches yet for that, son.

Growin' up, the Reeves had neighbors lived on a farm north of Hedley. His wife went all over with him, helped him all the time. Once, he was fixin' a windmill, and she was down on the ground, lookin' up at him. He was hookin' a chain up so he could pull the sucker rod out. Well, he's gruntin' and groanin', and she's down there, starin' hard up at him, and the clouds is rollin' by. When that happens, sometimes it looks like the thing that ain't movin' is movin' and the thing that *is* moving—them clouds—

ain't movin' at all. That's just what happened. Looked like the windmill entire was fallin' over.

She yells out, Windmill's a fallin'! Get off that thing!

He didn't think or do nothing but jump off that tower like it was on fire. Landed in a muddy hole—overflow from a stock tank. Broke his leg. Wonder it didn't kill him. Windmill never did come down on top of him. People are funny.

Annnnnnnyway, when Don got older and married, he hired out on the Renfro Ranch. One time, Don and Donnie Mack Roberts were over lookin' after some cattle on a ranch owned by a feller named Dale Martin. There was a big ol' bull on that ranch Dale wanted to sell. Don and Donnie Mack gone out to get him. But they couldn't pen him.

Donnie Mack finally says, I think I'll just rope that bull.

Don says, Donnie, that bull will jerk your horse down.

No, I'm gonna rope him. Won't jerk nothin'.

Donnie took off after that bull, caught him, and roped him. Didn't jerk his horse down, but almost. Bull weren't done yet though.

Donnie Mack was yellin', Heel him! Heel him!

Took some doing, but Don got a loop around his back legs and heeled him. Donnie Mack had the rope pulled tight around that bull's neck. They was chokin' him down pretty good to get control of things. Finally got him stretched out. All of a sudden, the bull went slack. They got on the ground and kicked on him a bit, but he was done. Wasn't movin' or even breathin'. Chest wasn't risin' nor fallin'.

They'd choked him to death. Donnie Mack was wide-eyed. Them bulls ain't cheap

He says, I'll tell Dale he got lightning-struck.

Don is still kickin' on that bull some, lookin' for signs of life.

He says, Donnie Mack, we ain't had a storm in two months.

It was gettin' late. They quit for the day. Left that bull lying there, dead. Talked about it all the way back to headquarters. What were they gonna tell Dale. He wasn't there, so they decided to wait until mornin' to figure it out. Both fretted most of the night, worryin' about their jobs.

In the mornin', Donnie Mack calls and says to Don, I seen a miracle!

What are you talkin' about, Donnie Mack?

That bull. He's alive. He's risen.

Donnie Mack gone out there early, and the bull was gone. Looked around and found him on another section of the pasture. His health was restored. After that, the bull was gentle as a kitten. Don says you would be, too, if you'd been resurrected. You could drive him anywhere. Don says they Christianized that bull.

One time, Don and Donnie Mack was down at a rodeo dance in Tulia with a third feller. Let's call him Lefty. Lefty was pretty tight. Joey Applegate, an old football player, was there. Lefty didn't like Joey for some reason.

Lefty says, See the situation here?

Don didn't see nothin' but trouble. He says, Leave it alone, Lefty.

Lefty says, No, I gotta get Applegate.

Don says again, Leave it alone. He'll kill ya, boy.

Lefty says, No, I'm gonna get him.

Music was playin'. It was the middle of a dance. Floor was full. Applegate was dancin' with the prettiest gal, the sheriff's daughter. Lefty waded in, took a crooked path from his drinkin', and bumped into couples all over. It was dark. Applegate don't ever see him. Just as Lefty reaches him and rears back his arm, Applegate is dancin' the light fantastic and swings his partner around. Lefty throws the punch and hits the gal square in the jaw. Sends her flyin' out of Applegate's arms, onto her backside, and slidin' across the dance floor.

All hell broke loose. Looked like a bomb hit. But it was dark, and ever'one's first reaction was to help the girl. In the second it took ever'one to recover and start lookin' around for what happened, Don and Donnie Mack had grabbed Lefty and were hustlin' him toward the door. Lefty wanted to go back in once they got him outside, but Donnie Mack offered to whip him right then and there if he didn't get in the car. He did. They left town in a hurry. Don was relieved to get home alive that night.

Everyone was huntin' 'em after that, but they didn't know who done it 'cause of the dark, the crowd, and the confusion. Them three was waitin' for the sheriff to show up at their doors the next day and many days after, but no one ever come.

Renfro bought the TO Ranch. Don was up there workin' for a few days. Was a pretty palomino there, as gentle as could be to look at. They called him Guaigüoa, a Spanish name. Don asked Billy Bateman, the cow boss up there, why no one was ridin' that palomino.

Billy just smiles and says, Well, let's catch him.

Every mornin' the wrangler's job is to rope the horse in the corral a cowboy wants to ride that day. So he roped Guaigüoa for Don. Saddled him, and he was still gentle. But after they crossed a hay meadow and got over a road, that horse went to buckin'. Don rode him three or four jumps and was gettin' along with him good, but then he turned and tossed Don head over heels. Landed on both shoulder blades. No damage but knocked the wind outta him.

Other cowboys were gettin' a hoot out of it. They knew all about Guaigüoa.

Don got himself up, dusted himself and his hat off, and says, That spoiled son of a bitch.

Spoiled is a horse weren't broke right.

Billy says, Don, he ain't spoiled. Never been ridden long enough to get spoiled.

Way it worked was, after they got their laugh, them other cowboys rode on. Didn't wait for Don. He had to rope another horse, get it saddled, and catch up. If you're a cowboy, you ain't injured and don't need assistance unless you're on the ground and can't get up.

Don's job at the TO was to figure out how to make the ranch more profitable. One thing, they plain had too many horses. Don got to thinkin'. Mr. Renfro was a good friend of Len Butler, a big shot in the RCA Rodeo.

So Don says to him, Jack, there's a horse up there gonna kill somebody. Buckingest horse I ever seen. He bucked me off, and I seen him buck off two other boys. He's a professional kind of buckin' horse. That Len Butler might want him.

An old boy out of Memphis name of Leonard McCravey worked for Butler. He was a rodeo saddle bronc rider. Well, Len come up in a brand-new Cadillac. Had McCravey with him. Leonard had his bronc saddle in the trunk. Ever'one was there to watch the bronc ride.

Remember, that ol' Guaigüoa was gentle when he didn't have a rider. Didn't have to run him down the chute. Just open the bucking gate and let him in.

Skeptical, McCravey turns to Don and says, You sure that horse gonna buck?

Don says, Yes, Leonard, that horse will buck.

You ever ride him?

Tried him once. That was plenty.

Don called out, Who's gonna pick him up?

A cowboy on horseback run alongside a bronc rider and picks him up when the ride is done. Billy had a saddle on a good horse and says, I'll pick you up, Leonard, when it's all over with.

Possum Brown was in the peanut gallery. He stuttered. He says, Hhhhhe wwwwwwon't nnnnnneed a pickup man. Hhhhhe wwwwwwon't gggggget that far.

They put a flank on them horses to really make 'em buck, kick high.

Leonard says, Who's gonna put the flank on?

Possum says, I wwwwwwill. Bbbbbbut you aaaaaain't gonna nnnnnneed it.

Leonard screwed down and called for him. He was gonna spur him rodeo-style. Really ride 'em. Opened the gate. Out come Guaigüoa a buckin' and a kickin'. McCravey rode him for about five seconds. Then he grounded ol' Leonard pretty hard. McCravey got up, dusted himself off, and says, Put him here. Let's try it again.

Billy says, The horse gets to rest fifteen minutes.

Sure enough, they tied him up. Everyone lookin' at their watches and each other for a while. Then Leonard got back on. Guaigüoa bucked him off again.

Len Butler seen enough. Wrote out a check for fifteen hundred to Mr. Renfro. He knew a rodeo buckin' horse when he seen one. Guaigüoa made it to the national finals in Oklahoma City one year. That's not exactly how Don planned to cull the horses on the TO, but he sure enough made some profit for Mr. Renfro.

After he cowboyed for a while, Don became the county extension agent. County agents work for land grant universities and provide all kinds of help for ranchers and farmers. One of Don's jobs was castratin' baby chicks. Ain't much to work with there.

Don says a brain surgeon ain't got nothin' on him after all them baby chicks he's castrated. It's called caponizin'. Them 4-H kids would show 'em at the fair. Those ol' capons get to weighin' twenty-five pounds. They're good eatin'. Better'n any regular chicken or turkey you ever ate in your life. Don would kill about one in six tryin' to caponize 'em. Wasn't exactly like headin' and heelin' a calf. You'd tie their wings and their legs. Stretch 'em out on a table. Then you'd lift the wing and cut in between the next-to-last rib. The testicles are right next to a vein. Hard not to hit that vein. They bleed to death in twenty seconds if you do. But it's something is done because any castrated animal more tender and tasty without all them hormones in 'em, includin' chickens. Don hated that job.

Don was a county agent for thirty years after he cowboyed. Worked with farmers and ranchers, crops, and livestock. Disease control mostly. Figured he'd be a ranch manager somewheres, but it just never worked out. Don's seventy-three and retired now. He and Blackie still run together.

Talkin' about them as kids, Don says, I couldn't wait to get to school every day to see what we's gonna do. We'd always have a plan of some kind.

Blackie's still up to his old tricks. Not too long ago, he had a feller out his place, diggin' a hole for a septic tank. Name of Bo. It was a pretty deep hole, ten foot at least. They hit hard clay. Bo had a pick down there. To give him room to swing it, Blackie pulled up the ladder and told Bo he'd haul up the loose dirt in a bucket when he come back, but he had to go into town a while.

Then he says, Oh yeah, I got a blind mule out here named Bess. She got a bell on her. If you hear that bell, just call out Bess, and she'll stop.

Well, Blackie waits about fifteen minutes and then he gets

to ringin' that bell some. Sound of the pick hittin' the ground stopped. Blackie moved a little closer, ringing that bell.

Now he hears, Whoa, Bess.

Blackie just kept a movin' closer and closer to the edge of the hole.

Bo starts hollerin', Whooooaaaaa, Bess. Whooooooaaaa, Bess!

When Blackie 'got back' about fifteen minutes later and poked his head over the rim of that hole, Bo got to cussin' him and yellin' for the ladder and wantin' out of that hole. He was hollerin', Damn you, Blackie! That mule of yours like to fall in this hole.

Yeah, Don and Blackie still good friends. If you ever see them two together, might think of your fellow man and alert the authorities.

The Dutch Dairyman

J akob Van Der Weg wanted to be a dairy farmer all of his life. His father owned, lived on, and ran a dairy farm in the north of Holland. All of his life. He had fifteen cows. Jakob was born and raised on the farm. When it was time for Jakob to become a dairyman, there was no land and no opportunity in the Netherlands, and his father wasn't ready to turn over the operation to his eldest son. In fact, his father discouraged the life. But Jakob always wanted to be a dairyman. Jakob moved to Texas. Jakob owns a dairy farm. Jakob has fifteen thousand cows. He's a success story, but there's a twist. A major twist.

Jakob left the Netherlands in 1991 and settled in Stephenville, Texas, about an hour southwest of Fort Worth. Started with thirty cows, but kept growing the herd. Leased three different farms in the Stephenville area. Kept outgrowing them. He married a Hispanic woman with four children, and they eventually had two of their own.

At a farm show in 2001, Jakob ran into an economic development guy from Hereford, a town in the Panhandle an hour southwest of Amarillo. Calls itself the Beef Capital of America. Development guy said they were looking for dairymen to start operating in the Hereford area. Jakob liked what he heard and decided to relocate his family and dairy operation. Local investors kicked in a half-million-dollar loan to get him going.

Things took off from there. Jakob lived the life he had dreamed of, a twenty-four-hour-per-day dream. He milks seven thousand of his cows. The rest are young stock. Takes two years before a cow starts to produce. Then they're good for two or three years. After that, they're processed for beef. So he basically has to turn over one-third of his cows every year. Bring in new producers and weed out the ones no longer producing. Most of Jakob's milk goes to a cheese plant.

It's an ultra-modern operation with two rotaries for milking. A rotary is like a Ferris wheel for cows, only it turns horizontally, not vertically. It's a rotating cement structure with fifty individual milking stations lining the perimeter of the wheel. A pusher moves the cows from their pen through a V chute, but he hardly has to do a thing. The cows know the drill and seem to like going for a ride. They push a bit, heads down, like bovine subway riders heading home at the end of the day. One by one, they load themselves into the individual stalls as the rotary turns slowly. One cow slides aside, and another open station appears. A worker attaches a milking apparatus to the new arrival. By the time the rotary has made one rotation, it is full of fifty cows, flank to flank. By the time a cow has gone round, it has been milked. A worker disengages the milking equipment, and the cow backs out. After a moment, another slides into place. The wheels go round and round.

'Dairy farm' doesn't quite capture what's happening. It's a business. The investment in the rotary, the cows, and everything else is based on 24/7 operation and production. Six to seven hundred cows per hour on the two rotaries. There's also a standard parallel milking operation in another barn. It takes eight hours to milk all of the cows and clean the rotaries. Then the process starts again. Round the clock. Three shifts, three milkings, twenty-four hours a day, three hundred sixty-five days a year. There are fifty employees. A truck of some sort, hauling in feed or hauling out milk, seems to rumble at all times down the mile-long dirt road to the farm.

Jakob was on the same schedule. Twenty-four hours a day. He lives in a trailer only a few steps from one of the milking barns and only a few feet from a railing that encloses one of the feed pens. If there was a problem at three in the morning, his beeper sounded, and he'd rise and walk a few paces from bedroom to barn and deal with it. His life was not divided into professional and personal. It wasn't even divided into work and home. And it was hardly divided into night and day. Dairy farming and his life were one big one.

His was the first dairy in the county and grew to be the largest in the county. Now the county is the third-biggest milk producer in Texas. Jakob says, If you like what you do, you never work a day in your life. And that's how I felt.

Then his wife walked out.

It was 2003. They'd been married for five years. Six kids by then: four hers and two theirs. She moved into Hereford, five miles away, with the three oldest. After the divorce was final, the three youngest lived with Jakob. He took them to their mother's place every afternoon and then picked them up each evening. One day, he went, and she wasn't there anymore. Hadn't said good-bye to the children. Took the three older ones with her back to Comanche, near Stephenville. Nakita was one of them. After a year with her mother, Nakita stayed with Jakob for a summer and never left. She was five when Jakob and her mother married, and Jakob was the only father she had ever really known.

When Jakob was younger, he didn't think he'd ever get married. Thought of himself as married to his job. He had no illusions about the amount of work it took to be a dairyman.

What he didn't figure out until it was too late was how much work it took to make a marriage successful. He knows in retrospect that he didn't pay his wife enough attention, especially after moving her away from familiar ground in the Stephenville area. He thought he could work around the clock and she'd be all right with it. But in the end, it was she who messed up. He got the kids. He wanted the kids. No comparison to cows, not even fifteen thousand of them. And the kids wanted to be with him.

Jakob carried on for five years after the divorce: 24/7 dairy farming and 24/7 parenting. But the numbers didn't add up with a wife, and they didn't add up without a wife. In 2006, he got a business partner, another Dutchman named Patrick Van Adrichen. Patrick was visiting from California with his girlfriend, now his wife. He was looking to get into the dairy business. He worked for Jakob for a couple years and then was going to start his own operation across the road. Instead, they partnered up, fifty-fifty. In addition to two hundred thirty acres where the dairy operation is located, they have seven other sections elsewhere to raise feed for the cows, a total of forty-four hundred acres.

Jakob kept at it for two more years. A partner helped, but he was still overachieving as both a dairyman and a single father. Then came the day one of his daughters got in trouble on the computer. That was it. It happened quickly. He turned over daily operations to Patrick.

Jakob wanted to be a dairyman all of his life. But now he knew he didn't want it to be his whole life. He is still financial partners with Patrick. They still strategize together. Jakob is there if Patrick needs him, but, otherwise, pushing fifty, he is a full-time father to four children, two of whom aren't even his biologically.

It wasn't easy leaving the dairy business, and maybe he has to bite his tongue now and then when his partner makes a decision he might disagree with, but he knows it's his partner's call the way they have things set up. And neither is it easy being a single father of four kids ranging in age from seventeen to nine.

Jakob's parents stayed together their whole lives. They had three boys and no girls. Jakob says he has an appreciation for his mother that few sons who haven't been single parents could possibly have. But he doesn't try to be a mom to the kids. Says he can only be the father he is.

He told them, It's just me. You can complain all day, but that's the way it is. We have to work together on this.

Nakita is Jakob's seventeen-year-old daughter. She isn't exactly the product of a nuclear family, although it's not necessarily an atypical American family these days either. A Hispanic young woman living with a big, strapping, middle-aged Dutch immigrant who isn't her biological father, along with three other siblings and no mother, in a trailer next to fifteen thousand cows on a dairy farm in the middle of the flat and nearly featureless Llano Estacado in the Texas Panhandle.

Yet she's as normal as the rising sun and just as bright. She works after school at the library in town. One evening, a stranger arrives to pick her up just after closing time at nine. An older woman is with her, standing outside the locked and dark library. Like most dads, single parent or otherwise, Jakob hadn't fully explained things to her. Nakita was under the impression that both her father and the visitor were coming to pick her up.

Still, her father had sufficiently briefed her, and she had no trouble with the idea of riding home with the stranger. But the woman, who was merely being responsible, looked on the stranger with suspicion. Talking out of the side of her mouth, she whispered to Nakita, loud enough for the visitor to hear distinctly. She asked if the girl felt comfortable going with 'this man.' She said she didn't need to get in the car, and told her to call immediately if there were a problem.

Nakita was smiling. Not an ounce of fear in her eyes. Not a drop of distrust. Got it worked out with mother hen and climbed in. The stranger took a chance and kidded Nakita that maybe he should floor it, make the tires squeal, and go in the opposite direction of her farm. Her response was an impish grin. She said, Maybe you should have offered me candy.

She talked freely about her life. Before Jakob quit dairy farming and Nakita was old enough to get an after-school job, he worked nonstop. Not only did Nakita play Mom, ironically, it was as if she were a single mom. She did all the cooking and cleaning. 'The kids,' as she calls them, were 'terrible.' They threw things at each other all the time. One can imagine the scene. Jakob arriving home at nine after a long day. Nakita all but shouting 'They're yours!' and storming out of the trailer for a few moments of peace and solitude.

Nakita says Jakob acts strict, but is basically a pushover. She says, He trips up sometimes because it's all new to him.

Now that Jakob isn't working and Nakita *is*, after school, he does most of the chores and the cooking. On Saturday, they all clean together and then go out to dinner in Amarillo. When she talks about the family trips to Amarillo, it's about what the younger ones like to do, which is what they end up doing, not what she wants to do. Like a mom. She says that, if she suggests they go to the Chinese restaurant she likes, her little brother quickly develops a stomachache.

And about the mother-abandons-a-Hispanic-girl-to-live-with-her-no-blood-relation-big-white-Dutch-immigrant-father-in-a-trailer-next-to-fifteen-thousand-cows-in-the-middle-of-nowhere thing? It barely registers with her. Except for the mom part. The only time she gets a bit subdued is when she talks about her mother. Nakita says her mom wants to be in their lives, but it's hard for her. She doesn't feel like she measures up as a mother, so she isn't in contact with the kids much. They send her Mother's Day cards and birthday cards.

Nakita says, It sounds mean, but I try to block her out.

She doesn't know how else to deal with it. There's pain there, for sure, but it's not holding her back from living her life and moving forward. It's the only life she knows, and she's happy with it. Happy with her father. Happy with her siblings. Happy with school. Happy with living in the country. Okay with the fifteen thousand cows. The joy seems to bubble up from within. External factors aren't allowed to call the shots.

An arriving car parks haphazardly by the trailer. The last trace of light is fading quickly on the western horizon. Three enormous 'guard' dogs are prone, sleeping close to one another near the front door. Stepped over, they stir not, exhausted from a day of chasing cows, kids, and an assortment of vehicles. Cows low near and far. Calves bawl. It stinks from fifteen thousand Holsteins within a half-mile. A vehicle leaves the dairy out on the dirt road. Equipment in the adjacent milking barn hums.

Nakita enters the trailer. Jakob watches her proudly and then asks if she 'cried like I told you to' when she talked to the visitor.

No pathos here. Just your basic nuclear family and a happy Dutch immigrant ex-dairyman living a different kind of dream.

The Coin and the Compass

There's lots of ways to define what it means to be a cowboy. There's the ropin', the ridin', knowin' horses, and knowin' cattle. But if you strip away the hat, the boots, the saddle, and the spurs, the quality that has always defined a cowboy best is freedom. Freedom from the tyranny of a cubicle. The freedom of an open pasture. The freedom of a timeless world. Bob Walters took that freedom to another level. He would hire on for a roundup, but, right from the start, he'd tell the cowboy boss, When the chuck wagon pulls in, I'm pullin' out.

Cowboys is a funny breed. They're thin-skinned. Could work on a ranch three or four years. Could live in a house supplied by the ranch and have a string of horses given them by the ranch. But, if they're slighted in any way, they'll gather their bedroll and saddle and head on down the road. Bob Walters wouldn't even last that long. Not that he was slighted. But after a few months campin' in the field and gatherin' and branding cattle, when the wagon come in, he'd pack his car and be history. Just the way it was. Just wanted to go, even though he had absolutely no idea where he was headed. When he come to the first junction, he'd pull out a coin and flip it. Heads, he'd head north. Tails, he'd head south. Was the ultimate freedom.

Most of the fellers I been tellin' you about been born and raised and lived their whole lives in Texas. Fact, some of their ancestors been in the country three or four generations. But there's others, transplants like Yankee Bob Walters who ain't from here, but he's still every bit a cowboy as them was homegrown. Grew up on his grandmother's farm outside of Menomonee Falls, Wisconsin. Couple of farms over was a horse dealer who let Bob ride all the time growin' up. Taught himself how to rope and ride. He rode dozens of different horses because none was around long. The horse dealer would buy horses cheap because it was the 1940s and tractors were comin' in and then sell the horses for processin'. For Bob, who took a likin' to horses, that wholesale slaughter was unsettling.

What brought him to Texas?

A Hudson car.

Funny, Bob. But what made you decide to come to Texas from Wisconsin?

They run me out of several states 'fore I landed here.

In fact, he left Wisconsin right after high school and headed for the West Coast. Went into the army. Looked like he was headed for the Korean War, but they sent him to Europe instead. Then the Korean War ended. He got out of the service and went to work on a seventy-two thousand-acre ranch near Maricopa, California. A good cowpuncher needs to know a lotta things, includin' ropin', but he mostly needs to know cattle and horses. Bob didn't know the first thing about cattle, but he did have the second part of the equation covered. In fact, when it came to horses, he could look at one and tell you what it was thinkin'.

They put him in a camp, alone, seventeen miles from head-quarters. It was a good thing and a bad thing. No one was there to see how little he knew about cattle, but, on the other hand, no one was there to teach him nothin' neither. He was supposed to keep the cattle on water, move them to different pastures, and doctor sick cows. Turned out he weren't totally isolated. He'd sometimes be with other cowhands. But whether it was California or Texas, a lotta them old cowboys wouldn't teach the younger ones. Just wasn't done much. Not sure if it was like a chef didn't want to give away his recipes too freely or what, but the new hands had to learn mostly by observin'. Bob picked a feller he thought was the best hand, and he just did ever'thing that feller done. If he took off his hat, Bob took off his hat. Eventually, by watchin' and imitatin', he got good at handlin' cattle. Only problem was, the feller he picked to shadow was the jealous sort. Havin' him as a role model proved to be a chore. If you got a new bandanna, he had to get himself a new bandanna. If you got a compliment from the boss, he had to get a compliment from the boss. It was like workin' with a bothersome younger brother.

One of the worst wrecks Yankee Bob ever had was on that ranch in California. Parts of the ground was rugged hill country, so they sometimes done their work muleback. One time they brought up a mule from the Central Valley. Was supposed to been broke by a feller down there. But when Bob got on him, he left. Just left. And there was no stoppin' him. So Bob let him run. But then that mule started down a hill that ended in a grassy ditch. Mule stumbled, but caught himself. Bob was startin' to swing his boot free of the stirrup to get off when the mule bucked and tossed him high up in the air. As Bob was reenterin' Earth's atmosphere, comin' down behind the mule, the critter bucked again and kicked out his hind legs. Caught Bob in the chest. Broke his back and seven ribs, and collapsed a lung. Lyin' on the ground, he could feel himself goin'. Thought he was gonna die right there in that ditch. But he rallied and managed to half-walk and half-drag himself a mile back to camp. A pickup was there. Was able to get in and start it. Drove to another camp where there was a house and a feller supposed to be diggin' a well. Bob honked his horn. The feller come to the door of the house and, real friendly, waved him in. Bob was sure he was takin' his last breath from his last lung. He couldn't do nothin' but honk, but then he couldn't even do that no more and passed out.

He woke up four or five days later in a hospital. First thing he saw, two beds away, was an older man with his wife and grown children by the bed, a doctor, a nurse, and a priest. Bob watched him die and realized they'd put him in the death ward. Not a pleasant realization to wake up to. But he had no immediate plans on dyin'. His journey just begun. He was out of the hospital and back to work in three weeks. In fact, he went right out and got back on that mule. No mule has more stubborn on him than Yankee Bob got.

One time on the MU Ranch there in California in the early 1950s, Elvis almost killed Bob. The foreman said Bob had to come over on a Sunday night and watch the *Ed Sullivan Show*. He says, There's a crazy feller on, sings and gyrates his hips. You ain't gonna believe this. He was on 'fore, and he's gonna be on again tonight.

So Bob decides he needs to see this on the new TV they got, and he drives the ranch's 1938 Dodge pickup seventeen miles from his camp to headquarters. He sees the show, sees Elvis and ever'one screamin', and then heads home. That pickup no longer had lights that worked. Bob was crawlin' along a bumpy ranch road that run alongside a steep canyon. He didn't realize the lip of that dirt track had washed away in a storm. The left side wheels slipped over the edge sudden and the car tilted that way. Bob bailed out of the passenger side door. Without his weight, the pickup stopped slidin' and hung there, half over the cliff. With his weight, it woulda gone over the side for sure. Hoofed his way back to camp in the dark. Had to winch that truck to safe ground the next mornin' from the top of the ridge above. Bob has always figured Elvis owed him one.

When he left the MU, a coin flip pointed him north, and he ended up on a ranch in the barren, rugged country of southwestern Idaho. Got a job on the Flying H Ranch in Riddle. That was when school started. Bob says, It was put in front of you, and you either done your job or got hurt bad tryin'.

He slept on the ground with one thin blanket and a tarp to cover him. They had two meals a day in the field, and it was bad eatin'. When he pulled out of Idaho, he figured on settlin' for a while in Montana. There was a job at a ranch in Missoula if he wanted it, but a coin flip pushed him south.

He ended up tourin' Texas in his old Hudson. Had his saddle and bedroll and not much else. He liked the look of Clarendon in the southeast portion of the Panhandle and stopped there at a boot shop. He ran into the owner of the RO Ranch who needed a hand real bad. The ranch was first put together by a British feller name of Alfred Rowe back in the 1870s. He was buddies with Charles Goodnight. Alfred went down with the *Titanic*. Bob agreed to hire on. He was twenty-four. Although his wanderlust would take him to other ranches in the Lone Star state, he'd found his home, Texas.

Sometimes he'd only stay on a ranch three or four months, sometimes three or four years. Sometimes he'd go back to a ranch a second time. All told, he worked at seventeen ranches in twelve years, including fifteen different ones in California, New Mexico, Arizona, the one in Idaho, and Texas. In Texas, he worked at some of the biggest ranches, including the JA, the four 6s, Bivens, the RO, and the Matador.

Yankee Bob was friends with an in'eresting cowboy by the name of Bigun Bradley, a stocky, handsome man. Bob broke horses for Bigun's dad, Shorty. The father was a cowboy's cowboy. Bigun gone off to the service. When he come back, he needed a job. Bob was workin' at the JA, but knew they needed a hand at the 6s and told Bigun about it. Carl, his real name, got the 6s job. One day, an advertisin' feller from Chicago come out to Texas and seen Bigun. One thing led to another, and Bigun became the first Marlboro man. Had his picture in just about every magazine there was with a rope in his hands and a cigarette hangin' out of his mouth. Bob says Bigun weren't no show cowboy neither. He was the real deal, a good roper, rider, and horse breaker. Funny thing though, he smoked Kools, not Marlboros. One day, they found him dead in a stock tank, drowned. Looked like he'd gotten bucked off a horse, but no one ever knew for sure. He was only in his mid-thirties. Left behind a wife and young child.

Life on the high plains can be fragile. One time on the Bivens Ranch, Bob was on a horse that run off on him. A lotta rivers and creeks in the Panhandle and West Texas have broad floodplains. Actual river channel, where water is flowin', can be fairly narrow, but that floodplain can be mostly bog, almost like quicksand. Bob was still tryin' to get the horse under control when it landed in a bog next to a narrow creek. The muck swallowed up the mare's forelegs and held them down. But the rest of the horse kept going. Its head slammed into the opposite bank. Bob was thrown off, but landed soft in the muck and wasn't hurt. The mare broke her neck and died instant. Even for a hardened cowboy, it give Bob pause. A horse runnin' full gallop one moment, dead and gone the next.

Bigun give Yankee Bob one of the best horses he ever had. Name of Geronimo. Bob was at the 6s, too, then. He was already settin' down for dinner one noon at ranch headquarters while Bigun was still out in a corral. Marlboro Man roped Geronimo, who was known for being bad to pitch. Horse reared up and fell over backwards, hit his head, and immediately lay still. Blood poured from a wound. He was killed instant. Bigun was bothered of course, but there was nothin' could be done, so he gone into dinner. Deal with it in the afternoon. When they come out, Geronimo was alive and on his feet. No accountin' for critters.

Bigun give the horse to Bob. Brought him down to the old Taylor camp where Yankee Bob was stayin'. Pitched like mad for him like he done for everyone else. Horse had a mind of his own. Bob had a discussion with Geronimo. It was mostly nonverbal and primarily involved Bob's quirt. A quirt is like a ridin' crop. He whipped that horse pretty good in the flanks and on the head. Made him pull his head back up, and made him get along. Went on for some weeks. Geronimo kept pitchin', harder and harder. One day, Bob finally quit. Stopped whippin' him. Last time Geronimo ever bucked. Seems he got the message and was willin' to cooperate, but only on his own terms, which were simple. No more whippin'. Became one of the best workin' horses Bob ever had. When he left the 6s, cowboys was lined up wantin' Geronimo in their string.

Speakin' of legendary old cowboys, want to tell you about Boots O'Neal. He works for the 6s, too. Was born in 1932 on a ranch in Clarendon. Went to work cowpunchin' full-time on the JA Ranch in Palo Duro Canyon after his sophomore year of high school. Need to tell you about the JA. Lotta well-known ranches in Texas, but the JA is pretty special. The Comanches ruled most of what is now Texas and parts of other states and Mexico for a couple of hundred years. By most accounts, they were the fiercest of all American Indian tribes. By the 1870s, their numbers had dwindled from disease and fightin' with federal troops, Texas Rangers, and other tribes. In 1874, the United States cavalry, led by Ranald Mackenzie, tracked what was left of the Comanches to Palo Duro. If you were a horse, what happened next weren't good news. But given all the bloodshed between Comanches and settlers in Texas the precedin' half-century, the last gasp of freedom for the People themselves was mercifully bloodless. Mackenzie slaughtered their horses. Without their mounts, the Comanche surrendered and was packed off to a reservation in Oklahoma. Within just a year or two of the Comanches being cleared out of the canyon, Charles Goodnight established a ranch there. Goodnight might be the most famous rancher in Texas history. First made a name leadin' civilian retaliatory raids against the Comanche, but he was probably best known being the first to drive cattle north out of Texas, right after the Civil War. The Goodnight-Loving trail is named after him. The ranch Goodnight established in 1876 in Palo Duro Canyon was the JA, and that's the one Boots worked on as a teenager.

Annnnnnnyway, Boots got an initiation early on at the JA. They were drivin' cattle through Palo Duro Canyon and runnin' three wagons. There was the chuck wagon, drug by a four-horse team, which the cook drove. There was also the hoodlum wagon, which hauled the water and the rope corral. The hoodlum drove that. And there was a third wagon with a two-horse team, filled with the cowboys' bedrolls. The newest cowboy, usually the youngest, the lowest on the totem pole, drove the bed wagon. When Boots first got to the JA, that'd be him. Movin' along the bottom of the canyon, you crossed back and forth over the creek there, the Prairie Dog Town Fork of the Red River. It was tricky, 'cause like I told you, creeks and rivers in Texas ain't real wide where the water flows, but the floodplain on either side tends to be broad and filled with something close to quicksand. Cons'quently, the wagons followed where the cattle and the remuda packed down the bog. When they done that, they rolled along well enough. But the bed wagon was drawn by two buckin' horses that was mean and give the driver hell most all the time. One fine day, Boots figured he had them under control good enough to roll a Bull Durham. When he tried, he dropped the reins. Them ornery ol' horses saw their chance, and they just left. Headed right down the bed of that river. Boots passed the four-horse chuck wagon like it was tied up at the barn.

The ol' boy runnin' that thing, the cook, hollers, Jump off, son! Jump off!

Didn't take much convincin'. Boots done what he was told. He bailed off that runaway wagon and hit the ground rollin'. Soft sand absorbed the fall, and he was fine, but it weren't a second later that wagon hit a log and threw all them bedrolls in the river and then went topsy-turvy. All hell come bustin' loose at that point. Spooked the remuda. And them runaways was draggin' the wagon upside down through the river. Cowboys was yellin' and cussin'.

Finally got them broncs on the bed wagon slowed to a stop. Boots thought for sure his career cowboyin' was 'bout to be terminated in its infancy. Wagon boss was none too pleased and give him a lecture on smokin', but, thing about punchin' cows, just too much going on. Too much to do. Too many critters to take care of. Had to put something like that behind you. Fix it, and move on. The wreck had torn up the harness, and they had to send a boy horseback to a line camp nearby to get some spare leather to replace it. Had to flip over the wagon, rescue all them bedrolls from the river, and gather up the herd and remuda. Fact, the wagon boss weren't the one who give Boots the biggest earful about all that. The older hands done some real chewin' on him as they pulled their bedrolls drippin' wet out of Prairie Dog Town

Fork. And they had a few more things to say when they got into 'em that night and yet additional comments when they got out of them wet beds the next mornin'. But that's the cowboy life. Most times on a weeklong campout like that, it would rain one or two nights. Get your bedroll wet. Sometimes, the next day, the area around camp would have a couple of dozen bedrolls draped over the biggest nearby mesquite bushes to dry out. Only it might rain that day too, so they'd be even wetter than before. Boys would just wring 'em out and sleep in 'em. Sometimes, cowboyin' is one part romance, one part freedom, and eight parts misery.

Boots wasn't the only one got special treatment as a newcomer. He cowboyed at a number of big ranches, was a brand inspector for a few years, too, and was later a wagon boss and a foreman. One June when he was foreman at the Waggoners, the ranch owner or general manager or somebody had a friend from the city who was a dignitary of some sort. He sent his kid out to the ranch to spend a summer workin' there. Bosses told Boots to take care of him and watch over him, but they wanted the boy to live in the bunkhouse and work with the crew. There are greenhorns, and then there was this kid. Boots takes him to the bunkhouse, gets him settled in, and then goes back to what they called the big house, where he and his wife lived. Boots was explainin' about the kid to his wife. Gonna have to take care of him. She was lookin' out the front window. She says, Well, you better start right now. They got him hangin' on the gate by his feet.

Boots couldn't believe it. He'd barely gotten through his front door. The overhang on the gate was about ten foot high. The kid was strung upside down on it and swingin' by his ankles. Boots never did figure out what happened. Lotta rules in them bunkhouses. Even though they's all unwritten, it's like the law. Ignorance of 'em is no excuse. Kid probably just asked too many questions too fast. Boots had to go cut him down.

One time, Boots and two other fellers, Eddie and Glen, were way out on the ranch in the middle of February. Had to bring in some steers. One thing they done occasional is rope 'em and tie 'em up by the horns to a tree overnight. They get to shakin' their big ol' heads in the night, and that rope burns 'em some—can get real tender. The next day, they'll go wherever you want to take 'em. That's the theory anyway. Boots and them was up on the Wichita River. Next mornin' Boots gone to work and pitched a rope over a seven-year-old steer. Eddie cut him loose from that overnight rope. Day was bitter cold. Plan was to lead that steer downriver a bit where there was a decent shallow crossin' and then load him on a trailer. That particular steer didn't make the briefin'. He turned direct into the river. Picked his own crossin'. Crashed right through the surface ice. Boots and his horse got jerked in. Wrong place to cross. Too deep. That steer was swimmin' soon enough. Boots' horse kept his footin', but his jeans was soaked to the waist. Now the bull snaps the rope. Boots tries to fashion a makeshift hondo while his mount is wheelin' and splashin' in that ice-cold river. Meanwhile, the cow is thrashin' and going nowheres in that deep pool. Boots gets soaked head to toe in what felt like glacier melt.

Glen is watchin' all this from the other bank. After a while, he says, I'll go make a fire.

That was Glen's contribution. He drifted out of sight. Eddie had already gone off for another stray. Boots manages to rope that steer again and half drag his carcass the rest of the way across the Wichita. Ties that ornery cow to a tree along the other bank. Barely able to walk, his clothes froze stiff, he takes off boots, hat, and every stitch of clothin' and tries to dry them by the fire Glen made. Glen and Eddie come by and then go off to get the other men and the truck so they could load the steer. Just left him.

Nowadays, say a teacher take a buncha kids on a school trip or something and one falls in an icy river, there'd be panic and fire trucks and ambulances and the FBI and hospitalization. And even if the kid come out fine after a few minutes in the drink, there'd be TV news stories with a headline in a little box over the news feller's shoulder. Hypothermia Near-Death Tragedy. Investigations, lawsuits, new rules governin' field trips, and the teacher findin' a new career. But not them cowboys. Just left Boots standin' out there stark naked in the February breeze, shiverin' like a refugee and dryin' his clothes by the heat of a prairie campfire. When they finally got to the wagon for noon dinner, Boots could still feel dampness from hat to socks. But neither Eddie nor Glen said a word. Grabbed their tin plates and buried their faces in their beans and biscuits. Just another day at the office.

Boots was probably best known over the years for breakin' horses. He run the bronc pen at Waggoners for eleven years. Broke forty or fifty horses every winter there. One time on the Matador Ranch, they give him a bronc no one else could ride. Ol' Floyd Brewer was by the wagon. They were in a pasture, middle of nowhere, about twenty miles from the town of Adrian. Well, not even Boots could handle that bronc at first, and the colt bolted on him. Took off at a dead run. Flew past the wagon. Boots was barely hangin' on.

As it galloped by, Brewer come out of the cook tent sudden and yells out, Hey, Boots, if you go through Adrian, could you get my mail?

Boots' father was named Boots, but everyone called the son by his real name, Bill, when he was real small. But his first day of school in 1938, he was waitin' for the bus.

When it stopped and them doors opened, the bus driver said,

Get on here, Little Boots.

Ever since then, he'd been Boots, too. It's on everything from his bank account to his driver's license.

Boots is seventy-eight now. Been a workin' cowboy for sixty-two years. He was married forty-four years. Nel passed on four years ago. Most days, he still thinks of something he'd like to tell her. He's back livin' in the bunkhouse. The afternoon we talked, he'd saddled a horse before daylight, ridden all day, and roped twenty calves. And he saddled a horse before daylight the next mornin', too.

Annnnnnnyway, I was supposed to be tellin' you about Yankee Bob Walters. He married for the first time in his early forties. Stopped flippin' coins and settled down, if you can call it that. Stopped day workin' as a cowpuncher and shod horses for twenty-five years. Didn't relocate as much, but he did travel around to a lotta different ranches. He finally retired a few years ago. His days of roamin' free are over now. His mind is as sharp as ever, but Parkinson's disease has tried to make him a prisoner in his own body. He lives in Dimmitt, a small town an hour southwest of Amarillo on the Llano. He lives on a pretty, quiet, tree-shaded street, but only three blocks away, the houses end and the plains begin. They roll, unchallenged by any obstacle, to the horizon. Freedom in all directions. Freedom tantalizingly close. Only a coin flip away.

The Trader

There's probably only one person in the entire world who has ever called Salem Abraham of Canadian, Texas, a dumbass. It was his grandfather Oofie. And he called him that a lot.

When Salem returned to Canadian in January 1988 after graduating early from Notre Dame, he was ready to go to work for Oofie, who had made a fortune in the oil and gas business. But Salem's heart, mind, and soul were in commodities trading. He'd written an algorithm while at Notre Dame that showed a lot of promise. Oofie had given each of his three grandsons a grubstake of fifty thousand dollars, and Salem started trading with it. His balance dropped to forty-five thousand after the crash of 1987 and the rebound, but he wasn't deterred. He wanted to start a real trading operation through the Chicago Mercantile Board of Trade. He went to his two brothers and got them to put in a total of twenty-five thousand. He now had seventy thousand, but wanted a nice round hundred thousand to start with, so he asked Oofie to kick in thirty thousand.

Oofie shook his head and said, Of all the dumbass ways to go broke, why did you pick the fastest?

Salem went through and showed him a simulation of how, if his system had been followed for the prior calendar year, his algorithm could have turned a million dollars into 1.8 million.

Mistake. Loud mistake. The show-and-tell lit Oofie's fuse.

You think with your fancy-ass Notre Dame degree the world

is going to roll out a red carpet for you? Why don't we just wrap up your algorithm and send it to Chicago with a bow on it? They can cut us a check, dumbass.

Salem insisted that what he was showing Oofie was a good statistical sample and it would work in the future. Old-school Oofie was not impressed. Probably to teach the kid a lesson more than anything else, he wrote out a check for thirty thousand. But there was a proviso.

Oofie said, If total assets drop below fifty thousand, we're going to throw your quote machine out the window and stop with the dumbass trading nonsense and get back to real business.

Salem started trading. Over the next four months, the original balance drifted down to eighty-two thousand. Then in May, it dropped quickly to seventy thousand. Those were the early days of facsimile machines. They spit out a fax on thermal paper, the kind where the ends would curl up. Salem was in his office early one morning, trying to read one of those Dead Sea scrolls. It was more bad news. He was looking a bit disheveled, even though the day was young, when Oofie happened by.

Where are we today?

Salem has a steel-trap memory for numbers. He recalls the exact amount. He said, $68,740.

Oofie's eyebrows arched up. Then he rubbed his hands together in glee and said, Just a matter of time.

Thanks for the vote of confidence, Grandpa.

But that was the bottom. The drought of 1988 hit, and Salem was long on corn, wheat, and soybeans. All three went through the roof. By the end of the month, Salem was back up to $100,000. By the end of the year, after he had taken his 20 percent commission, he had turned the $100,000 into $240,000.

Although Oofie wasn't one to admit the kid had done good,

Dumbass as a proper name was employed a lot less frequently around the office.

Canadian, Texas, is an isolated oasis amid the stark landscape of the northeastern Panhandle. Nearly two hours from Amarillo and three from Oklahoma City, it's approached through miles and miles of largely featureless high plains that give way to rolling ranch land dotted with gas wells and then more rugged canyon land before the highway drops down into the wide Canadian River Valley. Eventually the traveler is deposited in a mostly prosperous-looking burg with a brick main street, a smattering of fast-food joints, and a handful of handsome mini-mansions on tree-shaded back streets that hint at the town's vibrant past. With a population of 2,233, Canadian is quintessential small-town Texas.

On the corner of its busiest intersection resides the century-old Moody building, a three-story brick edifice majestic in its simplicity. Everything in the town looks like it belongs here and vaguely reflects the past: from the plethora of pickups with cowboy-hatted drivers to cattle trucks rumbling through town and struggling retail stores on Main Street. Everything except the third floor of the Moody Building. What's happening there looks like it was beamed in from a high rise on Wall Street. The brightly lit trading floor of Abraham Trading Company is a futuristic ménage of high-def screens and computer terminals, all displaying a striking pallet of color-coded charts and graphs, the latest version of Salem's algorithm hard at work. ATC has $480 million under management and trades in fifty-nine futures markets, everything from Australian dollars to zinc—including orange juice—while the cattle trucks rumble by not thirty-five feet away. Over the last twenty years, ATC has earned an average annual return of 20 percent.

Mild-mannered, forty-two-year-old Salem Abraham is the great-grandson of a Lebanese immigrant trader of dry goods, not commodities. Despite a net worth in the tens of millions of dollars that would allow him to live in the pricey suburbs north of Chicago, Greenwich, Connecticut, or even Beverly Hills or Aspen, where he has a home, Salem may be Canadian's most confirmed citizen.

His great-grandfather came from a village in Lebanon and made several trips to America with his brothers starting around 1906, while he was still a young teen. Sticking to the East Coast at first, he rolled cigars in North Carolina and even ventured as far as Brazil before setting his sights on Texas. The development of large parts of Texas and the West could be traced to the plotting of railroad lines, with towns springing up along the right-of-ways. When he was in his twenties and had a wife back in Lebanon, Salem's great-grandfather, Nahim Abraham Maloof, would stock up in Kansas City, carefully packing suitcases with clothes, shoes, and other dry goods. Then he'd head down the railroad tracks and peddle at every stop on the way to Amarillo.

When Nahim moved to the United States for good in 1913, bringing along his wife and two sons, Canadian was a booming cattle town and a prominent stop on the rail line. He decided to settle here. Nahim rented a building for six years. Then he bought one for a store and lived in the back of it for twenty-five years. Nahim's third son was the first born in America. A common name in Lebanon, Maloof was dropped as the family name, but given as a first name to the third son.

Maloof, or Oofie as he was known, grew up, married an Irish rancher's daughter south of town, and began a career as a bookkeeper. He eventually tried his hand at just about every occupation one can attempt in small-town Texas: real estate, insurance, restaurateur, and trading cattle. In 1952 or 1953, a deal went bad. He bought a bunch of cattle. By the time he shipped them to market, the price had dropped. He ended up going bankrupt, although he didn't welsh on any of his debts. When the oil and gas boom rolled into the northeastern Panhandle in the 1960s, Oofie, with his real estate knowledge and facility with numbers and entrepreneurial spirit, was well positioned. Plus, he'd been mayor of Canadian in the 1950s and knew everyone. The big oil and gas companies usually employed a local to help them arrange oil and gas leases. Oofie was their man, and he was able to buy into a bunch of deals. After his nascent political career sputtered, he refocused on business just as oil and gas boomed in the 1970s. He amassed what most people would call a fortune.

There was another oil bust in the 1980s, but Oofie had learned his lesson in the 1950s and was debt-free, so he was able to ride out the storm. One of Oofie's sons was a successful doctor who had three boys: Salem, Eddie, and Jason. Salem showed an entre-preneurial bent early on. He injured his leg playing high school football. After his freshman year in South Bend, he had surgery on the leg and knew he'd be hobbled most of the summer. He thought about what he could do with limited mobility to make a little money. He decided to buy a fixer-upper home in Canadian that he could turn around and rent. It would be something he, his girlfriend, and brother could work on over the summer. Because Oofie had kept his hand in real estate, even as he was becoming a mini-mogul in oil and gas, Salem went to him, described what he wanted to do, and asked his grandfather if he had any houses that qualified.

His grandfather looked him up and down, tossed him some keys, and said, I may have just what you're looking for.

Salem said, What do you want for it?

Oofie said, Twenty-six thousand.

Salem checked out the place. It was rundown, but pretty much what he wanted. Structurally sound, it just needed some light repairs, paint, and carpet. He came back to his grandfather's office and said, It's perfect, I'll take it.

A dark cloud filled the room. Oofie stared at him. He said, You'll take it? He paused a minute and asked again, You'll take it?

Salem said, Yeah, I'll take it.

At what price?

You said twenty-six. I'll give you twenty-six.

Oofie shook his head while grimacing. He seemed to experience something like physical pain at the encounter, wondering if genetics were a crock and if the same blood ran through the kid's veins as his own. In the best of times, he semi-affectionately hurled epitaphs at his grandson. Now he strung together at least a half-dozen dumbasses before he was through making his point, plus a few other expletives.

He said, You dumbass. Just like that, you'll take it for twenty-six. You're killing me. You have to bargain. Finally, Oofie said, Look, dumbass, you don't just say you'll take it. Because you're such a dumbass, I'm going to help you out. I'm going to sell it to you for twenty-five, but I would have sold it to you for twenty-four if you had just asked. So never forget I got you for a thousand, dumbass. And never forget to ask.

Salem has never forgotten. That summer, he paid his brother and girlfriend five dollars an hour to paint and repair the house. He got three years of rental income out of it before moving into it himself. His girlfriend, his high school sweetheart, eventually became his wife and mother of his eight children. That was the first house they lived in after graduation and marriage.

When Salem first went off to college, he and his brother had a plan. Salem would study finance. His brother Eddie, who was one year older, would get a petroleum land management degree from Texas Tech. Then they would come back to Canadian and work for their granddad. But they told Oofie, who was sixty-eight at the time, that he drank too much, smoked too much, and didn't exercise at all. Said he had to stay alive to keep up his end of the bargain.

Yeah, yeah, yeah, you dumbasses.

But in January 1986, as a college sophomore, with oil prices below ten dollars a barrel, Salem was trying to figure out how to hedge his bet some. Working for Oofie in a dead industry wasn't a welcome prospect. He started thinking about commodities trading for three reasons. First, he could do it from anywhere, and Canadian, Texas, is anywhere. Second, he could do it on the side while working for Oofie. And third, although Salem claims substandard achievement in a number of areas of academic study, math is not one of them. If there is a math quiz or contest, might as well etch Salem's name on the plaque before you even get started because he's going to win it. He knew he'd be flat-out good at trading. No ego. Just knew it.

In the fall of 1987, during his last semester at Notre Dame, he began trading using an algorithm he'd written and the fifty thousand from Oofie. His algorithm is based on predicting the behavior of people, not markets. If a hundred people are in a room and they're invested in a certain market that begins to move, their behavior is not entirely predictable, but it is predictable enough to give Salem and his traders an edge. He got up to sixty-six thousand before the crash of 1987 dropped him to thirty-three thousand. He took a week off from trading to clear his mind and then got his balance back up to forty-five thousand before taking a break for finals and graduation.

That was when he started the trading company and more than doubled Oofie's money in a year. His grandfather's way of acknowledging Salem's success was to toss a prospectus on his desk after the New Year and say, You did better than them.

It was a Dean Witter prospectus. They had a commodities trading fund. Salem had indeed had a better 1988, but, more amazingly, in retrospect, was that the random encounter with Oofie turned out to be the next career step for Salem. He picked up the phone and called Dean Witter in January 1989. Nine months later, they gave him a test account with $200,000 and then added another $200,000 six months later. In the summer of 1990, he became a full-time trader with them at age twenty-four. Before he turned twenty-five, the allocations ramped up very quickly. One time he flew to Dallas and needed to rent a car, but wasn't old enough. He tried to tell the lady at the counter that he was entrusted with $20 million of people's hard-earned money to trade as he wished for a living, so she could probably trust him with a $20,000 car. She wasn't buying it. Joe's rent-a-wreck bailed him out.

Maybe Oofie sensed Salem had the temperament to take his abuse and let it roll off his back. One of Salem's brothers once asked if it didn't bother Salem to be called a dumbass a half-dozen times a day. Salem knew Oofie's biting criticism was his teaching style. Positive reinforcement wasn't in his pedagogical quiver. He said to his brother, Just think of it as him speaking Spanish and he's saying that he loves you and would like you to do better.

For all of his sharp edges, Oofie was a brilliant businessman. Salem knew it was worth enduring a bit of Spanish in exchange for learning from him.

When the original trading partnership with Oofie and the

three brothers was broken up in 1990, prior to reforming under a more formal arrangement, Salem handed Oofie a check for $167,000, his gain on his original $30,000 investment less than three years before. Salem asked Oofie how much he'd like to reinvest in the new venture. Imagining that a 450 percent increase, along with Oofie's already considerable assets, would induce Grandpa to at least round up to $200,000, if not more, Salem was a bit surprised when Oofie said, I'll peel off $17,000 and give you $150,000.

Although Salem nearly doubled the fund over the next three and a half years, he was down 10 percent in 1992.

That's when Oofie came by and said, You know, you've had a good run with this commodities deal. Too bad it's over.

Whoa, Gramps.

Salem explained it was just a rough patch and he'd get through it. Indeed, it was one of only three down years in the twenty-year history of ATC. The tables finally turned a few months before Oofie died in May 1994, when his original one hundred fifty thousand, which was really his original thirty thousand, had climbed to two hundred seventy thousand.

Oofie came to Salem and said, You know, I'm thinking about adding a bit.

It was a sweet victory for Salem. He smiles when he tells the story. He said to Oofie, No, you aren't allowed to add. You've never been a believer. You cannot add. I don't need your money. What's in there is what you've got.

Remember, Oofie was not his poverty-stricken grandfather. He was worth millions, so the economic component of the discussion was relatively unimportant. It was all about giving Oofie a taste of his own medicine.

In the four years following Oofie's passing, stocks were the place to be, not commodities. With stocks gaining 20 percent annually, money flowed out of Salem's trading operation as if through a broken dam. Money under management had climbed to $132 million before tumbling in 1999 to $3.7 million, which was basically family and very loyal friends. But Salem was taking a close look at the chess board and spotting other ways to make money.

That same year, 1999, he closed a water deal he'd been working on for thirty months that was pure Salem. Because he, his brothers, and Oofie bought and sold ranches in those early years after Notre Dame and given Oofie's background in oil and gas, Salem knew a lot about property and mineral and water rights. A dam was built on the Canadian River in 1965 that supplies water to eleven cities in the Panhandle and as far south as Lubbock. The resulting Lake Meredith serves as a large reservoir, but the water drawn from it is brackish. The consortium that owns the lake, the Canadian River Municipal Water Authority, has had to buy groundwater from other sources to blend with Lake Meredith water to bring it into compliance.

Salem noticed in 1997 that an energy company, Southwestern Public Service Company or SPSC, had bought up water rights in the eastern Panhandle in the 1970s. That group was going to build a nuclear power plant and use aquifer water in the cooling towers. Long after the nuke fell through, CRMWA bought forty-two thousand acres of water rights from SPSC. Salem and his team crooked an eyebrow at that deal and began looking into long-term demand for water. Salem figured the water companies would need more water before the water companies made the same calculation.

It was vintage Salem. He has a technique where he researches a subject to within an inch of its life and talks to every expert he can find. Then, when he knows as much as any living human on the matter, the variables become like chess pieces. He is able to see several moves ahead and then capitalize, as a businessman, on his intuition. But in the past, people he respected, professors at Notre Dame and Oofie, would hear him out, but fail to agree with how he connected the dots. Eventually, Salem was proved correct. It's happened about a half-dozen times. He's not sure where the ability comes from, but he has learned to trust his instincts and act on them.

With the water deal, he went to numerous ranchers to get them to sell him one-fourth to one-half of their water rights. Because the ranchers only needed to water their cattle, since they weren't raising crops, they were happy to sell a portion of their water rights. In fact, it was the ultimate no-brainer for the ranchers the way Salem structured it. Salem was able to offer $250 per acre for water rights, even though the land itself at the time might be selling for only $200 hundred per acre. A rancher with five thousand acres pocketed over a million dollars, and Salem was taking all of the risk. He took a quarter of the deal for himself.

In the end, Salem put together seventy-two thousand acres of water rights around Canadian. By 1999, water demand had risen sufficiently for him to sell the water rights he had amassed. CRMWA didn't want in, but the city of Amarillo did. Salem ended up clearing $12 million. Dozens of people devote their professional lives to forecasting water demand in the Panhandle and planning for it, but Salem, who trades commodity futures and only briefly turned his attention to water, made a handsome profit predicting water futures. Salem figures he spent about five percent of his time over two and a half years making the deal happen. If you squeeze all of those hours together, he earned that $12 million in about six weeks worth of work.

It was right about that time Salem began playing chess for big dough on a bigger board, the Chicago Mercantile Exchange. In 1999, he bought fifteen seats and essentially owned 0.6 percent of the Merc. The seats were relatively cheap at the time, but Salem foresaw the rise of electronic trading and how that volume would translate into value for the Merc and the seats. Salem figured the seats, which were eventually converted to stock, would be worth four times what he paid for them. He eventually sold out for ten times the original investment.

His foresight paid off two ways. Not only did he successfully predict the rise of electronic trading and cash in on the resulting increase in value of his Merc seats, he also pioneered electronic trading itself on the Merc. He essentially created a self-fulfilling prophecy. With his traditional money management business slow, Salem figured, Let's use our computer expertise to fast trade on the Merc and replace the pit traders' skill set with our own. At the time, floor traders still handled trades on the Merc with their iconic hand signals and the ability to do math in their heads, translate it all to paper, and rapidly interact with others to execute trades.

Of the first fourteen Merc electronic trading machines outside of Chicago, Salem had the first one in Texas. He joined a roster of the world's leading capitals. There were machines in Tokyo, London, Paris, and Canadian, Texas. But the Merc still handcuffed electronic traders. By agreement, they wouldn't let the owners of the fourteen machines actually electronically enter an order. Nothing could be hooked up to the trading machine. Every order had to be entered manually. Well, it didn't take long for Salem and his crew to figure out what an advantage they would have if they could hook up and enter orders electronically, but they followed the rules. At the same time, they petitioned the board of directors of the CME to agree to allow full electronic trading.

At the end of two months, Salem said to the Merc powers that be, I get the impression you don't do this very often.

They said, You're the first to ask.

Salem got permission. For a few years, they minted money. Salem likens it to a game of slapdash where a bunch of ten year olds get together around a kitchen table. Following a signal, the first one to slap his hand down wins. But one day, one of the ten year olds brings an electronic robot friend to play for him. It has a computer brain, optical recognition, and an automatic arm, and it slaps its techno hand down faster than any of the other boys nine out of ten jacks. The robot's owner builds a pile of cash, but it also hacks off the other boys in a hurry.

It was a fascinating and fun time. They held futures contracts for an average of two tenths of a second. At the peak, Salem's operation accounted for 1 percent of the daily trading volume on the Merc. A group of guys in suits would fly down from Chicago in a private jet to meet Salem. They'd touch down at the airfield in Canadian, which is pretty much deserted most of the time, disembark from their Gulfstream, squint, and act like they'd landed on the moon.

Over time, others climbed the electronic trading learning curve, and the profit opportunity diminished. In 2005, Salem closed down that subsidiary operation and refocused attention on traditional money management. Now ATC holds futures contracts anywhere from two days to three months and does fifty trades a day rather than five thousand.

While in high school, Salem dreamed of owning ranch land, not trading, but when he returned home after Notre Dame, he and five family members only owned a section and a half. But they started buying and selling ranch land, as well as mineral rights, and would themselves buy ranch land that came up for sale at exceptional value. Now the family owns tens of thousands of acres. But Salem's two brothers are the ranchers, not he.

Younger brother Jason has the largest surrogate mare quarter horse breeding operation in the country, two thousand mares. When an owner wants to breed a racing mare, he wants the best of both worlds. He wants her to keep racing, but he also wants her to breed. A $300,000 mare will produce colts worth an average of $30,000. So they breed her, but when she's seven days pregnant, before the embryo has attached to the uterine wall, they flush it and place it inside one of Jason Abraham's mares, which carries it to term. Not only can the racing mare keep racing, she can also produce five embryos per year and only lose a few weeks of training and racing.

Salem's other brother, Eddie, is an accomplished marksman. He worked for Salem on the trading desk of ATC for ten years, but his plan from day one was to get enough money to buy a ranch and cattle and not have any bosses or employees. And that's what he did, worked for Salem for ten years. For the last twelve, he has been a rancher. He has also competed and done well in Old West quick-draw competitions, but is also skilled in extremely long-range shooting.

Salem's daughter recently graduated from high school and is headed for Harvard University. She had never shot a gun or shown an interest in shooting, but Salem decided before she went off to the Ivy League and they told her how the government could solve all problems, as a Texan, she needed to ask herself: what problems do we have that we can't solve? We can feed ourselves, he told her. We have our own energy. And we can defend ourselves.

So he took his daughter out to Eddie's ranch to shoot guns.

She shot about twenty different ones. After Salem gave her a basic lesson, a sniper friend of Eddie's spent about four hours with her. At the end of the day, she hit a man-sized target at nine hundred yards with a Barrett .50 caliber semi-automatic sniper rifle. Probably aren't too many Harvard freshmen who've done that.

Salem admits to not being much of a cowboy. He rides some, but, when he goes out to the family ranches, his brothers gently insist that he not work so he harms neither himself, the ranch hands, nor the livestock.

In the end, a lot ties Salem to Canadian. He may not be a cowboy or a rancher, but the land out here is still a magnet. Sometimes, the schools in a small town can weigh in the decision on where to live, but, with Abraham's daughter going to Harvard, the schools obviously aren't a negative. Certainly raising a family in a small town has inherent plusses. And his wife is from Canadian. Also, Salem has a rich Texas heritage on his mother's side. His maternal great-grandfather was Irish. He came to Canadian in 1888. Despite his Lebanese name, Salem is three-quarters Irish.

But it isn't just sentiment or family history that keeps him here. His personal and business lives are fully integrated. Salem went to high school in Canadian with Lee Haygood, who heads up ATC's oil and gas business. Lee's forefathers also arrived in the area in the 1880s, and Salem's great-grandfather and Lee's great-grandfather were friends a century ago. Those sorts of relationships and history just don't happen in large cities. When a big oil company out of Oklahoma or Dallas comes calling and it wants to drill in the Canadian area, the toughest part for them is making connections with local ranchers and signing a lease deal. The ranchers don't know the oil companies, and they don't trust them. Salem and Lee know everybody in Canadian. For them, brokering an oil and gas deal is doing business with their neighbors.

Enormously successful but still a young man, the dealmaker and trader from Canadian is focused for the moment on his core commodities operation, but he most certainly will tackle new and different challenges in the future. Whatever chess match he chooses to play, it's highly unlikely he'll make any dumbass moves.

The Renaissance Rancher

Jimbo Humphreys is about six-foot-four and built like a rectangle. Not a lotta cowboys did much funnin' with him when he ran a chuck wagon. Left him be mostly. Weren't just that he could throttle any scrawny cowboy with one hand while tenderizin' a steak with the other. No, way it is, the cook is God. And you don't want to rile God. To a cowpuncher, gettin' up 'fore the sun, ridin' and ropin' all day, freezin' in winter, sweatin' buckets in summer, swallowin' dust, sniffin' manure, and matchin' wits with bulls the size of small trucks—food is everything. Food is life. Fact, cowboys have a way of describin' death. They call it no breakfast forever.

Way Jimbo worked, had a stove built inside his cook tent. 'Fore he went to bed at night, he laid out all his wood for the mornin'. Had to be up 'fore four, get the fire going, and get the bread cooked. Wood makes the fire go. Fire makes the cookin' go. Cookin' makes the cowboys go, so the cook's wood ain't to mess with. Lotta them wagons was dry, but not all the ranches. One time, cowboys got to drinkin' and playin' poker all night, or at least until just before Jimbo started his day. While they was dealin', they kept feedin' the campfire with Jimbo's wood. He got up and looked to build a fire in the stove. There weren't no wood. Started to do a slow burn, like the embers from their leftover campfire. Weren't that far a walk out to the woodpile, but, then again, it was far enough. God don't want to stumble around in the dark at four in the morning, searchin' like a blind man for the woodpile after He had already laid out his blocks by the stove the night 'fore.

One of them poker-playin', wood-burnin' boys made his bed inside the cook tent by the canvas wall. Jimbo used a gasoline-diesel mixture to light his stove. On this particular mornin',' unlikely a trained terrorist could have made it any more combustible than Jimbo done. The door of the stove faced the bedroll of the unfortunate card shark, about six foot away. Jimbo circled behind the stove, swung his arm around the front, and tossed in a match. Mouth of that stove roared like a dragon in a fable. The flame that come out of that thing woulda burned Shadrach, Meshach, and Abednego to a crisp. It blew over the top of the cowpuncher and torched the wall of the tent. Feller swung up outta his bed like the trigger on a mousetrap, assessed the situation in less time than it took for the smoke to clear from his singed eyebrows, and run quick to the woodpile to replenish Jimbo's stock. The late-night poker games was mostly dark, chilly affairs after that.

Out on the edge of the Llano Estacado, there ain't much more than land, sky, and wind. The ground don't give up much easy. There's mesquite and sage, grass in patches, no timber. Have to drag the water out of the ground. If you own land, you have possibilities: cattle, and minerals if you're real lucky. Sometimes, these days, you can even sell the wind. But if you don't own ground, you have to scuffle. Have to make something out of not much.

Jimbo Humphreys has found more ways to squeeze a livin' out of the shortgrass steppes of Texas than most anyone, and not only has he had fun doing it, whatever it is, he usually becomes the best there is at it. He's been a cowpuncher and a horseshoer.

Ran a fencin' crew. Owned a lumberyard and cement plant. Ran a welding crew and a carpentry crew. Made bits and spurs. Built his own underground house. Built a chuck wagon from scratch, ran a chuck wagon for years, won chuck wagon cookin' contests. Trained horses, competed in ranch competitions, won ranch horse competitions, and manages a ranch.

Feller don't get much more Texas than Jimbo. Ranchin' runs through his veins. His father, Jim Humphreys, was the general manager of the Pitchfork, a one hundred eighty thousand-acre ranch east of Dickens. Even by Texas standards, that's a big spread. Jimbo grew up there, but went to high school in Afton. Didn't happen easy. He was the first kid in years to go to high school from ranch headquarters. In them days, they hired mostly young cowboys who didn't have a wife, not to mention babies or high school-aged kids. Weren't mainly to get more work out of a single cowboy. No, back then, ranch managers paid cowboys a modest wage, but fed them most meals and bought their other groceries. Those cheap some bucks hired single cowboys so they didn't have to feed a wife, much less a bunch of teenage eatin' machines. Pitchfork headquarters is on the edge of the Patton Springs School District. This is Texas, so it ain't like the school district is a few miles end-to-end. It was a seventy-five-minute school bus ride each way. In fact, it was so long that the school district bought a trailer house and parked it on the Pitchforks. Bus driver stayed there overnight on weekdays. Didn't make no sense for him to drive seventy-five minutes back to Afton after droppin' Jimbo off in the evenin' and then do the same thing the next mornin'.'

A lotta ranch families in the Panhandle sent their problem sons to the New Mexico Military Institute in Roswell to whip them boys into shape. Not sure if Jimbo got a bit broncy on his parents or if they just thought he'd get better schoolin' at New Mexico, but they decided to send him there. Jimbo's perspective on the matter was different. He thought Patton Springs School District had an admirable educational program. Course, he wasn't on the two-person committee makin' the decision. September of his sophomore year, his parents packed him up, hauled him to Roswell, got him settled in there, and left. When they got back to Pitchfork headquarters, over two hun'erd miles away, Jimbo was watchin' TV in the family room. He'd hitchhiked home and beat 'em. A rather audible parental discourse followed, and Jimbo ended up spendin' two years in Roswell 'fore going back to public school his senior year.

Back then, the local vet, Ed Murray, used to go over to the Pitchfork for Jim Humphreys every winter between Christmas and New Year's and worm their mares for two days. Miserable cold. Like I said, Jimbo is a huge man, about six-foot-four and broad-shouldered. He'd fit right up on a movie screen, walkin' side by side with John Wayne. Even as a kid, he was big and gangly. The wormin' was always scheduled for Christmas break because it was for sure Jimbo would be home from school then. He was the only one tall enough to reach across the chute and get a halter on them skittish mares.

Army got him after he graduated from high school, but the Vietnam War was windin' down. Jimbo was only gone six months. When he come back to Texas, he didn't see a future on the ranch. The last paycheck he drew for cowboyin' in 1972 was two hun'erd dollars a month. He gone into the horseshoein' business. After learnin' how at a school in Grapevine, he set up a mobile operation and traveled around to all the ranches in the Dickens area shoddin' horses. He was as good a man nailin' a piece of hot steel on a horse's foot as that country seen. But it's hard work manhandlin' a dozen horses a day every day, and he didn't particular like workin' alone. One day, after he been at it six or seven years, a horse give him trouble. He'd hobbled it and then ended up draggin' it down and hog-tyin' him. But somehow, in all the excitement, Jimbo got his own leg tied up with the horse's. He ended up alone in a barn with a horse floppin' around on top of him, tryin' to kick him into the next county. He escaped finally, but got to thinkin', There has to be a better way to make a livin' than this and cowpunchin'.

He didn't quit shoein' right off, just added another line of work—fencin'. Had a ranch circuit set up for shoein', so he knew everybody and knew they all needed fence work done. Put together a four-man crew. Personnel thing was the killer. Fellers he hired weren't exactly the cream of the workforce. Fact, when he gone to wake 'em up in the mornin', he could never be sure they'd be there. Not infrequent they'd pack up overnight and vamoose. Jimbo fenced with a wagon team. Usually two horses. Haul their posts and wire in the wagon. He traded a coupla soapers he had. Soapers is horses not long for the knackers and gettin' turned into bathroom bars. In return, got what may've been the sorriest two equines ever paired. They bucked like rodeo broncs. Not that that bothered Jimbo much. He was all confidence and nothing but. Knew them horses would be worth a lotta money after he broke them to fence. Didn't quite work out that way. It took the entire crew to hook them up every mornin', and you had to keep someone in the wagon at all times, or they'd take off on you. And I mean all day long. Someone had to eat his dinner in the wagon. If there weren't no one in the wagon, them two evil horses would leave. Just leave.

One time, Jimbo was runnin' the wagon, and a kid was ridin' with him. Them horses bolted. No tellin' what set 'em off. Maybe it was a noise. Maybe they seen a critter. Maybe just got a mind to be sportin'. It was on the Pitchforks. They stampeded east toward the 6s. Mostly flat ground out that way, but they hit a small gully. Wagon wheels dropped into the void and then slammed against the uphill on the far side. Jimbo braced for it, but the kid flipped out of the wagon like a pop top. So did all the fence posts. Kid rolled to a stop in the grass. All them fence posts piled on top of him like they was numbered. Buried him clean. Looked like a dang Saturday mornin' cartoon. Jimbo tugged hard on the right rein, which made them runaways start to turn in a circle. He got 'em slowed and under control. Kid was okay, but it was a sight seein' his head pop up like a prairie dog from under all them fence posts.

Then Jimbo bought a lumberyard. Ran good for five years. Then it took another five years for him to figure out how to get rid of it. In the meantime, he added a ready-mix plant and had two welding crews runnin', plus the fencin' crew and a carpentry crew. Calls it his ranch construction phase.

We was tryin' to get rich about that time, Jimbo says, smilin' under his dust-crusted black cowboy hat and long, white mustache.

But the economy turned bad, and ranches started buyin' direct, cuttin' out the retailer. Fact, Jimbo seen a lotta changes in how them big cattle operations is run. Huge ranches used to only have one pickup, and everything was done horseback. Every ranch had a chuck wagon that would serve meals out on the range. But then, horses got expensive to buy, train, feed, and harness, and the owners bought a herd of trucks instead. For a spell, they even used helicopters to gather cattle. Chuck wagons disappeared. Cowboys would ride their pickups back to headquarters and eat at the cookhouse.

After a spell, pendulum swung back some. Maybe nostalgia played a part, too. No more helicopters. Got to be more of a mix of trucks and horses. And the chuck wagon even made a comeback. That last one may have had a lot to do with Jimbo single-handed. He studies stuff. When he had that team for fencin', sorry as that pair was, he learned a lot about horse teams and wagons. And the way he set up his contracts, he'd fence three days straight, forty hours, which meant campin' out in the field with his crew. That way, they'd be there in the mornin'. Required him to cook for them boys.

So next thing you know, he built a chuck wagon from scratch. He was out of the fencin' business and into the chuck wagon business. Worked branding season for all the big ranches. For a week or two, sometimes more, they'd camp out on the range, round up cattle, brand the calves, give them shots, and castrate the baby bulls. Jimbo would cook three meals a day out in the field. Cowboys lived in tepees. Jimbo would start the season workin' for operations in Texas like the Pitchfork and Silverbrook Ranches. Then he'd follow spring north, runnin' the chuck wagon for ranches in Oklahoma, Kansas, and as far up as Nebraska. He'd be out for three or four months. Then he'd do it again for the fall season.

Just like Jimbo with the chuck wagon deal. Didn't settle for just cookin' a decent meal. Learned the heck out of it. Started cookin' for sport. Gone to all kinds of competitions they had special for it. Like the Western Heritage Classic ranch rodeo at Abilene. All the ranches brung their chuck wagons and had a cook-off. Usually twenty wagons or more. Jimbo won that thing two years in a row. Won most all of the big competitions at least once. Usually judge in several categories, pick an individual winner for each, and choose an all-around best cook. Might judge biscuits or bread, beans, meat, and dessert. After he won everything, then he was a judge for a few years.

Another thing he done when he wasn't doing the ranch circuit with the chuck wagon was makin' bits and spurs. Done it near full time when he wasn't cookin'. With his blacksmithin' experience, wasn't a huge jump. Made hundreds of spurs over a few years 'fore he got tired of it, too. Mostly couldn't get the know-how he needed to get really good. Them old-timers who done it kept their secrets to themselves. Had two or three years of orders prepaid when he hung it up. Give the money back, and turned the business over to his son. Now his son is one of the better known bit and spur makers in Texas.

After that was when Jimbo decided to get back into ridin' and cowboyin'. Never rode all through his construction phase. Maybe a dozen years. But one reason he gone into horseshoein' when he was young was because he loved horses and had a way with 'em. So he started day workin' at the Guitar Ranch south of Dickens, near where he lives. Gave him a new opportunity to ride. But again, this being Jimbo, he weren't happy just ridin'. Had to know it inside and out, and be the best at it—both ridin' and trainin' horses. Wanted to learn the little things. Finesse stuff.

Back when he was a kid, cowboys would break horses by manhandlin' 'em. Jimbo don't even call what he does breakin' horses. Calls it startin'. He'll start a colt. They're already halter broke when he gets 'em. Do that when they wean 'em. Spend a month on initial trainin'. Sacks them out, and then puts a pack saddle on 'em. That's different than a lotta fellers do. He's got panniers made outta old tires he loads on the pack saddle. Sometimes, he'll use regular panniers and fill 'em with fifty-pound salt blocks. Horse gets used to feelin' weight on its back. On horseback, he'll lead the colt on a long walk around his pasture. It gets used to seein' Jimbo above him and behind him. Also feels the sage brushin' against its legs and branches rakin' across its flanks. Jimbo usually buys and trains two colts a year. Keeps one and sells the other broke to ride.

For a while, Jimbo and Winona, his wife of thirty-five years, kept two buffalo at their place. Used them for horse trainin' some. If a horse can herd and cut buffalo, it won't have much trouble with cattle. Them buffalo got after Winona one day. She'd been feedin' 'em cubes through the fence. Later, Jimbo turned them out, and she ended up in the same little pasture as them. They probably didn't mean no harm, although they can get ornery. Just figured she had more feed for 'em. Whatever. They come lopin' over and got her hemmed up in a corner of the pasture behind a little ol' mesquite bush. Give her a rough time. Mighta been as long as half an hour. She was wavin' the scrawny limbs of that bush like a matador and dodgin' them critters. Buffalo finally gone on. Think they got tired of the dogs yappin' at 'em. She was a bit shook up. Come into the house where Jimbo was. He didn't know nothing about it, but made the mistake of grinnin' a bit as she told her story real fast, wheezin' for breath. Oh, she lit into him like she wanted to do to them buffalo.

Finally, she says, We're eatin' those two.

Fattened 'em up a bit. Then they went to town. Went to the processin' plant. Now they're in Jimbo's and Winona's freezer. There's a lesson there for all livestock.

Annnnnnnyway, the horse trainin' led to the next thing he done, Versatility Ranch Competition. There's variations, but usually five categories: ridin', obstacle course, cuttin', reinin' and ropin', and show. Get judged separate in them five categories, and give awards separate, too. But at the end of the day, they total your score. Declare an overall winner. Have to drag the info out of Jimbo, but he studied the heck out of all them events, trained like mad, and won a lotta them deals, too. Goes all over the country doing it. One year, he won all five of the individual events at the Tri-State Fair in Amarillo.

In the middle of all the stuff he done, he also designed and built his own underground stone house on some acreage he has south of Dickens. It's partly underground really. Two exterior walls are exposed. He built one like it for someone else during his construction phase. Thought it was pretty neat, so he acted as general contractor and made one for himself. Carved into the side of a low hill. Dirt was bulldozed back over the flat roof when the house was finished. Stuff growin' out of the prairie on top of his house these days. Done the underground thing for both insulation and the threat of tornados. Weather can change outside, and it'll be three or four days 'fore there's any difference inside. Rocks used to build the exterior walls were gathered only a few miles away. The town of Dickens is less than ten miles east of the eastern edge of the Llano. Ground there drops away from the caprock, creatin' a hundreds-mile-long north-and-south runnin' escarpment. But there's also a second drop-off, just east of Dickens, and only a couple of miles from Jimbo's place. It's called the Croton Breaks. Below it, red, scalded ground rolls away to the east. Jimbo's house is made of stones from the Croton Breaks.

Mason who built the rock wall exterior of the house was a piece of work. Feller was a master craftsman when he wasn't nippin' the hooch. He hauled in a trailer, plopped it on Jimbo's ground, and lived there for the duration. Surprise ever' mornin' seein' if he was sober enough to labor. Artists. Every few days, he'd sidle over to Jimbo, half-looped, and say, Man, I'm runnin' out of rocks. I need some rocks.

Jimbo would look around the yard and see hundreds of boulders scattered about. He'd lift his hat, scratch his shaved head, and wonder what the feller was talkin' 'bout. But they'd get in Jimbo's flatbed pickup and head down to the Breaks. Jimbo risked internal injuries liftin' eighty-pound chunks of the earth's crust and dumpin' them in his truckbed, upwards of two dozen sometimes. Meanwhile, the rock whisperer would careful select maybe two or three stones not much bigger or heavier than a toaster oven and gently lay them on the floorboard of the pickup. That happened about three times before Jimbo got to watchin' him surreptitious after they come back from one of their expeditions. Lotta them old masons would use balin' wire to hold rocks in place until the mortar set. But the rock whisperer wouldn't dream of employin' such a cheap trick. If a rock wouldn't lay perfect without mortar, he'd toss it. Finally dawned on Jimbo that, when the feller said he was runnin' out of rocks, he wasn't talkin' about volume. He was talkin' about the right rocks. Usually ones to finish a corner. The house is decades-old now. Rocks in the exterior walls still perfectly fitted, like pieces from a precut jigsaw puzzle been snapped into place.

What goes around comes around. Jimbo is cowboyin' again. And like his dad, he's managin' a ranch. Got promoted and runs the Guitar Ranch south of Dickens. Course, it ain't said like it's written. It's said the way a brayin' donkey would say it. Ghee-tar. Got two hun'erd fifty mother cows and another hun'erd or so yearlings. Jimbo has put together two sections of his own ground where he lives and trains his horses and himself for ranch competitions. Got one next week in Colorado. But ranch competitions probably ain't the end of him. If there's anything else a feller can do on the high plains to make a livin' or have fun, Jimbo will discover it and learn how. And if they score it, he'll win.

The Feud

Ed and Bud Brainard, son and father. You know how sons and fathers can be. Father expects a lot of a son and chews on him. Fours girls in the family. Ed was the only boy. Bud would chew on Ed 'fore he done anything wrong. And during. And after. A hired hand could screw up, and Bud wouldn't hardly say a word. Ed screwed up? Bud be on him night and day. Didn't give him no slack. Couldn't do nothin' right. Started when he was a boy. Still going when he was in his fifties. Every now and then, Ed had enough.

Like the time Bud was gettin' on Ed about his work ethic. Said, You need to start earlier. If you ain't up 'fore the light, you ain't up in time. The work is waitin' on you too long.

Rather than reply direct, Ed had a tendency to act out. Got together all the hired hands on the ranch well 'fore dawn. Hunted every weapon they could find, saddled up, and rode across the prairie east toward the faint mornin' glow. Just as the sun crested the horizon, Ed give the order, and that herd of cowboys stampeded the Brainard ranch house, all them pistols and rifles firin' and punctuatin' daybreak. They thundered across the pasture and into the yard, guns blazin'. They didn't stop 'til they was jerkin' their rides to a halt about an inch from Bud's window.

Ed shouted over the roar of them dischargin' firearms, By God, is this early enough for you?

Brainards have a long history in the eastern Panhandle, up there along the Canadian River, not far from the Oklahoma border. Back in the 1880s, Bud's father was partnered with a feller named Morgan who come down with smallpox. Only doctor in the area was in Mobeetie, about thirty miles away. Not much in a car these days, but back then on horseback, it was a ride, and Brainard done it straight through. When he got to the outskirts of Mobeetie and told his story, they wouldn't let him into town. Only one who took him in was a saloonkeeper. Eventually, a doctor come out to meet him, and they rode back to Canadian. Morgan was dead. Doc said to load up Morgan's wife and kids and get them to Dodge City in Kansas. Only big town at the time could take care of 'em. Brainard done it and saved the wife and a coupla kids, but lost one or two other children.

When you move cattle to a pasture and leave 'em, you want to make sure they know where the water is. Average cow don't have a high IQ. Can't be sure they'll find the water without gettin' it pointed out. One time, Ed hauled a bunch of weanin' calves from Canadian out to a pasture Brainards had near Higgins. 'Fore Ed left in his rig, haulin' the first load, Bud says, It'll be a week 'fore we see them calves again. Make sure you put 'em on water.

Cattle have a tendency to run as soon as they get out of a trailer. They don't like being cooped up. Well, that pasture near Higgins was squared off and wired, and the stock tank was in the southeast corner. Jimmy Shaffer was there. He says to Ed, Instead of droppin' them calves near the water and them runnin' off, just drop them by the gate at the northwest corner. They'll run down the fence line, make the turn at the southwest corner, and stop at the water.

Ed thought that made sense so that was what he done with that first load. When he come back to headquarters for the second load, Bud come up to him and says, Did you put them cattle on water like I told you?

Ed says, No, sir. Unloaded them up there at the gate.

Bud started fumin,' What part of *make sure you put 'em on water* didn't you understand?

Bud got to chewin' on him while Ed was fillin' the truck with the next load of calves. Ed's temp'ture was risin', but like most always, he don't say nothin'. When he leaves, Bud gets in his grill and says, Put ... the ... damn ... cattle ... on ... water. And he don't say it in a friendly way.

That bobtail was a pretty big rig with paneled sides. Probably fit fifteen head in there. Whole truck bed could tilt up at a forty-five degree angle. When Ed got back to that pasture near Higgins, he gone through the gate and drove straight across to the dirt tank. He backed up the truck, tipped up the storage compartment, and slid them calves right into the pond. They went to floppin' and splashin' around for a spell 'fore they made it out and scattered all over the place.

When Ed got back to headquarters, Bud come over. Did you put them cattle on water like I told you twice?

Ed said, By God, I put 'em on water all right.

It was weeks 'fore what happened got back to Bud.

Once, Ed was up on part of the ranch north of the Canadian River, in Roberts County, building a set of steel pens. Ed was nearly finished welding. His pickup was inside the pen when Bud come along. After he got old and weren't ridin' no more, Bud would go everywhere in a big ol' Caddy. He pulled up, got out, and looked things over a minute. Then he shook his head, at a loss to understand. He says, That gate ain't wide enough to get your truck through, pea brain.

Ed had had another long day. Weren't in the mood for

unsolic'ted input. He spiked the welding torch like it was a football and says, It sure the blazes is.

Ed hopped in the pickup, put it in first gear, and launched through that gate. Both sideview mirrors ripped off along with what chrome there was on both sides. But Ed didn't count them mirrors as a deal killer and yells through the open window at Bud, By God, did it fit through the gate or didn't it?

Just gone on like that one story after another. There was the time Pat Crouch was out at the Brainard's, about to start some doctorin' on their herd. Pat is the local veterinarian in Canadian. His assistant called and needed some health forms signed so he told her to come on out. He'd sign 'em there. There were cattle in a pen, and they was gonna move 'em. Well, another buncha cows was comin' in just then. The two herds was headin' for a mix-up. Cowboys formed a picket fence on horseback to keep them critters apart, but a few got tangled. Bud was sittin' horseback on a hill, watchin' all this. You could tell, even from a hun'erd yards, he's gettin' mad. After it all got sorted, he yells for Ed. They all watched Ed make the slow trek up the hill. When he gets there, they can't hear nothin', but they can tell by the way Ed is leanin' off his saddle, away from Bud, that he's gettin' his butt chewed for almost mixin' up them herds.

Eventually Ed saunters back down, gets off his horse, and comes over next to Pat in the corral. He's hangdog. He says, When does the next Greyhound come through Canadian?

Pat says, Why?

Ed says, Because I'm gonna leave that some buck and get as far away from here as I can.

Just about then, Pat's assistant arrives in her car, and Pat motions her over. She walks through the gate and starts across the corral. She's a cute little thing. Ed gone out to meet her halfway.

Ed was a bit slovenly. Plus he'd been cowboyin' all mornin', but he grabbed her in a huge bear hug and then give her a big kiss. She screamed and dropped them health forms. They scattered in the breeze and landed in the muck. She run all the way back to her car in her heels and drove off.

Ed come back over to Pat with a big smile on his face. Took a deep breath, let it out, and says, I feel a lot better now.

Another time, Ed says to Pat, Have you ever seen anybody work cattle the way we do?

Pat says, Ed, I ain't never seen anybody do anything the way y'all do.

Wasn't just Bud set in his ways. For the longest time, best way to treat cattle for scabies was to dip 'em—run 'em through a dippin' vat. Narrow chute filled with medicated water. Cattle swim across and rinse out. Well, along come some new drugs. Pat tells Ed all about it. Several times. But Ed don't want to inoculate his cattle, don't trust them pharm'ceuticals. Rather run them through the dippin' vat, which is a pain, hard to maintain, and a general bother.

Eventually, Pat breaks him down. Ed says, Okay, fine. We'll use the drugs.

Few weeks later, Pat was out there, and he seen what Ed considered progressive. He run his cattle up to the edge of the dippin' vat. Cowboys gave each of them an injection with the new drug and then jumped them into the dippin' vat and run them through.

No, Pat ain't never seen anybody work cattle like Ed and Bud.

One time, Ed called Pat out to a pasture they had quite a ways from Canadian. When Pat got there, he seen a figure settin' under a cottonwood tree by himself. Pat drove over. It was Ed in the shade under the canopy, surrounded by empty beer cans. It was clear he'd been sittin' there all afternoon drinkin' beer after beer, like he didn't have a care in the world.

Pat says, What's going on, Ed?

Ed says, The old man looked in the refrigerator, saw a case of beer, and told me to get rid of it. And by God, I'm gettin' rid of it.

That's what Ed done a lot to get back at Bud. Just done literal whatever Bud was chewin' on him to do.

Don't want to give the wrong impression. Brainards was a great family. Did a lot for the town. Bud's sister died in childbirth, and Bud and Sally raised their three kids. Sally was something else. She'd be up at four and have breakfast made by five ever' mornin' for all of the cowboys and Bud. And it weren't like she was wrapped in a frumpy robe. No, sir. She was a classy lady. She'd have on a pretty dress from Paris and high heels. Her hair was tied up real tight in a bun. Every day, just like that. Cooked lookin' like that. Looked perfect at five in the mornin'. Wore them heels ever'where. Gardened in 'em. Great cook. Bud had the same breakfast ever' mornin'. Big, thick steak, one egg, biscuits, jelly, and cocoa. Didn't drink coffee.

Sally was like clockwork. When she drove out to where the cowboys was that day to bring them dinner in Bud's Cadillac, you could set your watch by her. High noon. She'd park and open that trunk. There'd be a big ol' roast and all the fixins. Cowboys would want to work at Brainards just for those dinners. That was the only time she drove that Caddy slow, when she was deliverin' meals. Otherwise, she drove it ever'where 'bout a hun'erd miles an hour. Got tickets all the time. She'd cuss out the highway patrol like a sailor. They didn't pay her no mind.

She kept the family books. Knew where every penny was. When Pat Crouch would send out a vet bill, she would drive over the next day and deliver the check. One time, he was going through his accounts and seen where he double-charged them for something three months before, two bills for fifteen hundred for the same services. He'd gotten paid the three thousand.

So he called Sally right away and says, Mrs. Brainard, we overcharged you about three months ago. I just wanted you to know we caught it, and I'll make it right.

She said, I know you made a mistake. I caught it, too. I just thought I'd wait for you to catch it.

No tellin' how many people in Canadian the Brainards helped. They didn't tell no one. Didn't want no one knowin'. Didn't want it in the paper. Heck, one kid who worked for Pat, they put through law school, and no one but both families and Pat knew it.

Like I said, she was classy, but she was a terror, too. She could blister you. Didn't pull no punches. When she talked over there in town, they paid attention. She and another lady would collect donations for the charity bazaar. Go store to store. If you knew Sally and you seen her come in, you gone straight for your checkbook. No use puttin' it off. If Sally gone in a store and they made noises like they weren't donatin', or maybe they just wasn't puttin' enough in the hat, she had something to say. And it was loud and it was long. Ever'one in the store could hear it. The check was wrote out.

On their taxes one time, they deducted sixteen hun'erd dollars for all them dinners Sally would cook and deliver to the ranch hands at noon. Business expense. They got audited. Bud and Sally gone down to Amarillo and the IRS. Things was going all right, but that auditor started pushin' on that sixteen hun'erd-dollar deduction. Weren't allowed. They owed sixteen hun'erd dollars. Period.

Remember, Brainards had over sixty thousand acres and no

tellin' how many thousand head of cattle. Sally prided herself on keepin' the books just right. So she asks the revenuer what he done 'fore he started auditing. He said he run a small business but it gone broke. Well, that about broke something in Sally. Them high heels hit the floor, and she says, They got a some buck like you who can't keep his business above water tellin' us what we can and can't deduct?

Bud reached for his checkbook and wrote out a sixteen hun'erd-dollar check as fast as his hand could sketch. Got Sally out of there pronto 'fore the feller could tack on a surcharge.

For all that, she didn't have no airs. Jimmy Shaffer had a kid born blind and mentally retarded, and they were going down to Amarillo a lot to have him taken care of. One time he was going and mentioned it to Sally. Jimmy said he was worried about his ol' truck makin' it down there and back. She piped right up and said, You just bring your pickup over here and take our Cadillac down to Amarillo.

So Jimmy done that. When he come back to Canadian, he gone into town to gas up the Caddy. Sally had needed to go do some errands, so he seen her drivin' by in his beat-up 1955 Chevy pickup. Didn't matter to her.

Annnnnnnnyway, I was tellin' you about Ed and Bud. Ed loved ridin' around in his bobtail truck. He was braggin' on it all the time. Just as proud as a prince on a prize pony drivin' that thing. He'd always tell you something about that truck if you sat down with him. Not sure where that come from. Maybe he just felt in control when he was behind the wheel of that rig. Maybe just felt like he was lord of his own realm in that bobtail, away from Bud.

Them two. Tension would build over days, weeks, and months. Then just a couple of words might detonate an explosion. Like when the bobtail's windshield was once covered in dirt, smashed bugs, blood, and manure. Bud got to ridin' Ed about it. Ed, of course, did what he could to make it dirtier and dirtier and sure as heck never washed it.

Finally in the yard one day, Bud says, You can't even see out of that some buck windshield. Clean it up 'fore you have a wreck.

Between two other relations, it might've been considered a rational piece of advice, but it was one of them times when father and son tension been brewin' for a spell. The comment flipped Ed's switch. Power surged to his limbs. He gone over, grabbed a Steelson wrench, climbed up on the hood, and worked mayhem on that windshield. Swung and swung and swung some more. Just smashed that laminated glass to bits. Then he cleared all the debris with a sweep of his arm. Wind whistled through the gapin' hole he'd created and swirled around the cab. Standin' tall on the hood of that truck with his chest heavin', wrench held aloft like he was some sort of service station gladiator, Ed says, By God, you can see out of 'er now.

Bud made him drive around in the bobtail for quite awhile with that big ol' hole in it.

Sometimes, Ed probably deserved a bit of chewin' on by Bud. He could be forgetful. Brainards raised a lotta grain so they got a hog operation going. Put that grain to use. Ed hauled hogs in the bobtail for sale in Oklahoma. One time, he backed up to the chute at night and loaded the rig with hogs for auction. Drove half the night 'fore stoppin' somewhere shy of his final destination. 'Fore he bedded down around three in the morning, he checked on the hogs. Only a few was left in the truck. He hadn't closed the tailgate completely when he loaded. All night long, he'd been scatterin' hogs across the state of Oklahoma. Pigs was slidin' out the back of the bobtail and onto the road without him knowin'. He turned around and drove straight home, swervin' where he had to avoid hog carcasses. Loaded up the truck again in the dawn light, closed the tailgate, and headed back to Oklahoma. Bud wouldn't miss another load of hogs from the pens, but he sure would've missed the money if Ed only sold six or seven hogs instead of three dozen. Ed never did tell Bud he'd littered Oklahoma's highways and byways with Brainard pork.

When it come to decision-makin', Bud had a pretty tight grip on Ed. A cattle association was gonna put Bud in its hall of fame up in Kansas City, but Bud was in a wheelchair by then and self-conscious about it, so Ed gone for him to accept the honor. Bill Breeding, the vet from Miami, Texas, went with him. All-day drive. At lunch, Bill ordered.

Ed said, Same thing.

At dinner, Bill ordered first again. When waitress turned to Ed, he says, Same thing.

When she walked off, Bill says, Is it just a coincidence you like the same things I do and even cooked the same way, or is there something going on here I don't know about?

Ed told Bill that, when he was a kid growin' up, he and Bud would take their steers to Kansas and put them on grass there all summer. One year, they pulled into a restaurant on the drive north. Bud ordered a steak cooked a certain way. Ed ordered a different kind of steak cooked a different way. When the food came, they had the steaks mixed up, and they were cooked wrong, too. Bud had had a bad day, and he says to Ed, Damnit to hell! Next time, order the same thing I do. It'll make it impossible for them to screw things up.

Ed done it. And it got to be such a habit that, most times when he ate out the rest of his life, he just ordered the same thing as the feller he was with.

Like I said, when it come to anyone but Ed, Bud was easy-

goin,' more easygoin' than most. Pat gone up regular to one of the
Brainard's ranches where they was raisin' hogs and giving shots to
the baby pigs. But after a while, there was fewer and fewer baby
pigs. Soon enough, had the appearance of being suspicious. So
next time Pat gone up there to doctor them baby pigs, he put a
small tattoo on the underside of their flank. No one seen him do
it and you couldn't see that tattoo when them pigs was standin'.

Well, turns out some hands was stealin' them piglets. Law
caught up with 'em when they decided that, if they was stealin'
Brainard's pigs, might as well go ahead and take their feed, too.
Law tracked them to a big ol' house in Canadian they'd rented.
Had it full of feeder pigs. Tattoos made the case. When it was all
over, Bud only fired a couple of them and kept the rest.

He told Pat, Oh, they probably just needed the money.

One time, Ed and Riley Bradstreet and another hand was
comin' in off the pasture after a long day. The Outlaw wanted to
race back to the barn, but Ed was reluctant. There's a rule cowboys
have. You never run a horse home. Makes them barn crazy, or
barn sour. They don't forget it. See that barn again next time, and
they'll run off with you. Least that's what every cowboy's dad ever
told him. Riley knew all that. Just being ornery. So they raced.
Thundered across the pasture. Riley wins and his friend is next.
Ed's laggin'. Just as they rein in, Bud steps out of the barn. Think
he'd hid himself there. Riley thought for sure he'd be fired on the
spot. For some, runnin' to the barn is a dead serious matter.

Bud took off his hat, wiped a sleeve over his sweaty brow,
and looked disgusted. But all he said was, What's the matter, Ed?
Can't you keep up?

Bud never got on his hands about gettin' drunk neither.
Brainards have long memories. Because a saloonkeeper took in
Bud's father when his partner had smallpox decades before, back

in the 1880s, the cowboys on the ranch always had a free hand when it come to gettin' in trouble drinkin'. Like Roy B. Sessions. Known for downin' a few now and then. Often, really. He'd get drunk a lot. Folks would get on Bud to fire him, but he'd tell them, Roy B. is a better cowboy drunk than most of my other hands are sober.

Fact, Bud leaned toward a crew of heavy drinkin' cowboys. He found that, when he bailed out the drunk ones, in return, they worked hard for him, right up until they went on another bender.

Story about Bud and Roy B. One time, they was workin' a pasture near ranch headquarters. Bud stopped by the house, got dinner from Sally, and brought it over to the boys, along with a special pot of coffee he'd made. Remember, Bud didn't drink coffee. He drank cocoa. Bud poured out the coffee all around. Cowboys was used to coffee with some bite, but this was like tar. Couldn't hardly pour it, much less drink it or stomach it. Stuff oozed into their tin cups.

Course, Roy B. say anything to anybody, includin' Bud. He says, What the hell you do to this coffee?

Bud says, By God, I made it stout. I'm tired of you boys settin' around drinkin' two or three cups. I want one cup to do ya.

Roy B. used to go out and visit Jimmy Shaffer's nephews on the Isaacs Ranch. He loved those boys. Taught 'em some cowboyin'. They loved him back, too. Once when they were about seven and nine, he gone over to see 'em, but he also got to drinkin' some while there. When he gone to leave, wasn't able to fully consummate his departure. He'd climb up into the seat of his pickup, but, when he reached for the door to shut it, he'd tumble out. Done that a few times. This was long 'fore seat belts. One of the things Roy B. had taught them young boys was how to use a piggin' string. So, with Uncle Roy draggin' himself off the ground near their feet, the youngsters had a quick meetin'. When he next got himself into the cab, but before he could fall back out, the boys secured him to the seat with piggin' strings. With his Western-style seat belt holdin' him in place, Roy B. be on his way home.

Give you a short lesson. A steeple is a bent-over two-pointed nail. Looks like a thumbnail-sized wicket or an oversized staple. It's banged into a fence post to attach barbed wire. When a cowboy is steepling fence, he's basically stringin' new wire or repairin' old. One time, Roy B. been drinkin' some while drivin' cows. He was behind one, runnin' along a fence by a road. Happened to look over his shoulder. A car was comin' along. Roy B. was a good hand and always rode good horses. Just as he turned to look at that car, the cow took a right turn. Well, a good cuttin' horse don't wait for commands from the rider. He knows what to do, so that horse turned to head the cow. When horse went right, Roy B. went left and tumbled off to the ground. No self-respectin' cowboy wants the car-ridin' public to see him thrown off his horse, so Roy B. rolled over quick and up onto one knee. Grabbed the top of a cedar fence post. He said later, When them people drove by, they just thought I got off to steeple up that fence.

A bunch of good cowboys worked for Brainards. Besides Roy B., there was Joe Wheeler and Toots South. Told you some stories on Toots. He was cowboy boss at the time. Joe and another hand was always ornery and aggravatin' Toots. He got mad one time, got them boys out their saddles, and put 'em to work in a hay field. No sorrier sight than a cowboy off his horse cuttin' hay.

Annnnnnnyway, the cowboy crew always comes to noon dinner at the wagon, which was parked by the hay field. There was a hill beyond the pasture and sagebrush where the hay field

ended and the ground begun to rise. Well, Joe knew that, every
noon, when the cowboy crew come off the range, they'd line up
on top of that sand hill and race to the wagon. So Joe and that
other hand each got themselves horse blankets. They gone and
hid in the sagebrush just 'fore noon. There was a gruff, crusty
old cook name of Chris Blake. He was fixin' dinner and watchin'
them boys.

Sure enough, at noon, six riders showed up on top of that
hill. Whoop went up, and they come thunderin' down. It was
Ed, Toots, Roy B., and three others. Just before they got to
the sagebrush, Joe and the other feller jumped up and waved
them blankets. They bucked all six of them riders. Ever' dang
one. Cowboys will tell you themselves they ain't the smartest
bunch, and maybe buckin' cowpunchers ridin' full gallop downhill weren't the best conceived idea. Knocked out three of 'em,
includin' Toots and Ed. Total unconscious.

Like to scare the hell out of Joe and the other feller. They
was workin' on Toots and Ed, tryin' to get 'em to come to, when
Blake called out to them. He was standin' by the third guy, kickin'
at him some.

He says, Hell, you boys better come work on this one. He's
dead.

Well, that about put Joe and the other feller over the top, but
he weren't dead. He come to. When Ed got his senses back, first
words he said was, Please don't tell Dad.

Joe said, Hell, that ain't a thought crossed our minds.

Toots was mad. Maybe he was boss, but he wouldn't try Joe.
Joe was one of the toughest some bucks you ever run across. One
of the hands worked at Brainards said that, if he stayed the same
age and Joe got to be a hun'erd, he still wouldn't try him. Wasn't
a bigger-hearted man ever walked though. Give you the shirt off

his back. Took a lot to rile him. One time, a nearby rancher, someone he neighbored with, stole a cow and calf off him. Joe happened to be at a sale when he seen them come through. He got pretty mad. Could have taken the feller with one punch or done worse damage, or got him arrested. But he knew the feller had three girls and thought maybe they needed some new shoes or such. So he never said a word, ever. Even kept neighborin' with the feller.

Joe was real slow talkin', but he was fast enough with a comeback. He ended up workin' for the Brainards forever. After he'd been there a while, new hands would ride alongside and ask him questions. Knew his reputation for cowboyin'. Once, there was a young feller just got to askin' too many questions too fast, and Joe had had about enough of it.

Finally, the kid asks, How long you been in this country?

Joe held up his hand and curled his forefinger around. Tucked it into his thumb until only a pinprick of light shone through.

He says, Hell, I don't remember, but, when I first come here, the sun wasn't but about this big around.

Kid got the message and rode off.

Joe was in the cavalry in World War Two. Got sent over to Burma. Course they took away their horses and give 'em mules instead. Led them around more'n rode 'em. Joe said the first thing he learned over there was that, when the Japanese started shellin' and you dove in a foxhole, you damn sure better scoot over because that mule was gonna be right behind you. He told stories about Burma and India. Would've had to been a double-tough some buck just to survive what he been through, but he not only survived, he come back with three Bronze Stars. Lot of country boys gone over. They couldn't understand how them cows was sacred. Joe and them always makin' bull ropes and tryin' to talk the Indians into ridin' them sacred critters. Weren't no takers. But one time, they used bamboo to build a bucking chute and borrowed what they thought was a gentle Brahma bull from an Indian who got drunk. Joe's friend rode the bull while the rest of them country boys flanked it. Feller got bucked off. Joe said that the next mornin' Indians with bulls was lined up for a mile. Them cattle had suddenly lost some spirituality. Indians was all bringin' bulls to be ridden. Drunk feller had told his friends what a sight it was to see the American soldier get bucked off his bull, and all his friends wanted in. Joe and his buddies had managed to alter them Indians' culture and religious tradition overnight.

One of Joe's jobs for Brainards when he got back from the war was haulin' gravel with a mule team off the caprock, about a half-mile away from and up above the Canadian river. Joe wasn't payin' attention much while they was loadin' that gravel and rock the first time, but when he started down the steep grade, he noticed the wagon didn't have any britchin', a strap that goes behind the mules and keeps the wagon from outrunnin' the team on a steep hill like that.

Well, Joe was only halfway down that hill when the wagon starts creepin' up on them mules. The tongue was shovin' on their backsides. Joe snaps the reins like mad, keepin' them mules runnin' full tilt. Not only would there be a bad wreck in general if the wagon won the race and overtook them mules, but Joe was downhill from that funeral pyre of rock and gravel he was haulin'.

He got safe to the bottom, but was sweatin' through his shirt and blue jeans. Gone right over to the house to see Bud. Says to him, Mr. Brainard, ain't no britchin' on them mules.

Bud didn't look the least surprised. Fact, he was a bit put out. He says, Hell, I wouldn't have a goddamn mule couldn't outrun a wagon. If you run over one of them some bucks, go right out and get more. There's about thirty teams in the pasture.

Bud's expectations was high for man and beast.

Joe wasn't very big, but he'd just work. Day in and day out, year after year, just worked like an ox. When he got older, Joe got to wearin' a solid leather back brace Reed Errington made him. When he was in his late sixties, feller seen Joe without the brace one day.

He says, How's your back, Joe?

Joe said, Oh, it's fine. Got miracle cured. All I had to do was stop liftin' and haulin' cake.

Them sacks of cake weighed a hun'erd pounds each. Joe musta lifted them things for a half-century. Near ruined his back. Only give it up in his late sixties.

Errington also made heavy, thick saddles. Only two fellers ever plum wore them out were Toots South and Joe Wheeler. They'd take 'em in a few times and get them patched up, but Reed finally says, I ain't fixin' them no more. They're done.

That housing sits under your leg on them saddles. They wore that leather down thin as cigarette paper.

One time, Ed, Bud, and the hands had to drive cattle from a pasture on Pat's Creek, which is almost to Hutchinson County, to Horse Creek, just across the river in Canadian. Maybe twenty-five or thirty miles. They were shippin' 'em out of Canadian. But it'd gone to rainin'. Canadian River swoll up like you don't see no more since they put in the dam. It was rollin' a mile wide and bank to bank.

Bud come over to Ed and said, Cross them cattle.

Ed said, It's runnin' too deep. We'll drown them yearlings.

It was gettin' late. Bud backed off. They camped. That night, it clouded up and rained some more. In the mornin' Bud come across that narrow bridge they had for cars in them days. He was drivin' the big ol' Caddy.

He says to Ed, You cross them cattle.

Ed says, Can't do it. We'll drown 'em all.

Bud says, You throw them saddle horses in the river. If they make it across, you throw them cattle in next. Have to have them cows to the stockyard by tomorrow noon or the deal I signed ain't no good.

Ed knew there was no talkin' the old man out of it.

Bud says, If you boys was to get off in the river with your clothes wet, they'd pull you under. Tie your clothes and your boots to your saddle. And by God, tie 'em on tight.

So them cowboys did as they was told and gone into the river wearin' just their britches. It was Ed, Joe Wheeler, Roy B., and Toots South. Bud decides to mount up and he gone with 'em. Was dressed the same, too.

They'd barely gotten underway when they seen a boot go floatin' by.

Bud says, One of you dumb some bitches lost your boot.

Joe, Toots, Roy B., and Ed all looked around and seen their boots tied on. It was Bud's got loose. No one chose to point it out. Not even Roy B.

They was about in the middle when Toots hit a whirlpool and gone under. They said just his hat was afloat. Joe started turnin' to go help Toots, but Bud yelled out, Get the hell outta here. It's ever' man for himself.

About that time, Toots popped up and come ashore. Eventual, they all made it across.

As far as Bud was concerned, he'd proved his point. Didn't matter that Toots gone for a swim. Horses made it, so cattle could make it.

Bud said, Cross 'em.

So they gone back and crossed them cows, and every single one of them some bucks made it. Seven or eight hun'erd yearlings. Ed just hated it when Bud was right.

Bud would drive that big Caddy right out on the grass. One day, Ed was workin' cattle, and Bud thought he'd get to three or four pastures worth by the end of the day, but, when he drove up in that Caddy late in the day, Ed was where he left him in the mornin'.

Bud says, What in tarnation, son? You been here all day, and you only worked one pasture?

Well, Ed mighta been slow, but he was workin' hard. He was hot and sweatin', and now he was bothered, too. Been buildin' again for some time, and he plain don't want to hear it from his father.

Bud kept on. Finally, he says, What are you gonna do when I'm dead and gone?

Ed yanked off his hat, threw it down, and said, By God, I'll call Saint Peter and ask him what the hell you want me to do with the cattle!

One time, Bud and Ed were feedin' cows up at their place near Spearman. John's Creek, they called it. Wire was all over the pasture. It got wrapped around the drive shaft of the truck Ed was in and wadded up to the point where the pickup finally broke down. They had a devil of a time tryin' to get that wire unwound. It was hot, and Bud was chewin' on Ed, of course. One thing led to another.

Finally, Ed says to Bud, By God, that's it. I quit. What do you think of that, huh?

Now it was Bud's turn to lose it. He just reared back and threw a haymaker right at the center of Ed's chest. Would have flattened a horse. Hit Ed square in the sternum. Knocked him straight back and onto the ground.

I'm tellin' you all these Ed stories, and he might sound quick-tempered, but actually you couldn't hardly find a feller in the Panhandle didn't like Ed Brainard. He was funny and good-natured when Bud weren't chewin' on him. So after Bud flattened him, he got up slow, coughin'. Dusted himself off, stood up straight, and says, Well, I didn't know you wanted me to stay that bad.

One time in the fall, late on a Saturday afternoon, Ed showed up with his bobtail truck loaded down with cottonseed cake, a protein supplement for cattle. George Huff was there. Pretty typical ranch owners or cowboy bosses let hands off early Saturday afternoon so they could get cleaned up and go into town and raise Cain that night. Then they'd be off all day Sunday.

Ed gets out of the bobtail with that load of cake in back and George says, Ed, what are you doing comin' up here with a load of cake on a Saturday afternoon? I been workin' all week and I want to go to town. You're killin' me.

Ed says, Won't take us no time. Fact, it wouldn't take me but forty-five minutes to unload that cake all by myself.

George says, I'll bet you a case of beer you can't.

Ed says, You're on.

Ed grit his teeth and set to work unloadin' that cake. George sat down on a hay bale and watched the show. Ed finished in forty-five minutes exact.

George says, Well now, you got me, Ed. Here's your beer.

He handed over a case of beer. Only cost George five bucks to get an early start on his weekend.

Not sure if this story is true or not, but they say that, when Bud was dying in a hospital in Canadian, he called Ed in and gave him orders on how to run the ranch for the next fifty years.

Ed died in 1999 in a freak highway accident. Hired hand got stuck somewheres and Ed gone out to get him. Big oil field truck blew a tire, crossed over the road, and run right over the top of his pickup. Killed him instant. Biggest funeral in Canadian in a long time. Like I said, can't hardly find a feller didn't like Ed Brainard.

The Sure Enough Cowboy

Best roper Button Criswell ever seen was Ralph Reed. Never put down his rope. Carried it ever'where. Everyone else hung their rope on their saddle. Not Ralph. Carried it in his hand when he rode. Loved to rope. Roped everything, whether it moved or not. And talked about nothin' but ropin'. Most of the real ropin' is done in spring when you rope calves and drag them to the fire for branding. Roper throws a loop just ahead of the hind legs of a calf, and they step into the loop. Cowboy takes up the slack and knots up them back legs. The flankers guide it to the fire. Brand it, give it shots, and castrate the baby bulls. Usually rotate all them jobs. Maybe a roper would throw twenty or thirty loops and then switch off, but he'd do plenty of shifts ropin'. Hard to say what's average, but a decent roper, out of ten loops thrown, might catch both heels seven times, catch one leg a couple of times, and maybe miss complete the tenth time. If you catch only a leg, ain't the enda the world. Sometimes you slack out and throw again. Sometimes you drag to the fire with just that one leg roped, but makes it a bit tougher on the flankers because they have to deal with one free leg that could kick 'em.

Annnnnnnyway, one time when Button was young, he seen Ralph throw seventy-five straight loops without missin'. About like a basketball player hittin' seventy-five straight free throws. And none of them throws was one leg. Double-hawked ever' one.

Boys started what they called the Wildlife Roping Club.

Now, you got to understand, a cowboy out on the open range never seen nothin' movin' he didn't wanna rope and nothin' movin' he *couldn't* rope—at least in his own mind. They'd get to talkin' around the campfire, and one feller would say he roped a deer a couple days before. Another roped an antelope. Usually, the critters got smaller and smaller as the night wore on. By the time the fire had turned to embers, someone had roped a mouse the week before. The next guy, an amoeba the week 'fore that.

So they started the Wildlife Roping Club and assigned points for different critters. More dif'cult to rope, the more points. An antelope might be twenty points, a coyote five, and an elk ten. Anything they ever seen with four legs had a point designation: bears, deer, you name it. And you either had to have a witness or a picture. Couldn't just say you done it. No tall tales. No windies. Had to have proof. Weren't no time limit or nothin.' Whenever them fellers got together, at a rodeo maybe, they'd swap stories and evidence and tally up the points and see how ever'one was doing and who was leadin'. Whenever they met, Ralph would be quiet, sittin' off to the side and playin' with his loops. When they got to him, he'd say, I roped this, and I roped that. Someone would say, Yeah, I seen him do that. Uh-huh, I seen that, too.

When they got done, Ralph always had 'bout twice as many points as anyone else.

One day, Ralph, Button, and a coupla other boys was out trottin' along a pasture on the ranch. A jackrabbit jumped up. What they do is they'll run a spell, stop still, run again, and stop still. Keep doing like that. Soon as that jackrabbit popped up and ran, Ralph blowed to him, rode him down, and roped him on the first throw. Roped a jackrabbit. They all seen it. Didn't even have points for a rabbit. Had to call a special meeting of the Wildlife Roping Club to figure out how many points to assign to a jackrabbit.

There was another time Button was alone with him. Figures Ralph was in his sixties. He'd been married to Ruby forever. They come up on a dirt tank, a man-made pond with an earthen dam to water stock. They were below the dam, so the water was on the other side. Ralph motions for Button to be quiet and dismount. Ralph led them, and they crept up to the lip of that dam. On the bank next to the water were some mallard ducks. Ralph run over there by them ducks and roped one. Button seen it with his own eyes.

Button says to him, Golly, how in the world you get to where you could rope a duck?

Ralph says, Been practicin' on Ruby's chickens.

Had to have a special meeting of the club again. But this time they gone ahead and disbanded, dejected. Weren't nobody gonna come close to Ralph, much less beat him.

Button is a fourth-generation cowpuncher. Hired out his whole life. Where he is now in the Panhandle, owner supplies the house he lives in on a pasture in the middle of a treeless ranch outside of White Deer. Too far out for mail to be delivered. Gives him the pickup he drives, pays utilities, and gives him plenty of beef to eat. Button don't own a thing except his saddle and horses.

Button don't hardly know when his ancestors first come into the country, but it was early in Texas history. Says he has quite a bit of Native American in him. Says some of his ancestors was there to greet the others when the newcomers arrived. His granddad come up into Texas from New Mexico for a time, before World War One. Worked at the Matador Ranch. In Button's heyday, he slept under the stars two or three weeks a year, in spring and fall. His granddad was out with the wagon and sleepin' on the ground year round, twelve months. Never slept under a roof.

Button come from a dysfunctional family 'fore they ever called 'em that. His father was a trader. Horse trader mostly, but he'd trade anything. Cheated people. On just about every deal. He was known around. Put ads in the paper. People would call and say, I need a horse.

He'd say, What kind you need?

They'd say, A steer ropin' horse.

He'd say, That's just the kind I got.

But he didn't have a steer ropin' horse. Might not've had *any* horses just then.

Or a feller would call and say he needed a horse for the kids to ride. Button's dad, Eldon, would have a wild bronc, but tell the feller he had a horse that was gentle for man, woman, or child.

Like I say though, more often be Eldon wouldn't have no horse at all. He'd tell the feller, I'm real busy, but, if you'll come out Wednesday, I can show you that horse I got.

So Eldon would run around the country lookin' for a kid horse. If he found one, he'd tell the owner he wanted to ride it for a day. Brung it home. Feller lookin' for a kid horse would come out. Say he and Eldon agreed on six hun'erd dollars. Eldon would say he needed to think on it a day and then go call up the owner. If the owner said he'd take five hun'erd dollars for him, Eldon would buy the horse, sell it to the feller answered the newspaper ad, and pocket the surplus hun'erd.

Button would say, Is it right to do it that way, Daddy?

Eldon would say, Don't pay to have a lotta inventory.

If Eldon couldn't find the right horse, he'd do the deal anyway. Sell a feller a buckin' bronc when they wanted a child's horse. Feller's eight-year-old kid would get catapulted like a medieval projectile. People got mad and wanted their money back and hospital bills paid. End up in a big fight.

Button's momma was different. She might not've been strict honest in other walks of life, but she was when it come to business. She was the daughter of a cowboy, and the cowboy ethic run strong in her.

She said, Son, you can shear a sheep time and time again, but you can only skin him once.

Course, that's all Button's dad done his whole life—skin sheep right and left. Never quite grasped the concept of satisfied repeat customers.

When his dad was old, Button asked if he could sell a horse without tellin' a lie.

His father said, No, ain't hardly possible. If'n you wanna make a profit, you have to lie.

His mother was beautiful, fiery, and wild. Had a restless spirit. By the end of winter, she'd get cabin fever. Every single spring she'd run off, usually with a boyfriend she'd found. Occasional by herself. Gone to her sister's place times she run off alone. But most times, it was to parts unknown with the new boyfriend. There were five kids. Sometimes Rosetta, or Rose, would take two or three of them kids with her. Most times, she'd leave 'em all behind.

By March, she'd be baitin' Eldon. She'd say, I'm gonna find me a truck driver. Run off with a truck driver.

Them little kids of hers be listenin' and wonderin', What the heck? Why she gonna leave us for a truck driver?

Other kids' mommas be bakin' cookies and makin' cupcakes and bringin' 'em to school. Button shakin' his head when he seen that and thinkin', My momma ain't bakin' no cookies. She's fixin' to run off with a truck driver.

She'd usually regain her senses after a month or so and come home.

But not always. When she didn't, Eldon would ship them kids out to grandmas and neighbors and go lookin' for her. Sometimes it would take all summer. Eldon would find her. They'd patch things up, head home, gather all the kids from outlying regions, and usually move to another town and start a new life that fall. Had to move. People was talkin' too much. Things would be good again until late winter, but then, sure enough, about April, Rose would blow the plug, get spring fever like always, and run off with a new boyfriend.

One spring, Button's momma run off to her sister's house in Fort Worth. Gone a few weeks, but come home on her own. Found out Eldon been hoppin' the back fence with a neighbor lady. She got so mad she was gonna kill him. Button was about ten. Her big deal was to get a butcher knife. She was always gonna kill someone with a butcher knife. Rose got to chasin' Eldon around the house. All five of them kids was watchin' wide-eyed, but they knew to hold still when trouble was brewin'. Try not to be noticed. Eldon could outrun Rose and put some air between himself and the butcher knife. Hightailed it into the bedroom. Gone into the walk-in closet where all the guns and rifles was kept. Half-dozen firearms. Wanted to make sure she didn't trade in the knife for a gun and make quick work of him. Was gonna hide them weapons. She come into the living room with that knife raised over her head. Kids all in there, backs up against the wall, lookin' straight ahead, neither right nor left. She heard rustlin' in the bedroom and run in there. Them kids raced after her to the doorway to see the climax of the spectacle. Just as she reaches the closet, Eldon come flyin' out of there, hell-bent for leather with the family arsenal clumped this way and that in his arms. They collided head-on. The barrel of a rifle smashed into Rose's forehead, and she went down in a heap, unconscious. The knife gone flyin'.

Eldon called for them kids to help carry their momma to bed and cover her. Eldon lifted her arms. Older kid grabbed her feet. Rest of them kids was underneath, their arms raised high to support the effort, but barely reachin' her. Just as they was layin' her in bed, she come to. She was rubbin' her forehead where she got conked and says, Kids, y'all are my witnesses. Your daddy pistol-whipped me.

And that was it. Marked the conclusion of that particular spring event.

One time when he was twenty, Button was cowpunchin' on a ranch in New Mexico. His mother hadn't seen him for a while, so she come out to the bronc pen one mornin' to visit with him while he was workin'. Bunch of four-year-old horses there he was supposed to break. They never been touched but twice in their lives: once to get branded and once to get castrated. Otherwise, they run wild that whole time. Button had cut out a big, mean colt and had it in a round pen with his saddle layin' on the ground. His mother was settin' up on a rail, smokin' and watchin' him out of one eye.

Button is a tough ol' cowboy now, but he was a little scared of that horse back then. He was no sooner in the pen than that colt run straight for his saddle, picked it up in its mouth, and started shakin' it like a dog killin' a snake. Button weren't likin' what he seen and devised a go-slow strategy. Finally got a rope on him and then a hackamore, a kind of bridle the old-time cowboys use when they're first breakin' horses. Got a leg tied up on him. Then got the saddle on him. All that took the better part of a half hour. Then he flopped a blanket at him. Told you about that. It's called sackin' 'em out. Flop that blanket around, and rub it on 'em.

Colt like that is flinchy and scared. Blanket helps get them over it.

Annnnnnnyway, he'd been visitin' with his momma off and on, but she'd been quiet for a spell, smokin' cigarette after cigarette. Finally, after about a half hour of sackin' out that colt, she says, Son, why don't you just get on that horse?

Button says, Momma, gonna be honest with you. Bit scared of this big ol' colt.

She was havin' none of it. She coughed a disapprovin' cough and said, Son, that horse can only do two things to you. It can hurt you, but no matter how bad it hurts, it'll eventually stop hurtin'. Or it could kill you. In which case, you won't feel a thing. Now quit being a sissy and get on the damn horse.

He done what his momma said and mounted that horse. Colt didn't do nothin'. Never bucked. Just ran around in the circle for a while.

Rose didn't say a word, just dragged on a cigarette and let out a cloud. She could roll a Bull Durham in one hand with them long red fingernails of hers.

Eldon would come visit, too. When Button was grown and had his own family, parents would visit separate. They could live together, barely, but they couldn't travel together. Especially in a car. Drove each other plum loco. Actually, they divorced, and Rose married another feller, but she divorced him and remarried Eldon. Annnnnnnyway, Button didn't like it when his father come to visit. Done his tradin'. Just plain had it in his blood. He'd drive around the ranch lookin' at things. Then he'd go to Button's boss and say, See you're needin' some new fence posts. I can get you a deal on a thousand.

Button's boss would get talked into the deal and Eldon would rip him off somehow. Eldon would be long gone by the time the boss figured it all out and he'd get mad as hell at Button.

Both his parents passed years ago. Button loved them despite all. Don't matter what Rose was like, what she done or how many times she run off. Button loved her and loves her to this day and misses her all the time.

She mighta got her temper from her dad. Way back when her father, Button's granddad, Walt, was a married man with a family and livin' in Buffalo Gap, Texas. His father, Button's great-granddad, got into an argument over a team of mules right in the middle of Main Street. Two fellers had Great-Granddad on the ground and were workin' him over with a monkey wrench. Walt had a Colt .45. He come on the fight and shot them two fellers. Didn't kill 'em, but the sheriff come out later to the ranch to talk it over. Rose was real little then.

Sheriff says to Button's granddad, Walt, why'd you shoot them two fellers?

Walt said, They had me outnumbered.

He got off, but Walt stayed short-fused right up to the end of his days. Most cowboys don't retire. Just work 'til they die. But Walt got cancer, and the owner of the ranch where he'd worked for years bought him a place in town and kept his salary going. As a gift, they give him his pick of any horse in the remuda. Course, Walt gone for the orneriest one, a big four-year-old colt he fixed on breakin'. Named him Rattler.

Most fellers dyin' of cancer might be mellowed by the experience both in body and spirit. Not Walt. Button was settin' on the porch, just a kid then, and watched his granddad try to train Rattler to load in the pickup. Had stock racks on pickups back then. Rattler was havin' none of it. He threw his head from side to side, lunged forward, and reared back. Walt tried his darnedest to get that horse snubbed up in there, but Rattler was pawin' ever'thing. He knocked out the taillights. Tore up the whole back

end of the truck. Finally, Walt lost his temper. He threw his hat
on the ground and stomped on it, cussin' a lick. Then he stopped
a sudden and stormed into the house past Button. Boy didn't
say a word or move a muscle. Knew about Granddad, and them
fellers in Buffalo Gap seen the hollow end of his revolver.

Walt come outta the house, wavin' the same Colt .45 that
saved Great-Granddad. Only Rattler wasn't Granddad. Rattler
was the two guys with the monkey wrench. Walt stormed over to
Rattler, comin' up on him from behind, and put the revolver to
his head. He pulled the trigger. Just as he did, Rattler flinched,
whippin' his head away. Instead of the bullet going direct through
his head, it entered at an angle and shot out an eye. Horse went
down and was bleedin' through its eye socket and nose. Didn't
kill him. Walt was so angry he'd screwed up shootin' Rattler that
he tossed his gun on the ground, kicked it like he done his hat,
and cursed a blue streak.

When his temper, heart rate, and blood pressure all subsided
to levels normally associated with sanity, he come over to the
porch and sat down heavy next to Button. Huffin' and puffin', he
says, Button, let that be a lesson to you.

Button, settin' next to madman Walt with the horse down
and bleedin' bad and eyeball missin', was thinkin', I wonder what
the lesson is here?

Button says, Yes, sir?

Walt says, Don't ever lose your temper. I used to have an
ornery horse. Now I have a one-eyed, ornery horse.

Button was wonderin' to himself, Why don't you just finish
him off?

Instead, they nursed Rattler back to health. Sort of. He was
never quite the same after that. Can't imagine. When Walt died,
they sold Rattler. Never did get him in a pickup.

Button was born at home on a ranch just west of Las Cruces, New Mexico. Raised there, too. Old-time cowboys used to call a young boy a button. Family had three daughters before Button come along. When he was born, his dad give him his own name official, Eldon, but, when he seen he got a boy instead of another girl, he says, Finally got me a button.

When Button started cowpunchin', the older cowboys on the ranch kept callin' him Button, and the name stuck.

Growin' up, first day of school, he didn't know nothin'. Couldn't count to ten. Didn't know his ABCs. Course, wasn't like Rose was gonna drive into town, enroll him, and kiss him on the forehead and cry as she left back for home. Just put him on the bus and told him to make his way.

His best friend was Mexican, Pepe Archuletta. When the bus rolled up to school, they had to go in and get enrolled first thing. A teacher set him down. Button is five years old and don't know nothin' about the world.

Lady says, What race are you?

Button had no idea. And he wasn't sure what kind of race she was talkin' about, a horse race or a foot race.

So he says, What race is Pepe in?

Teacher says, He's Hispanic.

Button says, Well, that's what I am because we're best friends. We do everything together.

She says, You're not either. You're white.

Button is gettin' a bit flustered now. He's Rosetta's son, remember, so he says, If you know the answer, why you askin' me?

Got in trouble for sassin' the teacher. Got himself in trouble 'fore the bell rung first day of kindergarten.

Button can't remember first time he was horseback, almost

before he could walk. He first rode buckin' horses when he was nine. His horse-tradin' daddy would mount him up to see if a colt was gentle enough for kids to ride. Even if Button left a spur track across his saddle and got thrown off, his father could look direct in the eye a skeptical customer who wanted a gentle horse and say, impatient-like, Hell, my kid's been ridin' that horse.

Button's first real job cowpunchin' was on a ranch the summer he was fourteen. Rancher didn't pay him a thing, and Button didn't ask for nothin.' Just happy to be there, eat free, and get a bed in the bunkhouse. The next summer, he was paid fifty dollars for three months work. Was tickled to get it. He credits his friendship with Pepe with his gettin' along good with the Mexican cowboys he worked with. The headquarters on the big ranches were like little towns. They had a bunkhouse for whites and one for Mexicans. While his mother and father might not've been award-winnin' parents, he wasn't raised that way, to live separate. He bunked with the Mexicans. They taught him a lot.

Taught him how to tail cattle. Not many Caucasians learn it. Lotta Mexicans know how. Fact, it's pretty common in Mexican rodeos. If a steer is real bad about breakin' out of the herd and runnin' off, just let him go. Fact, build a fire in him, and get him to sprintin'. Gotta have a good horse for tailin'. Has to get right up on that steer so the cowboy can lean down and grab its tail. Then, while horse is gallopin' and cow is stampedin', cowboy has to throw his leg out and over the tail and then curl it over and brace it against his leg. No one's strong enough to hold that tail freehand. Then you give your mount a little spur and angle off, and that steer goes sideways. Let go of the tail and momentum and gravity done the rest. Cow starts to roll like a tumbleweed in a storm. Don't hurt 'em, much. Button done it a buncha times and never broke a cow's leg. Point is, when they get up, they run straight back to the herd. Fact, after that, you couldn't drive 'em out of the herd with the best cuttin' horse alive.

All the cattle Button is workin' now, yearlings, come up outta Alabama. They're wild. Never seen a man on horseback 'fore. The cowboys, if you even call 'em that, do everything afoot down there. Button loves to tail them Alabama steers when they run off. After they're through rollin' like an empty aluminum can in a stiff breeze and they're up and racin' back to the herd, he yells at 'em, Welcome to Texas, you son of a gun! This is my world here!

Kevin Burns, who worked with him for a while, calls Button El Vy-enny. Knows his real name is Eldon. Started callin' him that after he seen Button tail a cow. When that cow got to rollin' on the ground, Burns said it looked like a giant Vy-enny sausage, by which he meant Vienna sausage.

Mexican cowboy name of Nestor Navarrete taught Button how to break horses. He was the best hand with a horse Button ever seen. He could talk to 'em. He'd breathe in their nostrils. Button does it to this day. Went like this. When Nestor first caught a bronc, the very first time he ever handled him, blew in his nose. When two horses come together, you see 'em do that. They're talkin'. They establishin' what's what and who's boss. When a human done it, it establishes his dominance over the horse. That's what Nestor said.

Fact, Nestor and other Mexicans and fellers like Yakee Tatum taught Button a whole bunch about horses. So now Button has a routine for breakin' 'em. After he ropes 'em, gets a halter on 'em, and blows in their nose, something else Nestor done is grab the halter and the tail and spin 'em real fast. Then double back and go spinnin' the other way. Don't hurt them none, but they get a little disoriented and confused. That's when they start to submit to you.

That's all just groundwork. Then you got to tie up a hind leg and get a saddle on. Button then lets the leg down and sacks him out. Then he makes the colt lay down by using the halter to pull his nose over his shoulder. They go right down. Then Button steps on the saddle horn. Horse can't get up when you're standin' on that horn. They can thrash and fight all they want, but they ain't going nowhere. Terrifies a wild horse. They think of a cowboy or any people as predators. When they know they're helpless, but they also figure out you ain't gonna hurt 'em, they stop fightin'. That's when you start pettin' 'em. Pet 'em all over. Be their best friend. They'll let you because now you're the dominant force in the herd. Then you get in the saddle while the horse is down and ride him up off the ground. If you done everything right, and all that takes days and weeks, then, when that horse gets up with the cowboy on him, won't be no buckin'. Course, you can only ride around that pen, and maybe you got to repeat some steps, but after that, you can get to the real training—stoppin', startin', and turnin'.

Button been blessed. Worked with some sure enough cowboys when he was younger. One was Steve Robinson. Was in his eighties when Button got to know him. Button was in his mid-twenties. Robinson been friends with Walt, Button's granddad. Robinson admired Walt. Loved him. Walt was a hero to him. Robinson would talk to Button because Button was kin to Walt. Taught him plenty. But he wouldn't say two words to any of the other young cowboys.

One day, a feller come into the bunkhouse and asked Button if he'd seen his bridle. Button heard it come up missin' and the feller was lookin' for it.

He says, No, I ain't seen it.

Feller walks out. Robinson says, Well, you sure ain't nothin' like your granddad.

Button says, What do you mean?

He says, Walt woulda beat the hair off him for insultin' him that way.

Button says, What insult?

Robinson says, He come in here and accused you of stealin'.

No, he asked me if I'd seen his bridle. Didn't accuse me of nothin'.

Robinson says, Yes, he did. And Walt woulda beat tar outta him for that.

Lot of them old cowboys had hair-trigger tempers, all right. Button just shook his head.

Best rider Button ever seen was a feller I just mentioned, Yakee Tatum. He was wild as a kid. Yakee was the name of a drug, like peyote, that Indians took that made them wild, so they called him Yakee. When he was older, in his sixties, he was the wagon boss on the Spade Ranch, the cowboy boss. They put on extra help in spring for branding. One time, they hired a feller from one of the big ranches. Best cowboys got some swagger in 'em, but they ain't cocky. Swagger is confidence. Cocky is over-confidence, and it might get you hurt out cowboyin'. This young kid was cocky. They cut him a string of horses. Should probably tell you about that. Every cowboy got him a dozen horses or so. During spring, the cowboys might ride forty miles a day. Horse can't hold up to that day in and day out. So they usually saddle up a different mount every mornin' and afternoon and maybe only ride a horse one day out of four or five, dependin' on the horse, what it could do, and how hard it been rode.

Annnnnnnyway, ended up there was one ol' brown horse in the cocky kid's string that would buck. Told the kid that. Weren't tryin' to pull nothin.' Just tellin' him. Didn't buck like a rodeo bronc, but he would buck, sure. Usually when you got a horse like that in your string, you ride him in the afternoon. For some reason, when it's cold in the mornin' and they don't wanna go to work, that's when they're most ornery. They get humpy and go to buckin'. Well, you weren't gonna tell this young feller nothin' and he picks that brown horse first mornin.' Name of Poco. Cowboys had to get up on top of the mesa to gather that mornin.' Poco bucked the kid off six times before they ever got to the cattle.

Sixth time he got bucked off, horse and rider had almost reached the top of the mesa. Kid could hardly get off the ground by then.

He says to Yakee, Ah, Mister Tatum …

But that right there's an insult. Never call a fellow cowboy like that mister.

He says, Mister Tatum, if you'll trade horses with me, I'll quit when we get back to headquarters.

Yakee says, Kid, if I trade horses with you, I know you'll quit when we get back to headquarters.

Meanin', I'll fire you.

Kid says, I can't talk it no more. Horse is too rough.

So Yakee traded with him. Told you Poco bucked, just not like a professional bronc. But now his ego was so boosted from throwin' that kid a half-dozen times that he was plum out of control. Yakee got on him, and Poco went to jumpin' and jerkin'. Yakee was sixty-four at the time. He dug his spurs in hard every time Poco bucked. It was a show for twenty minutes, but Yakee never got thrown. Poor kid. Just hung his head in shame. When Yakee finally got Poco reeducated, he was gentle as a kitten the rest of the day.

Way the routine works is the cowboys gather by the corral in the mornin'. All the horses from all the strings is in there. Only person allowed inside the horse herd is the wrangler or sometimes the wagon boss. Cowboy tells the wrangler which horse he wants that mornin'. The wrangler ropes it and walks it toward the cowboy. Cowboy comes in with a bridle, meets the horse, and replaces the wrangler's rope with the bridle. Then he gets himself and his mount out of the way so the next cowboy can call for his horse.

One time, Button was at a ranch, and the wrangler was Mexican and didn't speak English. There was a cowboy there didn't speak Spanish. Most ranches, the American cowboys can speak a little Spanish, and the Mexicans can speak a little English, so everything gets worked out. New cowboy already had a string of horses cut to him, but he didn't know nothin' about any of 'em.

This particular mornin' Mexican wrangler says, *¿Qué caballo quiere?*

What horse do you want?

Cowboy just shrugged his shoulders. I don't know. Had no clue what the Mexican was sayin'.

Wrangler says, *No le hace?* It don't matter?

Cowboy says, Okay.

Thought *no le hace* was the name of the horse. Wrangler weren't being mean really, but he got a job to do and a lotta horses to get assigned. They was burnin' daylight, so he give the tender-foot the orneriest buckin' horse in his string.

Horse bucked him off four or five times that mornin'. Bucked him off hard on the rocks and cactus. By noon, the guy was prayin' for a quick death. But he made it through the day. Next mornin' they go to catch horses again. The new feller was all skinned up. His hat was smudged and got a few dents in it.

The wrangler says *¿Qué caballo quiere?* Which horse?

Cowboy shrugs his shoulders again. Don't know what that Mexican is sayin'.

Wrangler says, *No le hace?*

That cowboy been drooped over, bridle in hand, beat up from the day before. But he perked up instant and said, No! Hell no! Give that horse a rest.

Them other cowboys sure got a laugh out of that. Named that horse *No Le Hace* after that.

Funny about the cowboy ethic. A hired hand is a hired hand, and a boss is a boss. But certain things expected of both. If the boss don't act the way he's supposed to, then the hands get on him some. Like one time when Button was still workin' over in New Mexico. Ranch was all spread out. Had pastures everywhere. One they was workin' was eighty-five miles from headquarters. They'd put the horses in a trailer and camped out up there a few days. It was hot. Summer hot. Melt a cowboy hot. Once they'd finished up, the boss took off in his truck. Just like that. Left his horse for them boys. Still saddled up. Wanted to get himself home quick so he could sit next to the air-conditioner.

Boys loaded that horse up in the trailer with the saddle still on. Weren't about to take it off. Weren't hired for that. Trailer was a big one. Held about twenty head. Boss' horse was the nicest one on the ranch. Probably worth five thousand dollars. Well, them cowboys gone by a bar near Logan on the way back to Tucumcari. It was called the Road to Ruin. Couldn't resist the road to ruin, so they stopped and drank whiskey. A horse trader named Gene Cox come in.

He says, You boys got any horses in that trailer you wanna sell?

Cowboys looked at each other and says, Yes, and he's a good 'un.

They led out the boss' horse with that saddle still on it and let the trader ride it around.

Cox says, Man, this *is* a good horse. Probably can't afford it.

What do y'all want for him?

They said, Four hun'erd dollars will do you. That's with the saddle included.

He said, What?

Gene could tell there was something fishy, but them boys was standin' right there with the horse and saddle, offerin' up the package deal. He peeled off four hun'erd-dollar bills from his billfold, loaded up that prize colt real quick and got outta there.

When they finally got back to Tucumcari, it was almost dark. They was late, and the boss was standin' out by the barn, tappin' his foot and waitin' on 'em. Them cowboys played it straight. Didn't say a word. Just started to unload the horses. Boss' horse's name was Dan. They got about done, and there ain't no Dan.

He says, Where's Dan? Where's my horse?

They said, Oh, well, we sold him to Gene Cox over in Logan. Got four hun'erd bucks for him. Here's your money. We didn't spend a dime of it.

He grabbed that money, jumped in his pickup, and flew outta there, dust flyin'. Left so fast didn't even chew on 'em. Had to drive forty or fifty miles to Logan. Got it straight with Gene. Gene says he knew it was too good to be true and someone be welshin' on it.

When he got back, boss got on them boys. Gave it to 'em pretty good.

But after he was done, they said, Well, don't leave us your horse no more. We ain't your servants. We're ranch hands.

That ended the insurrection. Mighta been the boss done the chewin', but it was also him learned the lesson. Never did leave his horse behind after that.

There's two other young ranch hands Button worked with— his daughters. When his kids was little, Button would take 'em out on his rounds. One time, had his oldest daughter with him. Haley was only about four at the time. He was feedin' cake to cattle. Remember, that's a supplement comes in feed sacks. Big pellets, high in protein. Button would load up the truck with them sacks and head out to the pasture. When he got near the cattle, instead of turnin' the engine off, he kept the pickup in gear. Then he'd jump out, run back, and hop into the truckbed. Then he'd dump out them sacks. With the pickup rollin' along at a coupla miles per hour on its own, it'd create a line of feed across the pasture, and the cattle would fall in along that line. All have room to eat that way. Make it easy, too, to double back and count 'em while they's all gathered neat in a row.

Sometimes, he'd let Haley drive while he was unloadin'. She'd think she was drivin' anyway. Truck would be in gear, bouncin' along on its own with gas pedal untouched. Button would let her stand on the seat, holdin' the steerin' wheel with both hands, like a sea captain ferryin' a schooner across the prairie.

Button says, See that tree over there, Haley? About two miles? Drive straight for that tree. Don't turn for nothin'. Understand?

Yes, Daddy.

Button got her situated in that movin' pickup, jumped out the door, and hopped up in the bed. Started dumpin' feed. He forgot there was a two-foot dip in the middle of the pasture. Haley seen it, but she couldn't reach the brake pedal even if she knew what it was, and she didn't have permission to turn. Hit that dip like they'd dropped in a well. Flipped Button clean out of the truckbed and onto the grass. Cake pellets was flyin' ever'where. Didn't hardly hurt Button. Been thrown off broncs a hun'erd times. Haley smashed into the steerin' wheel, but she wasn't really hurt neither. Truck took a lickin' though. Button got up and brushed himself off. He was mad and gone over to the cab. She was bawlin'.

He says, Why the heck did you drive into that hole?

Tears was streamin' down her face. She says, You told me not to turn, Daddy!

Dad gum, he thought. I did say that. They reconciled.

Haley would help him count cows, too. At age four, she could only count to seventeen. Anything beyond that was pretty much infinity. There'd be two hun'erd, maybe three hun'erd cows in each of a dozen pastures. Button had to count 'em every few days. Make sure there weren't any strays, or maybe there'd be one down somewheres needed doctorin'. After the cattle gathered 'round the feed he'd spread, he'd raise his hand and poke his finger in the air as he counted up to two hun'erd head or more. Out of the corner of his eye, he could see Haley pokin' the air, too, countin'. When they was done, he'd ask her how many she got.

She'd say, I got seventeen.

Yeah, that's what I got.

They kept goin'. Every pasture they come to, they'd count, and every pasture had exactly seventeen cows.

Girls are grown now. Button's slowed a little. Maybe that's a good thing. His wife says you don't want to marry a cowboy until he's in his mid-forties. Ain't worth a pinch of snuff until then. Got too much hot sauce in 'em.

Button still in his fifties. Has a lotta cowboyin' ahead of him. Don't plan on retirin'. Most cowboys don't. Can't afford to, for one thing. He'll get along fine. He's one of a special breed. Lotta different kinds of cowboys. There are rodeo cowboys. There are feedlot cowboys. But cowboys who work on ranches have a name for each other. Call them kind sure enough cowboys.

One thing for sure, Button Criswell is a sure enough cowboy.

Afterword

This book is not easily categorized. It isn't journalism. It isn't history. It's not straight oral history either. I wouldn't call it folklore, although I regularly refer to it as lore. It's just a collection of funny and engaging stories. Labels aren't important. While the book is unarguably a commercial venture, a genuine desire to preserve these stories also motivated my effort. They document, in lighthearted fashion, a way of life that is quintessentially American, but also fast disappearing. I'm sure many relatives of those profiled in the book have thought about writing down Uncle Fred's stories or tape-recording them. But it rarely happens. For one reason, the magic of oral storytelling is lost in mere transcription. Hopefully, this book will help save these stories, which are not significant enough to constitute recordable history, but nevertheless deserve preservation.

One thing for certain can be declared when describing this book. It is nonfiction. It is clearly a creative technique to turn around and tell someone's story, which they themselves have related, in a third person composite voice. But the creativity does not extend to adding fictitious material. Very early in my writing of a previous book of lore, before I had settled on an approach, I toyed with creating fictional anecdotes to complement the ones I was hearing from sources. In my judgment, the experiment was a clear failure. My fictional anecdotes were obviously so while the anecdotes from sources rang true. I abandoned the idea of creating fictional anecdotes for that book, and it was never a consideration for *Texas Stories*. The content of each story is accurately represented as it was told to me.

Now, if a reader had access to the transcripts of the interviews I conducted and compared them to the finished stories, they would see a vast difference between the two, but it would be in the area of presentation, not core content. Oral stories are not told in a manner polished for print. They have to be structured around some sort of theme, fashioned into some sort of order, given transitions, enriched with stylistic flourishes, and so forth. But that metamorphosing of raw oral material into consumable literature is simply my value-add as a writer. It does not alter the authenticity of the stories. My essential point is this. None of the just-described massaging of the material alters its state from nonfiction to fiction.

I am inching toward a second point. The stories herein are an accurate retelling of the anecdotes as related to me, but, in most cases, I have no idea how accurate the stories were as they left the mouths of the sources I interviewed. The primary intent here is to entertain. If Uncle Fred entertains at family gatherings with war stories, it's every listener for himself in terms of how much credibility to give Uncle Fred. This book is a collection of Uncle Fred's tales. My "windy" radar was certainly in operation throughout the interview process. I heard a couple stories that sounded like whoppers to me, and they weren't included in the book. This volume does not purport to be history. I have no interest in verifying the details of personal anecdotes with legal certitude. The stories are what they are. I heard one anecdote about the Brainards (*The Feud*) five times … from five different sources. And yes, the same story was told five different ways. I couldn't possibly determine which facts from which version were "true" even if I were inclined to do so. So I simply chose the version I liked best.

Let me turn to a brief discussion of the narrative voice I use to tell most of the stories. It is an amalgamation of the dozens of voices I heard while doing interviews. I hope readers intuitively understand what I am attempting to do with the voice. It certainly was not a momentary decision to employ it. Most editors advise not to write in vernacular. I would both take and give that advice myself in most cases. But not in this one. The voice is not just words and phrases. It provides context and even creates an entire environment. Anyone who would deem it "fake" is missing the point by one hundred eighty degrees. The very reason I employ the voice is its authenticity. Indeed, telling the stories in proper English is what would render them "fake," in my opinion. Substituting a cowboy's words and phrasing with proper English would literally be putting words in their mouth.

In a previous book of lore I wrote that employed a similar narrator, the latter was once referred to as a "hick" voice. Allow me to address what I believe to be the unspoken complaint in that reference: that the voice makes fun of those portrayed in the stories or condescends to them. I can't imagine anyone who has read this book through could think the author, by employing the voice, is condescending to those profiled. On the contrary, I have the utmost respect for those I was privileged to interview. The book honors them.

Allow me to reiterate. The voice is simply an attempt to communicate the stories in as engaging and authentic a manner as possible. That said, the reader probably noted that, in several of the non-cowboy/rancher stories, the voice disappeared. In those cases, yes, use of the voice would have appeared contrived and detracted from, rather than enhanced, the storytelling. I initially worried about a whiplash effect for readers moving back and forth between the voice and straight narration, but, hopefully, in telling each story in a narrative style natural to it, the difference was hardly noticed.

Interviews for the book were conducted between April and August 2010. Any time reference in the book reflects the date of the interview. In other words, if someone mentioned in an interview that they were traveling the following week, and that information for some reason found its way into the story, I wrote it that way, in real time, even though the trip might have already taken place by the time I finished writing the story.

Acknowledgments

This book is basically a retelling of others' stories. It wouldn't exist but for those people who generously spent time with me and related their tales. I met with sources in their homes, offices, or in restaurants, and all were remarkably friendly and forthcoming. While I invariably used the name of a friend or acquaintance as an introduction when I first called, it is still a testament to the openness and generosity of people in general that, with only a short briefing regarding the nature of my book, they would take time to meet with me and be interviewed. I conducted approximately sixty interviews for *Texas Stories* and only recall four people turning me down.

For the sake of some sort of organization, I've divided the acknowledgments into four categories.

- Those who are profiled in the book generally served as the primary and, in some cases, sole, source for their own story. Each deserves special mention.
- There were interviewees who weren't profiled, but provided valuable anecdotes that were included in other's profiles and/or provided names of other possible interviewees.
- A lot of networking is required in order to identify appropriate interview candidates. A number of people assisted with this. These individuals were not inter-

viewed for content, rather they were spotters, suggesting others with whom I might speak.

- A number of people helped with various aspects of the book aside from content, such as design, editing, and so forth, and they will be acknowledged.

I am very grateful to Button Criswell, the *Sure Enough Cowboy*, whose profile is the longest in the book. I was also able to peel off one of his stories and make it the freestanding lead story in the book. I spent a very enjoyable afternoon with Button, first driving around the ranch he manages and then additionally at the kitchen table in his remote ranch house. For an author in search of storytellers, Button was nothing short of amazing. He had one story after another, all interesting and/or funny. My thanks to him for taking the time to speak with me and share his stories. Jason Pelham was profiled as *The Prankster*. We met in a backroom of the Bucket, an eatery in Canadian. Fortunately, we met between meals. Otherwise, I think we would have emptied the place. I haven't laughed that hard in a while. When I write, rewrite, edit, polish, and proof theses stories, I may go over any given profile a dozen times, maybe two dozen. But I still crack up every time I read the story about Jason catching his spurs on the electric wire. I appreciate his willingness to tell me his stories.

Stanley Marsh 3 has generally been treated fairly in the media, but there have certainly been negative stories. Rather than being gun-shy about being interviewed, Stanley readily saw me twice. He also gave me the names of several of his friends and had a couple of his young artist collaborators escort me to Toad Hall so I could see it and meet his wife Wendy. I was certainly going for laughs with Stanley's profile, but I hope it is clear I am laughing with him and not at him. Despite his prankster reputation, Stanley is a man of considerable accomplishment and certainly has my respect and gratitude. Our rather staid world needs more Stanley Marshs, not fewer. Thanks to Wendy Bush O'Brien Marsh, who gave me a tour of Toad Hall and sat for an interview. Her grace defines her. It was a pleasure and privilege to meet her. Wendy related the history of Toad Hall, the Frying Pan Ranch, and her family. She also gave me a book about her grandfather, and I used it to double-check some of the names and dates she provided. The book should be acknowledged here, *Empire Builder in the Texas Panhandle: William Henry Bush*, by Paul H. Carlson. Phillip Periman is a friend of Stanley's as well as a successful oncologist and noted photographer. Phil provided some great stories about Stanley, but would be worthy of his own profile in a book with a slightly different cast than mine. Although I poked some fun at Stanley's artist friends and young assistants, the three I dealt with couldn't have been more helpful: Michael, Drew, and LBK.

It was my original intent to meet with another of Stanley's friends, Bill O'Brien, solely to gather additional material on Stanley. While I accomplished that, Bill turned out to be someone else worthy of his own profile. He ended up inviting me out to his ranch. He was incredibly generous with his time, and our adventure on four-wheelers resulted in *The Stone*. Bill's considerable knowledge of the history surrounding his ranch and Tascosa turned into a significant portion of his profile. I'm indebted to him for sharing his time and knowledge and arranging such a fun day. Riley Bradstreet was one of the most interesting people I interviewed. While a lot of Riley's stories were funny, the reader may recall the accidental shooting that marked his youth. The relating of that incident could not have been easy, and I appreciate his willingness to share the difficult details of that experience as a precautionary tale.

The kind of individuals I most enjoy meeting are the ones who not only have led interesting lives, but are also characters and storytellers. CE Trimble, appropriately enough *The Horse Racer* in the book, wins the trifecta. He's every bit the lovable, but crusty, old character and storyteller the reader might have imagined as they read through his story. I thank him for seeing me and telling me his history. Thanks also to Joy Trimble. I generally like to meet sources alone. It can be uncomfortable trying to ask personal or probing questions with others either sitting near or hovering close by. The exception is The Wife Who Prompts Well. If there were a prize in this category, Joy would certainly be the recipient. As CE told his stories, Joy would gently, yet quickly and decisively, insert a clarifying date or name or explain a country colloquialism, all without ever interrupting CE's flow. I wish she could give lessons in the art.

When I describe to friends the kind of people I interviewed for this book, the term "salt of the earth" often comes to mind. To me, it is someone who is humble, honest, and hardworking and neither whines much nor grandstands. That roster would certainly include Weldon George, profiled as *Lindy's Wing Man*. He is a gentleman, self-effacing, witty, and at ninety-three, still able to charm a twentysomething waitress. All that and I came to find out at the end of our interview much of it was a brave front. His wife of decades was home, dying of cancer, and he was bearing the burden of that. Weldon is a remarkable man. I much appreciate Jerry Cates (*The Spur Maker*) taking the time to see me. Jerry is having some health challenges and yet spent close to two hours with me. He even gave me a tour of his shop. Dave Lane (*The Straw Boss*) is another straight shooter. Although Dave is not a large man physically, he has a self-assured manner and commanding presence that I'm sure made him an excellent cowboy boss. We talked for several hours in a roadside restaurant in Groom, bridging breakfast and lunch. Not only did his stories result in a profile about him, but Dave provided a number of contacts in ranch-rich Dickens and King Counties that led to several other profiles. I'm grateful.

Jack Patterson (*The Veteran*) is a poster boy for the Greatest Generation. He is an ideal example of the kind of individual whose story I am pleased to have a hand in preserving. Jack is a regular guy, but also every bit a hero. I'm honored to be able to tell his story. Chumpy Cates (*The Special Texas Ranger*) was another interview that was just plain fun. All I had to do was turn on my tape recorder and ask a few questions, and away went Chumpy. We talked for over two hours, but Chumpy probably could have gone on for two days or two weeks. Thanks to him for sharing his yarns. Lowell Stapf (*The Carny*) was another source who was very generous with his time. Not only did we have a lengthy interview, but Lowell also showed me around his warehouse, which is chock-full of memorabilia. Like many of those profiled, Lowell has led such a long, rich life that any attempt to capture it in a few thousand words is destined to fall woefully short of adequate representation. The format I have chosen for this book can only provide a snapshot of a life. My thanks to Lowell.

Bob Conatser (*Waiting on the Big Score*) was also a delight to talk to. I find it works best when writing a profile to establish a theme. It creates narrative focus and guides the reader. But it can also exaggerate one aspect of a subject's life over another. I focused on Bob's ancestral ranch and his attempts to hold on to it, but Bob is highly accomplished in many ways, including being an outstanding horse trainer. My gratitude to Bob for sharing his stories. There are many sources I interviewed I wish readers could meet. Don Reeves (*The County Agent*) is definitely one of them. Don is a quintessential Texas character and storyteller. His manner of expression is priceless. His voice and the narrator's are very similar. I met him in his home with his wife Katherine. I much appreciate their hospitality. Don was also very responsive in terms of helping set up a second meeting with the specific intent of including Blackie Johnson. I met Blackie with Don at a roadside café in Clarendon. Blackie probably comes off as a prankster-terror in *The County Agent*, but you couldn't meet a nicer guy. I appreciate his willingness to share his stories. Yes, the two of them together, despite their advanced age, is trouble waiting to happen.

My initial interest in Jakob Van Der Weg's story (*The Dutch Dairyman*) was straightforward. While there are literally millions of Hispanic immigrants in Texas, a Dutch dairyman immigrant to the Panhandle sounded unique and inherently interesting. It was only when I began interviewing him and his domestic situation became apparent that the story turned. I think Jakob sensed the direction in which I was taking his story, and I very much appreciate his willingness to discuss personal matters. And thanks to Nakita, a delightful young woman. I'm grateful she got in the car with the stranger and submitted to his questioning. I'm most grateful to Bob Walters (*The Coin and Compass*) for sharing the story of his remarkable life. As someone who has spent a lifetime in white-collar jobs, I have immense respect for a man like Bob who not only followed his dream of living the cowboy life, but also worked physically hard—as opposed to attending endless meetings in air-conditioned office buildings and calling it hard work—virtually every day of his life. Obviously, those qualities mark many people profiled in the book.

A number of times while interviewing Salem Abraham (*The*

Trader), it occurred to me that he was almost too good to be true. I couldn't help but think: there has to be something negative about him. I never did find it. Not only is he enormously successful in a professional sense, he is also genuinely humble. He's also a good family man and a good citizen. I didn't even mention his philanthropic endeavors on behalf of his hometown. Salem generously met with me twice and patiently explained the arcane details of commodities trading to his finance-challenged interlocutor. Jimbo Humphreys (*The Renaissance Rancher*) was another highly unique individual it was my good fortune to meet. He is as Texan, cowboy, and outgoing as they come, yet there is definitely a different quality about him. He is not a passive participant in his own life. He appears intent on making the most of virtually every moment and experience. My thanks to him for meeting with me.

My gratitude and apologies to Mary Eminy and Linda Lloyd. Well after the profiles had been written and this book compiled, as I was nearing the final edit, I pulled a story about Mary and an ecoVillage she and Linda are building. The decision is no reflection on Mary and Linda. The story just didn't seem to fit with the tone and subject matter of the rest of the stories in the book. I knew it was an issue from the start, but Mary and Linda were among the first I interviewed, so the discrepancy wasn't entirely apparent until the book began to take final form. Their story is probably more important than any other in the book, but therein may lie the problem. Important connotes serious, and this book just isn't all that serious. Both Mary and Linda gave me tours of the project. I am grateful for their time and again apologize that their story did not make it into the book. I have included their story on the Website and wish them and Mariposa ecoVillage enormous success.

I interviewed the following people who provided anecdotes that made it into the book and/or pointed me to other sources. I am grateful to each and every one: Jack Howell, JR Taylor, Marion Kinsey, Helen McCartt, EH Little, Harold and Avis Carpenter, Van White, Bill and Doris McClellan, Lorene Mason, John Lott, Hunk Hermesmeyer, Billy George Drennan, Keith Slover, Lee Haygood, Ann Arrington Webb, Bill Arrington, George Arrington, Bill Burkholder, Bill Philpott, and Janice Groneman.

Jimmy Northcutt identified Button Criswell for me. John Foster suggested I speak with Jerry Cates. Thanks to Leonard Zielke, who let me tell the story on him about the lady of the evening and his lost billfold. Thanks, too, to Rose Helen Zielke, who took the initiative and contacted me to set up the interview with Leonard. Harold Rector was my very first interview and quite helpful in terms of giving me the lay of the land in Amarillo. Three veterinarians I spoke with all happened to be characters in their own right and probably any one or all three could have been profiled. Pat Crouch in Canadian told some great stories about the Brainards. Bill Breeding in Miami provided several key names and a couple of anecdotes I was able to use. Ed Murray in Spur also had some wonderful stories and pointed me to Jimbo Humphreys.

Charlie Coffee invited me to his home for dinner and couldn't have been more hospitable. Charlie had some great stories about Joe Wheeler, which I included in *The Feud*. He also recommended I talk to Bob Conatser (*Waiting on the Big Score*). Jimmy Shaffer also provided some wonderful stories about the Brainards. He was the principal source for stories about Sally. Boots O'Neal is another one of those storytellers you could spend a few days with and not hear it all. He is imminently worthy of his own profile. I shied away from that because Boots has been written up elsewhere and been on some radio programs. It was my hope not to include stories previously published. I'm glad I was able to slip in some of Boots' stories. When it comes to cowboys, he is the genuine article.

I had a great time with Ron Cromer. We met on a Friday afternoon at the end of my seventh of eight trips to Texas. By then, I had a list of close to two dozen names I ran by Ron, who knows everyone. Even though Ron wasn't profiled in the book, I had as much fun talking to him as anyone I met with. Running through those two dozen names, we wasted a whole late afternoon gossiping like a couple of old women. Ron gave me Bob Walters name (*The Coin and The Compass*), and I was able to include Ron's buffalo drive story in the book.

Gathering raw material for a book such as this is all about contacts and networking. It requires a lot of phone calls and sleuthing to identify the right people to interview. I had a lot of wonderful spotters—friends or even people I met spontaneously—who were very helpful in either identifying or pointing the way to profile subjects. The networking for this book, if illustrated graphically, would look much like a family tree. I am hugely indebted to John Caldwell, who in a sense represents the base of the trunk of that tree. John has lived in New England for many years, but grew up in Bovina and tapped me into both the community there, through Troy and Lillie Christian, and the Amarillo network through his Bovina boyhood friend Alan Rhodes. Troy and Lillie were the first to mention Jack Patterson to me. Alan is a prominent lawyer in Amarillo. The day we went to lunch was a day he already had lunch planned with a friend, Joe Bob McCartt, a developer and husband of the incumbent mayor. Over barbeque, as I explained my mission, they broke out their smart phones and gave me innumerable contacts in Amarillo and beyond. Alan and I communicated several times early on, and he was extremely helpful in jumpstarting by networking effort. He and Joe Bob both mentioned Stanley Marsh, and Alan suggested Jakob Van Der Weg (*The Dutch Dairyman*). I also spoke with Alan's parents, Tom and Virginia Rhodes, who mentioned CE Trimble.

In order to both acknowledge some individuals who provided assistance, but also give the reader a sense of the degrees of separation that have to be bridged in order to find compelling stories, allow me to detail the sourcing of one profile. When I started to work the Lubbock area, I again called John Caldwell, who put me in touch with his cousin there, Bill Caldwell. Bill gave me the name of a longtime resident of the area, Andy Hurst. While meeting with Andy at a senior living facility, a friend of his, John Abney, stopped by. Andy and John bounced some names off each other, including that of Van White. I met with Van, an accomplished acrobatic pilot. Van suggested I talk to another pilot, or ex-pilot, in the Lubbock area, Weldon George. That meeting, of course, led to *Lindy's Wing Man*.

Two college friends who happen to have been born and raised in Amarillo also played a crucial role in jump-starting my networking: Doug Moser and Robert Baker. Both of their mothers were also helpful: Ruth Moser and Phyllis Lively. Doug and Robert both mentioned Royce Mitchell. Royce provided some key assistance. Not only did he point me to Lowell Stapf (*The Carny*) and then later provide some stories about Lowell (Royce was on the road with him for a short time), he also mentioned my project to a friend of his, Wes Reeves. Wes, a media relations executive for an energy company in Amarillo, grew up in the eastern Panhandle. His father, Don Reeves, is profiled as *The County Agent*. For various reasons, I had trouble reaching Don at first. Wes was very helpful in making sure the connection was made. And thanks to Wes' mother, Katherine Reeves. Like Joy Trimble, Katherine is a wonderful prompter.

I sometimes identify a source who is a strong candidate for profiling, but discover the source is too modest to tell stories about himself. If I am lucky, there are friends and colleagues around who can fill me in. That was the case with Lowell Stapf. Jack Sisemore, a very successful businessman in Amarillo, and Robert Witherspoon (T-Spoon in the story) both traveled with Lowell at various times and had fun adventures to relate. I appreciate their willingness to meet with me and tell those tales.

I happened to run into Monty Points at a wedding in St. Louis—Monty is from outside Oklahoma City—and told him about my *Texas Stories* project. He said I had to meet Kent Pinson, who was attending the same wedding. Kent owns an oil and gas company in Edmond, Oklahoma, but has an office in Canadian, Texas, and roots in Lubbock. Kent put his office staff to work, and they came up with a half-dozen names in Canadian and basically opened up that area to me. Kent's father, Maxey Pinson, a retired seismologist and wonderful storyteller, will be profiled in *Texas Stories 2*. Harrison Hall, a longtime rancher from Wheeler, was on Kent's list. He and his wife Cherry were the ones who pointed me to Riley Bradstreet (*The Outlaw*). When I explained to Harrison and Cherry the kind of person I wanted to interview and profile, Cherry mentioned Riley. Husband and wife looked at each other, and the smiles that came over their faces convinced me before I heard a word of description about Riley that he was the kind of character I had to meet. Harrison is in his late eighties, successful, distinguished, responsible, and fairly serious-minded. When Riley, in his mid-sixties, calls the house and Cherry answers, Riley asks if "the contrary old sh** is home."

You can see why I had to talk to the Outlaw.

Ellwood Towle, a St. Louis resident, called me at home one day to ask me about a matter totally unrelated to this book. I mentioned I had been in Amarillo and had read about a relative of his. Ellwood is named after Isaac Ellwood, co-holder of the first recognized barbed wire patent, along with Joseph Glidden. Although from Illinois, Isaac Ellwood bought ranch property in Texas, as did Glidden. Descendants of Isaac Ellwood, one of whom is Ellwood Towle's cousin, still own the ranch, the Render-brook Spade, the headquarters of which is located near Colorado City, though the cousin lives in Lubbock. The timing of Ellwood Towle's call was striking because I was planning on heading to Lubbock for the first time the very next week. I ended up having lunch with Ellwood's cousin and her husband, Jenny Ellwood Chappell Way and Edson Way. I hope it is clear to readers how much I enjoy meeting and talking to regular cowboys and how much I respect them, but it was also a delight and a privilege to spend a meal with the educated and cultured Ways. They opened up the Lubbock area to me in general and specifically gave me the name of a hand on one of their ranches up in the northeast corner of the Panhandle they thought I might like to talk to. My conversation with Jason Pelham turned into *The Prankster*.

Thanks to Colin Haynes, who gave me the core idea for the cover design. Almost from the first conception of the book, I started thinking about various Texas icons I might incorporate into a cover illustration. During my first trip to Texas, I was talking to Colin on the phone. He lives on the East Coast, but has traveled extensively, including to Texas. He suggested a Cadillac with longhorns. The idea had instant appeal. In later contemplating the concept, I decided an old pickup truck with horns might best capture the feel and spirit I was seeking. Caitlin

Heimerl, a recent graduate of the Rhode Island School of Design, did a cover for me for a previous book, and there was absolutely no doubt in my mind that I would engage her on this project. She again delivered a masterful watercolor illustration. It mirrors the whimsical, humorous, and fun, yet not overtly comedic, tone I was aiming for in the text. Caitlin also did the graphic design for the front cover. That is, she designed the title and integrated it with the illustration. She also painted the back cover illustration.

A special thanks to Rick and Drew Gillum, who fed me every other Friday night in Oklahoma City (and lodged me when the hour was late) on my long drives home to Missouri from Texas. But food and lodging are a small part of it. Their steadfast friendship has been a gift of incalculable value.

Thanks to Sara Diakabana for her help in translating some phrases. Three people read and commented on the completed manuscript. Susan Sebbard and Caitlin Carpenter were very helpful in spotting both specific miscues and offering strategic suggestions. A very special thanks to Pat Barber, who performed the same function. She has been a writing coach, editor, friend, and supporter for many years. Her comments on the manuscript, as always, were very insightful. Thanks also to marketer extraordinaire Brenda Goodsell.

About the Author

Craig Savoye was born in New Jersey and raised in California and Connecticut. He has had careers in journalism, government, business, public relations, and academia. He was a staff writer for the *Christian Science Monitor* in Boston, a corporate relations manager for a mainframe computer company in California's Silicon Valley, a public information officer at Lawrence Livermore National Laboratory, and an assistant professor of mass communication at Principia College in Illinois. He lives in St. Louis with his family.